M000098575

The Jews of West Point in the Long Gray Line

"... swifter than eagles, ... stonger than lions."
– Samuel II, 1:23

The Jews of West Point in the Long Gray Line

by

Lewis L. Zickel, Colonel, USAR
USMA Class of 1949

KTAV Publishing House, Inc.

Copyright © 2009 by Lewis L. Zickel

Library of Congress Cataloging-in-Publication Data

Zickel, Lewis L.
The Jews of West Point in the long gray line / by Lewis L. Zickel.
p. cm.
ISBN 978-1-60280-117-2
1. Zickel, Lewis L. 2. United States. Army--Officers--Biography. 3. Jewish soldiers--United States--Biography. 4. United States Military Academy--Biography. 5. Military cadets--United States--Biography. 6. United States Military Academy--History. I. Title.
U410.M1Z539 2009
355.0092'3924073--dc22

2009001275

All rights reserved. This book may not be reproduced, in whole or in part, in any form (beyond that copying permitted by U.S. Copyright Law in Section 107, "fair use" in teaching and research, Section 108, certain library copying, and except in publishing media by reviewers in limited excerpts), without written permission from the publisher.

Manufactured in the United States of America

Published by
KTAV Publishing House, Inc.
930 Newark Avenue
Jersey City, NJ 07306
Email: bernie@ktav.com
www.ktav.com
(201) 963-9524
Fax (201) 963-0102

To my brothers and sisters in the Long Gray Line
and to Yael, of course

CONTENTS

IN MEMORIAM

Lew Zickel, my beloved husband, died on May 13, 2007 content in the knowledge that he completed the first history of the Jews of West Point, an undocumented piece of West Point history. He was proud to have been a member of the original group that conceived and built the West Point Jewish Chapel, a home away from home for the Jewish Cadets. Like the prophet Moses who led our people in the desert to the Promised Land for forty years, Lew was there from the first meeting in 1965 to discuss the idea of a Jewish Chapel at West Point, until he became the President of the Jewish Community Council and in 2005 began writing this book.

This book was written for anyone interested in West Point, Jewish history and American military history; the Jewish American community who is still surprised to learn that there are Jews at West Point; and last but not least, the new Jewish cadets who join the Corps every year. Hopefully, this book will provide them with inspiration and encouragement.

ACKNOWLEDGMENTS

In the course of reading this book you will meet many individuals who made Jewish life vibrant at West Point. At this time particular thanks go to Lou Gross, Herb Lichtenberg and Dick Rosenblatt, who made this publication possible. Many others helped in writing, editing and publishing this book; most of all the 222 graduates and cadets who completed the survey. Lew would have thanked these individuals by name. Since I am personally unable to do so, I would like to thank you all on his behalf and express my deepest gratitude for making this book a reality.

Dr. Yael N. Zickel

PREFACE

Writing this book has been a labor of love: love for my Jewish heritage, love for my alma mater, love for the United States Army, and love for my country. They all go together very well.

I cannot recall when I first got the idea to write this account of the Jewish graduates of West Point. However, my dormant idea was awakened when one of our Jewish alumni, William Schwartz, Class of 1959, urged the West Point Jewish Community Council to memorialize all the Jewish members of the Long Gray Line by creating a display to be placed on a wall of the Jewish Chapel. We undertook the project, as will be described in detail further on in this book.

Sometime later, after the display was in place, Irving Schoenberg, Class of 1948, a retired Air Force colonel, spoke with me about the need to write the history of the Jews of West Point. In response to this, my wife Yael, said, "If anyone should write this book, it is you. Now, do it!" The time had come to take action. I thank them all for having been the catalyst in my literary effort.

I did not want the book to be merely a compendium of numbers and percentages. Jews, like all minorities, are interested in such statistics, and some appear in this book. However, I hoped to produce a readable book, to breathe life into the statistics and to tell the human stories behind them. In order to accomplish this objective, I needed input from alumni, cadets, and survivors of deceased alumni. I sought human interest material. A survey of living graduates was in order.

I prepared a questionnaire for distribution to every known living Jewish graduate who could be located. In addition to the request for statistical information, I asked that they provide one or more vignettes or stories about their cadet lives. I submitted the questionnaire with a cover letter to our rabbi, Chaplain (Major) Carlos Huerta, Lieutenant Colonel (Retired) Harry Garten. and Ms. Elaine McConnell of the West Point Cadet Library for their comments. I shall tell you more about these three outstanding people later. I then fine-tuned the documents based on their critiques and sent them out to 660 known Jewish alumni in mid-February 2005. Forty were returned "Address Unknown." I received 224 questionnaires (including mine), and more kept trickling in. I polled members of seventy-one classes from 1938 through 2008. Although the returns do not represent a random sampling, they have considerable statistical validity. They represent more than a 36 percent return; enough to provide a reliable picture of Jewish life at West Point during those years.

All the stories and data in this book were provided by the responding graduates or have been footnoted as to source. None of the stories have been inflated or modified. What you will read here is what was submitted to me, spelling and grammatical errors as written. None of the information or stories is a product of my imagination. I have made every effort to avoid personal bias in writing this book. It is a documentation of the Jewish experience at the United States Military Academy as told by those of us who lived it and as related to me by the graduates who returned their questionnaires and by those I interviewed. Wherever contributors are identified, they granted me the authority to use their names. Where stories appear without the contributor's name, authority was given to use the story without the author's identification. Some also volunteered information about their experiences after they entered active duty in the Army or Air Force. I owe all the contributors a debt of thanks. I could not have written this book without them. Grip hands!

This book is not an official publication of the United States Military Academy, the United States Army, or the United States Department of Defense.

INTRODUCTION

The young boy stood on the Plain in awe of the overwhelming panorama of stern military gothic buildings, somber monuments, relics of past wars, and rugged terrain all overlooking the majestic Hudson River. Neither a cadet nor a uniformed soldier was to be seen. It was the mid-summer of 1936 and the boy was nine years old. His father made it a practice of taking the family on one-day trips from their home in the all-Jewish Weequahic section of Newark, New Jersey. Today's trip was to the United States Military Academy at West Point, New York.

During the long drive home to Newark, the boy announced to his parents that he wanted to go to "that place." That boyhood desire survived and thrived throughout elementary and high school, reinforced by more compelling rational reasons than merely the impressive scenery of the Academy and the Hudson valley. His parents supported his desire to pursue a military career and all stops were pulled out to compete for an appointment.

And so I entered West Point in July 1945 and graduated in 1949, 147 years after the first Jewish graduate, Simon Magruder Levy, Class of 1802. Levy's class consisted of only one other cadet, Joseph Gardner Swift. These two men comprised the first class to attend the new military academy on the Hudson. Swift's Cullum (sequence) Number is 1, Levy's 2. Mine is 17,289, the 208th known Jewish graduate.

The history of Jewish graduates of West Point ever since those Cullum Numbers is an interesting story worth telling. More than sixty years have elapsed since I entered West Point as a cadet, and fifty-six years since I graduated with relief and pride. However, I continue to be asked, now as then, "How come a Jewish boy—?"

That question urged me to write this book. Perhaps it will answer the question for the reader.

Lewis L. Zickel
Colonel, United States Army, Retired
Dobbs Ferry, New York
2005

PART 1

THE WEST POINT STORY

Birth of the Academy

The "shot heard around the world" fired at Concord, Massachusetts, in 1775 came from the muskets of untrained colonial rebels. The professionals wore red coats. It was the start of a war against the strongest military power of the time, waged by untrained leaders and soldiers from General George Washington down to the men in the line. Neither Washington nor his generals and officers had any formal education in the military arts, the sciences, or engineering. If not for foreign volunteers such as the Marquis de Lafayette, the Polish patriot Thaddeus Kosciuszko, and the Prussian officer Baron Friedrich Wilhelm Augustus von Steuben, the Continental Army and the Minutemen might have been hard pressed to defeat the British and to win the American Revolutionary War.

The eighteenth-century colleges of higher learning in the American colonies (later to become the newborn nation) offered courses only in the liberal arts, theology, and some science. American education was devoid of engineering courses and military science. Schools specializing in these studies simply did not exist, nor were there teachers qualified to teach them. General, later President, George Washington was painfully aware of these shortfalls, which plagued his efforts all through the war. By the time he became president, he was convinced that the nascent nation needed a school, or a series of schools, to educate officers, engineers, and scientists. He envisioned a single school combining all of these courses of study. He sought support from Congress to open and fund such an establishment, and he selected the fortified ramparts of West Point on the Hudson River for its location. Alexander Hamilton wrote a curriculum for the new school. However, neither Washington nor John Adams, his successor, was able to persuade Congress to authorize such a school in the postwar environment. Ironically, success fell to Thomas Jefferson during his presidency. The irony stems from the fact that Jefferson had always opposed the establishment of a federal military academy, but for an unknown reason, he moved rapidly to have it approved by Congress. Finally, on March 16, 1802, Congress authorized the establishment of a Corps of Engineers consisting of ten cadets, with provisions to double that number. This marked the birth of the profession of engineering and the profession of arms in the United States. The new academy formally opened with two cadets, Joseph G. Swift and Simon Magruder Levy. As Swift observed in his diary, Levy "was from a prominent Baltimore Jewish family."

The early years of the Academy were less than ideal until a member of the Class of 1808, Sylvanus Thayer, became its fifth superintendent. Recommended for the post by then Chief Engineer Joseph G. Swift and appointed by President James Monroe, Thayer served in that capacity from July 28, 1817, until July 1, 1833.

Thayer realized that the Academy needed proper textbooks, qualified faculty, and a system of discipline, teaching, and learning. In 1816 the president authorized him to travel to France to seek the first two items on his list. He and Lieutenant Colonel William McCree (initially offered the assignment of superintendent, but who had turned it down) were dispatched with a letter of introduction from the president to the aged Marquis de Lafayette, asking him to introduce Thayer to Napoleon. Thayer was excited by the prospect of meeting the great Napoleon Bonaparte. Unfortunately for Thayer, the emperor had been defeated by the British at the Battle of Waterloo and sent into exile before he arrived in Paris.

Thayer's mission was to "study the military schools of Europe and coastal fortifications of France, considered the best in the world, and to purchase books and scientific equipment for the Academy." Thayer visited bookstores, Saint-Cyr, the French military academy, and the Ecole Polytechnique, the French school of engineering. With Napoleon gone, King Louis XVIII was in power, wreaking revenge on all he could find who had been enemies of the House of Bourbon. One of those being hunted down was General Simon Barnard, a talented engineer from Napoleon's staff and his aide-de-camp. Barnard willingly accepted an invitation to emigrate to the United States and become a professor at West

Point. The president approved the appointment despite a firestorm of resentment from the current superintendent of West Point, the Corps of Engineers, and others in the Army. Thayer prevailed. He returned with Barnard and more than 1,100 engineering and science textbooks, a French encyclopedia, and an array of scientific instruments. He now had the materials and the nucleus of a faculty to create an effective institution of higher learning.

In 1817, Thayer proceeded to redesign the system of teaching and reorganize the academic structure of West Point. Many of those innovative changes survived and are in use to this day. Small classes of ten to fifteen cadets are still part of the West Point system of pedagogy, and every cadet was required to recite in every subject and to be graded daily. This system had little tolerance for lazy students and those prone neither to study nor to participate in the classroom. Coupled with frequent examinations in each subject, the cadet was exposed to the material three times. This enhanced learning and retention of the material. America was now in position to properly educate its officers as engineers and military leaders trained to wage war. In time other American schools of engineering opened. Sylvanus Thayer founded one of them, the Thayer School of Engineering at Dartmouth College.

The Class of 1823 graduated thirty-five out of the eighty-nine who entered the Academy in 1819. The first man in order of merit in the class was Jewish, Alfred Mordechai, born in North Carolina. Upon graduation, Mordechai was appointed assistant professor by Major Thayer. He held this post until 1825, when he was assigned as an assistant to the chief engineer of the United States Army. His son, three great-grandsons, and a great-great-grandson followed in his footsteps and became West Point graduates. The last of the line known to me graduated in 1946, when I finished my plebe year. As of the graduation of 2005, more than 823 Jews followed Simon Magruder Levy as graduates of the Academy.

Two noteworthy cadets of the nineteenth century were James Abbott McNeil Whistler and Edgar Allan Poe. Whistler, a renowned artist, failed to graduate with the Class of 1855. He failed chemistry and later quipped, "If silicon were but a gas, today a general I would be." The portrait of his mother is internationally known. Poe, the distinguished American poet, made a sterling start during Plebe Year, then became a disciplinary problem and was dismissed from the Class of 1834 on February 8, 1830.

West Point, as the first engineering school in the country, produced graduates who were at the cutting edge of technology. They were instrumental in designing and building the transcontinental railroads. They mapped and surveyed large and small parcels of land along the east coast and throughout the Midwest. General Egbert L. Viele, Class of 1847 of the United States Army Corps of Engineers, among other projects, mapped all of the underground streams and the locus of the original banks of the Hudson and East rivers in New York City in 1854 and he upgraded these maps in 1876. I use his maps, as do other engineers, whenever I investigate basement water-intrusion cases in New York. The originals are in the New York Public Library and I kept a complete set of full-scale copies of those maps. General Viele also contributed to the design of Central Park and Prospect Park in New York City. The foregoing were just some of the notables of the period, the Civil War officers and generals, members of the Long Gray Line who fought on both sides of the conflict, notwithstanding.

The notable graduates who rose to fame in the twentieth century are familiar to most Americans: Generals Pershing, MacArthur, Eisenhower, Bradley, Arnold, Patton, Abrams, and Schwarzkopf to name a few. There are others not as well known to the public and often forgotten, such as George Washington Goethals, Class of 1880. He built the Panama Canal. Leslie R. Groves, Class of November 1918, directed the Manhattan Project, which produced the atomic bomb before Nazi Germany could accomplish that monumental task. Many of the astronauts who made space history deserve recognition here: Frank Borman, Class of 1950; Buzz Aldrin, Class of 1951; Michael Collins and Edward H. White II, both of the Class of 1952. Two of our graduates have served as president of the United States; Ulysses S. Grant and Dwight D. Eisenhower. Alexander M. Haig, Jr., Class of 1947, served President Ronald Reagan as chief of staff of the White House and was appointed supreme Allied commander in Europe. He ultimately became Secretary of State of the United States. Many graduates became members of Congress, mayors, governors, judges, lawyers, physicians, engineers, architects, captains of industry, cabinet secretaries, advisers to the president, diplomats, educators, and served in many other honorable professions. One of the many graduates who became captains of industry was the founding chief executive officer and chairman of America On Line, James V. Kimsey, Class of 1972. He was a major donor for the construction of the athletic center at Michie Stadium that bears his name.

All of America has benefited from the graduates of the school for soldiers envisioned by President George Washington and realized by President Thomas Jefferson more than 200 years ago. Because West Point is today considered to be the premier leadership school in the country, if not the world, its graduates will continue to serve our nation with distinction in future generations.

Service to nation and society is a noble pursuit, particularly to this nation and particularly by Jews. We came here more than 350 years ago with the earliest explorers and colonists. We are not here at the largess or whim of some ruling monarch who could decide to expel Jews from "his" country. We are here because we helped to create the nation; we are here because we helped America to rise in revolt and wrest itself from British rule, helped it to grow and flourish, and, above all, helped to defend it. With the exception of the creation of the State of Israel in 1948, never since the commencement of the Diaspora has Jewry been so undeniably a part of the birth and growth of a new nation as in America. It is certainly worth defending. To do so is to answer the highest calling. This is our obligation, and that is why young Jewish men and women have chosen to attend West Point.

The Jewish Warrior

"And he gave Joshua the son of Nun a charge and said; 'Be strong and of good courage; for thou shalt bring the children of Israel into the land which I swore to them; and I will be with thee' " (Deuteronomy 31:32).

Thus Jewish military history was born. Joshua was the first Jewish warrior. In 1451 B.C.E. he conquered the armies of the five kings of Canaan and "the walls came tumbling down" half a millennium after Abraham left the city of Ur in Mesopotamia and settled near Shechem in the land of Canaan. Close to 3,000 years later, the Jewish warrior was memorialized at the United States Military Academy side-by-side with Christian and pagan warriors of note. There are nine statues on the a massive stone mantle located in the academic board room in the Headquarters Building, carved by Lee Oscar Lawrie (1877–1963), a renowned German-born sculptor, "of the world's nine greatest warriors: three worshippers of ancient gods, three Jews, and three Christians—Hector, Alexander the Great, Julius Caesar; Joshua, David, Judas Maccabeus; King Arthur, Charlemagne, and Godfrey de Bouillon." I first saw the memorial to these warriors, described as quoted above in the 1945 volume of *Bugle Notes*, a handbook about West Point presented to each new cadet, when I entered the Academy as a plebe. It had been there for many years, twenty-five years or more prior to 1945. According to Robert Pinsky, in his book *The Life of David*, Arab poets credit David, the biblical warrior-king, with inventing the coat of mail, the metallic chain-link light body armor worn through the Middle Ages by most armies. David conquered lands from the Euphrates River to the Nile in Egypt during his warrior years.

The Book of Judges in the Holy Scripture ranges over 271 years of Judaic history beginning in 2901 B.C.E.—and ending in 2630 B.C.E.. This is about 900 years after the death of Abraham.

Toward the end of that period, as recounted in Judges 20:1–48, a conflict arose between the tribes of Israel and the tribe of Benjamin over the murder and dismemberment of the concubine of a man from Benjamin. Both tribes boasted hundreds of thousands of swordsmen. One of Benjamin's generals was left-handed and he reasoned that a battalion of left-handed warriors would offer great tactical advantage, so he organized a force of 700 men.

Opposing right-handers they held their swords in their right hands and shields in their left, "Every one could sling a stone at a hair-breadth and not miss!" This is analogous to a left-handed boxer.

The carnage was so great that the tribes of Israel prayed for God to intervene. He apparently did! The tribes of Israel prevailed.

This is but one example of the ingenuity of the Jewish warrior in biblical days.

War and Peace

HaRav Avraham Yitzhak HaCohen Kook was the chief rabbi of Palestine during the early years of the twentieth century. Rabbi Kook was a highly respected Jewish scholar and philosopher. At the height of World War I he wrote a series of essays on war and peace. Until recently, these essays were available only in Hebrew. Recently, they were translated into English in the Orot Series by Rabbi David Samson and Tzvi Fishman.

In the book Rabbi Kook cites Exodus 15:3, which declares that "Hashem [God] is a man of war." According to Rabbi Kook, the sin in the Garden of Eden and the creation of the Golden Calf during the Exodus angered Hashem into condemning mankind to evil, hate, war, and violence. Rabbi Kook came to this conclusion through meticulous research in Judaic literature: the Five Books of Moses, Prophets, Psalms, Rashi, Talmud, Gemara. "Wars are acts of God; not only their outcomes, but also their unfolding and design." As to participation in war by Jews, he writes:

> In Russia, the question arose whether a Jew should serve in the Russian army. Students of the Chafetz Chaim [a prominent rabbi of the nineteenth century] asked his opinion. He answered: in a short time, the Mashiach [Messiah] will come, and we will have a state, and a state needs an army. Will you wait until then to learn how to be soldiers? . . .
>
> Suddenly we realize that we can be soldiers too. During World War I the Hebrew Brigade, HaG'dud HaIvri, helped the British conquer Israel from the Turks. This is the first appearance of Jewish fighting units since the soldiers of Bar Kochva's rebellion against the Legions of Rome.

Every year since 1999 the Jewish cadets at West Point have hosted an event called the Jewish Warrior Weekend. The guests are Jewish students from colleges and universities in the Greater New York area, upstate New York, and Connecticut, as well as cadets of the Air Force, Naval, and Coast Guard academies. The weekend commences with a Friday night Shabbat service in the Jewish Chapel. At the commencement of one of these weekends, I addressed the group after the service. On one side of the sanctuary sat the civilian guests, representing the entire spectrum of Judaic practice and the cadets sat on the other side of the central aisle.

I opened my talk by saying, "The Jewish warrior may be an oxymoron to many of you, but as students of the Torah you must be familiar with our history as a people." The Jews of the biblical period, I explained, were a warlike people. They fought for survival and for conquest. In the last half of the twentieth century, I continued, the Israel Defense Forces certainly proved the point many times over again that Jews are excellent soldiers. The problem is that Jews in the Diaspora find this hard to believe or even accept as being applicable to them. The Jewish American warrior is just as capable and has proved it in every war from the American Revolution to Operation Iraqi Freedom, not to mention the "MACHAL" (overseas volunteers for Israel) and Colonel David (Mickey) Marcus, the American Jews who fought in the Israeli War of Independence. Jews in America are of the same heritage as the Israelis. I often remind those who cannot understand the concept of the non-Israeli Jewish warrior that we all came from the same continent, pointing out that "The difference lies with the destinations of migration; some went west, some went south. The only differences between these two groups are attitude and self- perception."

Many years ago I visited the curator of the Diaspora Museum in Tel Aviv. We discussed the subject of the Jewish warrior. He described a joint research project underway at that time by his museum and Tel Aviv University to determine whether there were Jews in military service during the Middle Ages. Much to their astonishment they were uncovering historical evidence of Jews serving in the professional military during that period of history.

The first Jews who settled in America 350 years ago in Peter Stuyvesant's New Amsterdam fought for the right to serve in the guard unit defending the settlement. In November 1655 Asser Levy petitioned the New Amsterdam court to grant Jews the right to participate in the colony's military defense. It took two years to win the privilege. This willingness of Jews to serve in the military continued through the American Revolution to the present.

Mark Twain wrote an article in *Harper's Monthly* in 1899 in which he expressed his deep admiration for Jews but implied that they had not helped in the struggle against England and added the stereotype, "The Jew is a money-getter." This was contradicted by Rabbi M. S. Levy in an article in the *Overland Monthly* that caused Twain to write a postscript to his article titled "The Jew as a Soldier." In the postscript Twain corrected himself and related a fairly accurate history of the service of Jews in all of our wars up to that time. The American Jewish Historical Society has in its archives a letter from President Theodore Roosevelt to Jacob H. Schiff dated November 16, 1905. Jacob Schiff was the chairman of the Committee on the Celebration of the 250th Anniversary of the Settlement of the Jews in the United States. In that letter, the president cited the outstanding military service of Jews in the American Revolution and the Civil War.

Melvin A. Young, Class of 1952, devoted many years of his life to researching the Jews who fought in the Civil War for both the Union and the Confederacy. He published several books on this subject. In 1860, at the start of the war, the Jewish population in the entire United States was 139,000. It grew year by year during the war until it reached 176,000 in 1865; an average wartime population (both Union and Confederate states) of 156,000 over six years. Young's research revealed that close to 8,000 Jews served in the war, counting those on both sides. They represent about 20 percent of the eligible Jewish males.

In 1946 Captain Sydney G. Gumpertz, a World War I Medal of Honor recipient, published his extensive research on Jewish participation in wars from the American Revolution through World War II. He found that among the 8,000 Jews who served in the Civil War were 9 generals, 18 colonels, 8 lieutenant colonels, 40 majors, 205 captains, 325 lieutenants, 48 adjutants, and 25 surgeons. Many of the Jews of all ranks who served were awarded the Congressional Medal of Honor. Most of the Jews who served were volunteers. The great majority of them were in the combat arms—infantry, cavalry, or artillery. Gumpertz identified seven of the Jewish generals by name: Major General Frederick Knefler, Brigadier General Edward S. Solomon, General Judah (probably a brigadier), General L.C. Newman (probably a brigadier), Brigadier General Leopold Blumenberg, Brigadier General Philip J. Joachimsen, and Brigadier General Marcus M. Spiegel. All listed were combat commanders.

The early Jews in America were Sephardim from Brazil. They were the descendants of Jews who had been expelled from Spain and Portugal in the era of the Inquisition. Most people are unaware of the fact that the Inquisition continued in one form or another into the nineteenth century. This migration was followed by the German Jews, beginning around 1825. They left Germany for the New World primarily because of constraints imposed on their education, restrictions against joining a profession, limited rank in the military (corporal was the highest grade open to them), opposition to their being accepted as one of the many German "tribes," and for economic reasons. Several German-Jewish activist leaders maintained a correspondence with Mordecai Manuel Noah, the former United States consul to Tunisia and cousin of Samuel Noah, Class of 1807 at West Point. He envisioned a land for the Jews on an island near Niagara Falls and Buffalo, New York, a project that never materialized. Both of these groups, the Sephardim and the German Jews, served in the American military in about the same proportions as the non-Jewish population.

The East European Jews migrated to the United States during the last two decades of the nineteenth century and into the twentieth century. These Jews were fleeing from the pogroms inflicted upon them by their neighbors and by the Russian tsar's Cossacks. They were also running from a forced draft into the tsar's army, a lifetime sentence to a cruel life. They brought with them an antipathy, distrust, and fear of anything military or anyone in uniform. Because of the overwhelming numbers of East Europeans in the migration, they became the stereotype of the American Diaspora Jew, a stereotype reinforced by many, including many Diaspora Jews, that unfortunately survives to this day. However, these same Jews with East European roots turned out in droves to serve in both world wars, for they saw these wars as crusades against evil. This appeals to the Jewish sense of justice and in keeping with talmudic teachings. It is noteworthy that this is true in all free societies, especially among Americans of all origins; the "popular" wars are those that fit the philosophy so elegantly framed in our National Anthem: "Then conquer we must, when our cause it is just . . ."

A number of authors have written interesting accounts of Jews in the military. Professor Debra Dash Moore of Vassar University wrote *GI Jews*, personal accounts of a group of Jewish veterans of World War II. I had the good fortune of attending her lecture at the Museum of Jewish Heritage in New York City on Veterans Day 2004. The veterans appearing in her book personally described their experiences as soldiers and sailors. An excellent summary of the Jew as a warrior appears in Max I. Dimont's *Jews, God and History*, in which he effectively describes the history of the Jewish soldier. He wrote:

> During his first thousand years, the mask of the Jew was that of a nomad and tiller of the soil, living by his wits, preferring peace, and taking to the sword only when forced to do so. In the second millennium of his history the nomadic mask was discarded. He became a man of war, intrepid in battle, unmatched in valor. Like the Greeks, the Jews had their Marathons—magnificent victories in the face of incredible odds. But unlike the Greeks, who remained passive after their defeat at the hands of the Romans, the Jews rose time and again in armed rebellion against their oppressors striking for freedom and religious liberty. *The stereotyped mask of meekness was later fitted on the Jew by Western civilization* [emphasis added].

I have never seen or heard it better expressed. This stereotyping plus the all-too-common belief that Jews cannot fight infuriated me as a youngster (and still does as an adult). It was one of the compelling reasons for my aspiration to become a professional soldier via West Point.

Dimont went on to relate that after the reigns of David and Solomon, Palestine was virtually destroyed by civil strife and conflicts between the kingdoms of Israel and Judah. A series of ineffective kings followed for several hundred years. Israel was saved by King Omri in 866 B.C.E. He put down the civil strife and destroyed the armies of six hostile nations attempting to invade Israel. Dimont named him the Napoleon of his age. He conquered a number of surrounding nations, arousing fear throughout the region. The Assyrians referred to Israel as "the land of Omri." Archaeologists found a monument so inscribed by the Assyrians. Subsequently, Omri's son Ahab decisively defeated the Assyrians at the Battle of Karkar in 854 B.C.E when they launched a war of conquest against Egypt. In order to get to Egypt they would have had to conquer Israel first. The battle resulted in 20,000 deaths and set back Assyrian conquests one hundred years. There are many more examples of successful Jewish warriors. Worthy of appearance here are some statistics to compare with the performance of Jewish forces listed by Dimont:

> Alexander the Great carved out his empire with 35,000 men.
> Caesar conquered Gaul and Britain with 25,000 men.
> Hannibal crossed the Alps to defeat Rome with 59,000 men.

But Titus required 80,000 soldiers and four years to defeat 23,400 Jews in Jerusalem. He tried to intimidate the Jewish defenders by parading his 70,000 foot soldiers and 10,000 cavalrymen beneath the city's walls for three days. He was jeered by the Jewish defenders. Titus pounded the city for two weeks, attacked, but was driven back. The Jews held out for another year—the fourth year of the war. This action showed the world that the Romans were not invincible, thus resulting in a decline of Roman power throughout their world of influence.

Bringing the story closer to modern times, I would add that Jean André Masséna, one of Napoleon Bonaparte's marshals, widely considered to have been the most outstanding field commander of his time after Napoleon, was Jewish, at least by descent (his father's original name was Menasse). And Sir John Monash, the commander of the Australian Corps in Europe in World War I, was also a Jew. According to Field Marshal Bernard Law Montgomery, the victor of Alamein in World War II, Monash was "the best general on the western front."

Racial and Ethnic Prejudice

My close relationship with West Point began when I entered the Academy as a cadet in July 1945. After graduation in 1949, my personal contact with the Academy was limited to that of an interested but geographically removed alumnus. In the 1960s this began to change to a closer relationship as the Jewish Chapel project got underway. My involvement with the project grew, and I once again became a close observer of cadet life. In the last decade, as an active volunteer and as president of the West Point Jewish Community Council, I have become more intimately familiar with life behind "the old gray walls of our rockbound highland home." These activities have provided me with considerable exposure to the many aspects of the Corps as a group and as individual cadets.

Note that I have not titled this section "Anti-Semitism." In the first place, as reprehensible and unacceptable as anti-Semitism is, there are many other ethnic and racial groups represented in the Corps of Cadets, and, in addition, since 1976, both genders have been part of the Corps. Second, I want to dispel any perception that only Jewish cadets may have been or may be the targets of prejudice. Any one or any number of minorities could be or could have been subject to prejudicial acts. Prejudicial and racist behavior is not condoned at the Academy, but it must be realized that every cadet arrives at West Point bearing the baggage of eighteen or more years of exposure to anti-minority attitudes that may have been prevalent in the youngster's home and community. Any such learned prejudices reside in the memory bank of each new cadet. Despite the official prohibition of racial, anti-ethnic, and anti-gender remarks, some of it may bubble to the surface on occasion. After all, the Corps of Cadets is a demographic sampling of every corner of the country. Cadets are America's best and brightest young people, and, though we should expect better behavior from them, they, after all, are human.

It is not my intent here to be an apologist for racist acts that occur or have occurred in the Corps from time to time. To deny their existence would be unrealistic and a departure from the truth. I can only report my own experience and the experience of the Jewish graduates who responded to the questionnaire I sent them, seeking their experience in many facets of their cadet lives, including anti-Semitism. I also recognize that not all confrontations between a Jew and non-Jew are anti-Semitic. Very often, the labeling of such confrontations is in the eye of the beholder and a function of individual sensitivities.

Personally I cannot recall one incident of any shade of anti-Semitism directed at me during my four years as a cadet. There was some good-natured bantering involving a few specific ethnic groups. For instance, cadet slang for a Catholic was "fish eater." The Catholic cadets referred to themselves as "fish eaters." I am unaware of any resentment or ill feelings arising from this bit of cadet slang. I was also unaware of any similar slang expression for Jewish cadets during my four years at West Point up until recently, when I learned from younger grads that during their time as cadets, Jews were referred to as "ham chasers." None of the respondents to my questionnaire cited this appellation as offensive to them. I polled every known Jewish graduate and cadet from the classes of 1938 through 2008, a span of seventy-one years. Of those who responded, between 16 and 16.5 percent reported some degree of anti-Semitic experience while cadets. There is more detailed information on this survey later in the chapter, including word-for-word reports of such incidents by those who reported them.

Herb Lichtenberg, Class of 1955, to this day carries the nickname "Kelly." That came to pass when an upperclassman in his company had trouble remembering his name. One day he announced, "From now on you are Kelly." I do not consider this to be an anti-Semitic act, and neither does Herb. Today, there is such a wide mix of ethnic groups at West Point that there is more "literacy" and agility at the Academy in pronouncing "non-Anglo" names.

My cadet platoon leader during my plebe year was of Irish lineage and, for an upperclassman, was unusually pleasant toward plebes. One day he asked me to obtain some information for him. When I went to his room to report to him, a number of his classmates were present and there was somewhat of a jovial atmosphere in the room. Standing in the traditional brace of that time, exaggerated rigid attention, I reported,

"Sir, Mr. Zickel reports to Mr. Flaherty with the requested information."

He responded in an Irish brogue: "Oh, 'tis Mr. O'Zickel, is it?"

I responded, still at rigid attention, also in an Irish brogue: "Aye, 'tis Mr. O'Zickel reportin' to Mr. O'Flaherty as ordered."

Our full discussion from that point through to the end of my report was in brogue. One of his classmates said, "Ed, he has a better brogue than yours." Today, the rules of behavior would most likely not condone such bantering. However, I never looked upon the incident as anti-Semitic.

From that point on, Ed Flaherty could not look me in the eye without smirking. This became a problem for both of us during inspection in ranks. Whenever he stood in front of me to inspect my uniform, shoes, brass, and rifle, he had to fight back the urge to break out laughing. I had the same problem, but mine was worse than his; laughing in ranks was and is a punishable offense that I somehow managed to avoid.

A member of the Class of 1950 is a native of Brooklyn, where handball was a popular sport in the Jewish community. This young man became a seasoned handball player, good enough to qualify for the A Squad (varsity) team at West Point. Included among the usual competing college teams were a number of civilian athletic club teams willing to challenge the Army team. One of the athletic clubs invited to compete with our Army team had a reputation for being notoriously anti-Semitic. Our Brooklyn boy was appointed the cadet host for one of the scheduled matches with the club. The assignment as host included escorting the visiting team to lunch in the Cadet Mess Hall. As they entered the hall, one of the visitors noticed an African-American cadet. He turned to the host and said, "I didn't know that you have niggers at West Point. I guess you have Jews too."

The host cadet's response was right on point. "If not here, mister, where the hell else in the United States?"

This was a remarkably astute, incisive response for a young man barely out of his teen years. This response, without question, foreclosed any further discourse on the subject.

The history of African-Americans at West Point had an abysmal start in the last half of the nineteenth century. The unacceptable treatment of and unwarranted charges against Cadet Henry Ossian Flipper, Class of 1877, and others have been documented and dramatized, highlighting the extreme racial prejudice suffered upon these young pioneers of their race.

Recently, through congressional action, the Army rescinded all the charges against Flipper and others and awarded rank posthumously to these victims of hate. These first young African-Americans were faced with the post–Civil War southerners still smarting from the surrender at Appomattox in 1865. The war ended only eight years before Flipper entered the Academy. This is not an apology for the unacceptable treatment of Flipper, it is only an observation about what may have been part of the reason for these acts.

Two of my classmates were African-Americans. I was unaware until recently of any racist acts perpetrated against them. However, I am not privy to the details of their cadet experiences. Today there are a substantial number of African-American cadets and officers on the staff. One of them, Brigadier General Leo Brooks, was a recent Commandant of Cadets. His brother, Major General Vincent K. Brooks, Class of 1980, was the first African-American First Captain of the Corps of Cadets.

In July 1976, the 200th birthday of the United States, 119 women were admitted to West Point, ending 174 years of an all-male bastion. This was the result of a congressional mandate. It was not warmly received by the male cadets or by many of the officers. Some time prior to the arrival of the first women, I had lunch with Major General Sidney B. Berry, Class of 1948, superintendent of the Academy at that time. He had the responsibility to make the gender integration work. He explained that he was preparing for the women's arrival and declared that in the face of all the opposition, he would make the integration a success; and indeed he did!

However, the first women faced hostility, resentment, and some denigration from their cadet brothers. It took a few years before these negative attitudes subsided into a degree of remission. Several women cadets have indicated to me that some of that resentment still exists. By the Class of 1990, the Corps had its first female First Captain: Kristin M. Baker. Recently, one of the first women graduates was promoted to brigadier general. As with the Class of 1802, when the first Jew graduated, the first Jewish female to graduate was a member of the first class of women: Danna Maller, now Danna Rocque. Well done, Danna!

Muslims have also begun to join the Long Gray Line. A few have been attending Jewish services, though provisions have been made for their worship. One is currently the leader of the Jewish Choir. Of the six who entered in 2004 with the Class of 2008, three were foreign cadets. I am not aware of racist incidents perpetrated against the Muslim cadets. Here, once more, I am not privy to the details of their lives. Though Muslims have been members of the Corps for some time, I have not heard of any conflict between Muslim and Jewish cadets. Our Jewish chaplain has a warm relationship with the Imam.

This chapter would not be complete without some mention of the relationship between Christian fundamentalist cadets and other religious groups. There have been a few reports of attempts by certain fundamentalist cadets to convert Jewish cadets, or to convince them on the idea of conversion. A unique incident arose out of the West Point National Prayer Breakfasts held each year. These events bring together all of the Academy's religious groups: Protestants, Catholics, Jews, and Muslims. They are attended by cadets, civilian employees of the Department of the Army, and uniformed Army personnel from the superintendent, commandant, and dean to the men and women in the ranks. The breakfasts are planned and orchestrated by the cadet chaplain, who oversees all religious activities at West Point. All chaplains, including our rabbi, attend these events. Lay members or clergy from each religious group recite a portion of their liturgy. All get equal time.

After one of these breakfasts, a fundamentalist cadet wrote a memo to the cadet chaplain berating him for allowing the non-Christians to perform their sectarian portions of the program. This young man's fervor and the strength of his beliefs overrode all the military protocol he had been taught. It is obviously inappropriate for a cadet to berate a senior officer, particularly a colonel. One can imagine the fervor and force of his dealing with his peers of equal military rank—Protestant, Catholic, Muslim, Jew, or agnostic—and even more with his subordinates.

As I pointed out at the start of this section, cadets arrive at West Point with the beliefs and prejudices of their upbringing and community. They are trained and educated on tolerance from the moment they arrive at West Point. I attended R-Day (the day new cadets report for duty) for the Class of 2009. Before the first week ended, the entire new class of cadets was herded into an auditorium for orientation. Part of the program was presented by Father Edson Wood, brigade chaplain. He described the availability of religious activities and delivered an outstanding speech on racial and religious tolerance. Among other things, he stated emphatically, "Your religion is no better than the persons' to your right and to your to your left." His talk was being taped. Unfortunately, the recording equipment malfunctioned and he was speaking without notes. It was such a powerful speech, I had hoped to include it in its entirety in this book. This speech must have had an impact on any home-grown prejudices.

An interesting example of these mindsets from a cadet's early life occurred in a class on Judaic history taught by Major Iris Cowher of the Department of History. The major was teaching a class on the Holocaust. One of the female cadets raised her hand and announced that her grandmother said that there was no such thing as the Holocaust. Major Cowher spent extra time with this young cadet, who finally realized that her grandmother was wrong.

Despite such incidents, West Point is the one school in America to which we can send our children with the comfort of knowing that they are not likely to become individual targets of anti-Semitism or group targets of virulent anti-Semitic rallies or student movements as prevalent at many colleges and universities today. The tradition of strong leadership by the superintendents, commandants, and deans is reinforced by the Respect Program introduced by a commandant in 1992. It is at the same level of importance at West Point as the Honor Code. Honor and respect are the stated bedrock values of the Academy. The Respect Program educates cadets at all levels in the Corps on tolerance toward others of different races, religions, and gender. Details of this program appear later in the book.

Comments on Anti-Semitic Experiences

The following comments from Jewish graduates regarding their experiences as targets of anti-Semitic acts against them or against other cadets have been reproduced here verbatim, as submitted to me on their questionnaires. All Jewish graduates from the seventy-one classes between 1938 and 2008 were polled. The classes of 2005, '06, '07, and '08, still cadets, were included to obtain up-to-date information. There was no response from anyone from the classes of '74, '91, and '95. The specific question posed was: "Did you encounter or experience anti-Semitism during your cadet years?"

My survey was not a random sampling. All 660 known living Jewish graduates and cadets were polled. Some did not respond. Out of 660 questionnaires mailed, only 617 were presumed to have arrived. Forty-three were returned "Address Unknown" by the postal service. We were unsuccessful in finding them. Of the 617 presumed to have arrived, 222, or 36 percent, responded. Of the 222 responders, 37, or 16.5 percent, reported a range of anti-Semitic incidents from minor to overt and outrageous. Of the 37, ten (4%) were classified by the responder as "minor," the remaining twenty-seven (12%) were classified as "overt." The minor acts were described as "jokes, slurs, etc." Some reported acts were presumed to be anti-Semitic. A number of those who reported "No" described ignorance or lack of understanding of basic Judaism and/or Judaic culture by non-Jewish cadets. They also reported encounters with cadets who had never met a Jew. There were no "spikes" in the reported acts with regard to any year or period.

Many "No" responses were emphatically expressed by underlining or reinforced with an additional negative, such as "no-never!" rather than a mere "No" to the question. Some of the emphatic responses are included here. All "Yes" comments are included no matter how "mild" the reported incidents were. The perpetrator of almost every reported incident was either a peer or an upper class cadet. The sequence of reported incidents recorded here has no significance. They are presented in the order that questionnaires were received from those polled. And as mentioned earlier, I have made no effort to change the original spelling, capitalization, grammar, or syntax.

I have made every effort to avoid bias in my reporting. There was no editorializing, and no effort to minimize or embellish these reported acts including my personal experiences as a cadet. An evaluation of these reported experiences is left up to the reader. However, I can reasonably conclude from the responses to my questionnaire that anti-Semitism has not been and is not now institutional or widespread at West Point. Nevertheless, I will say that any percentage of racial or religious bias is unacceptable, and how many incidents are considered "widespread" may be in the eyes of the beholder.

Individual Responses

Larry Waters, '62 wrote, "Yes. Whenever a Mid East problem arose, a Yearling (Sophomore) on my floor would play Nazi Storm Trooper music on his phonograph. I was used to slurs so it did not bother me as much." Larry offered the following experience that occurred twice after he entered the Regular Army: "On a sad note my uncle, the Colonel, told me to put under 'Religion' 'None Stated.' It was a big mistake. I was recommended for Junior Aide de-Camp of Lieutenant General Watson. His wife was very religious and when she saw 'None Stated' on my 201 (Personnel File), she vetoed my selection. I heard this from Watson's Senior Aide, a West Point grad. I was nominated for another general's aide and was turned down for the same reason. My uncle had always hid his religion and thought that this was best for me. It was a bad decision. Well, I did what he said. I went to Jewish Chapel and sang in the choir only because I didn't know where else to go. My roommates knew I was Jewish."

Larry served for six years. He was medically discharged in 1968 because of an injury incurred during a parachute jump during his service with the 82nd Airborne Division, where he was a jumpmaster. He also was a Ranger. In an e-mail to Cadet Isaac Greenberg, he wrote that he loved every minute of his military service.

Dr. Paul Kantrowich, '65 responded, "*Yes,* but I was too stupid to consider it anti-Semitism. I thought I was just a lousy cadet . . . which was true... . . . I was a terrible cadet!"

Richard E. Entlich, '63 described an all-too-common experience. "Plebe year I had a roommate from Georgia who had never met a Jew."

When Richard was ten years old he was inspired to attend West Point after reading a catalogue from the Academy that he had picked up at a rummage sale. He was commissioned in the field artillery, fought in Vietnam, became a Ranger, earned a variety of decorations, and served on active duty for 26 years.

In Beast Barracks, one of his roommates was Jewish out of twelve Jews of the 760 cadets in his class. This cadet "reached under his bed and pulled out his suitcase and started packing. I asked him where he was going and he said 'Home!' My roommate and I finally talked him out of going AWOL on the first night. He actually made it through four years and was one of five Jewish cadets to graduate in 1963 out of a class of 504."

Norman M. Smith, '55 gave a response that was typical of most reports of anti-Semitism submitted as "minor." He wrote, "Nothing specific. Slurs, comments. Never anything similar to events which had occurred to me during World War II years." He went on to report, "Out of sheer desperation, armed only with inspiration and no training, I led the Jewish Chapel Choir for over two years, on many trips. One of my stalwarts was a Mormon who joined up because he liked every Sunday breakfasts."

Norman became an infantry officer, fought in Vietnam, received many decorations. He served on active duty for 30 years.

Matthew D. Lampell, '49, my classmate, was one of twenty-one Jewish classmates who responded to the question as follows: "No—none. Quite the reverse—I always felt that there was total acceptance of all cadets by all cadets."

Matt subsequently sent me additional stories that will appear elsewhere in this book. Two of them deserve to be related here because they are examples of Army interfaith relationships and cooperation.

> First, when Muriel and I were married (on June 26) we had the usual 6 ushers—2 of whom were not Jewish. One (if memory serves me correctly, Ray Klemmer) was Catholic and told me afterwards he had gone to his chaplain to ask if he could participate and the chaplain told he [*sic*] that if he didn't "I'll break your neck . . ." And, a couple of years after I left active duty a classmate asked me to get back into uniform and be an usher at his wedding. I told him I probably couldn't because he was probably going to have a marital mass. He told me that he only had two Catholic Ushers . . . when we got there and met with the chaplain, the chaplain asked, "how many fisheaters do I have?" Two held

> their hands up. The chaplain continued, "OK, here's how we'll do it. . . . You'll stay outside the altar railing . . . 3 ushers on each side . . . 2 heathens with a fisheater in the middle . . . and if you're standing and hear me click my cricket, kneal [*sic*] . . . .if you're knealing [*sic*] and hear it, stand . . . .if you get lost, watch the guy in the middle . . . let's go.

(Where there's a will there's a way!)
George M. Dell, '47 relates the following:

> My experience with anti-Semitism was during my Plebe year with one first classman whose room was not in my division but near another Jewish classmate. This upperclassman was the only cadet who had me do push-ups in his room, which in itself was not such a big deal, and he never said anything expressly anti-Semitic. But he had a way of pronouncing words, including my name, which is hard to describe, but left no doubt in my mind. Both of the two roommates of my Jewish classmate had no doubt that this upperclassman was anti-Semitic and still believe it. But time passed, the push-ups ended, and he went away to complete his aviation training.

George entered the Army Air Force upon graduation. He left the Army because his eyes kept him from flight training. He went to law school, eventually was appointed municipal court commissioner, and went on to serve as judge on the Superior Court until he retired eighteen years later. He still hears cases as an arbitrator, mediator, referee, and temporary judge.

Gideon E. Sinasohn, '82 is the son of a retiree from the Army, then Air Force. He responded, "Yes. My first roommate in Beast Barracks. It was not easy to forget, since I was the smallest/lightest cadet and he was recruited as a defensive end on the football team. One of the first things I remember him saying to me was, 'You f—g Jew'. Other experiences were more subtle."

Norman R. Rosen, '47 reported minor experience with anti-Semitism: "I had one roommate who occasionally made a remark. Beyond, I never knowingly experienced any anti-Semitism."

Norman was lay leader for services at sea on a troopship en route to Korea, led services in Japan and Korea, and was lay leader of a congregation in Alaska. He organized and led a military/civilian congregation in Mons, Belgium.

Norman served on active duty for more than twenty-five years in the U.S. Army Corps of Engineers. He fought in Korea and Vietnam. In addition to service medals, he was awarded the Silver Star, Legion of Merit three times, ARVN Honor Medal 1st Class, Navy and ROK Presidential Unit Citations, plus a number of lesser awards. He was named Distinguished Member of the West Point Society of Washington, D.C. He went on to state, "Received far more recognition for contributions to Judaism than I ever received of anti-Semitic problems."

An *anonymous responder* wrote, "A few upperclassmen were openly anti-Semitic. They were a distinct minority and were very poor cadets. One I met on active duty barely made captain before he resigned."

Marvin S. Weinstein, '46 reported, "Probably. Dealt with it as I did before entry. Only direct confrontation was with classmate who [*sic*] I decked and who later apologized."

Marvin served in the Signal Corps for twenty years, served in Korea, and was awarded the Bronze Star.

Isaac Greenberg, '05 had particularly overt experiences. He reported, "Yes. I had been called names such as Hymie, Jewberg and even Kike. During the High Holy time people gave me a hard time for observing my holidays and missing classes. People have a hard time understanding the importance of our holidays and feel free to make a mockery of them."

This was the most overt and outrageous case reported from the cadets of 2005 through '08.

Mark M. Weiman, '71 responded to the question with an interesting comparison, "When I speak to Israelis about their situation they usually answer along the lines of 'you must understand that we live in a tough neighborhood!!' West Point was *not* a tough neighborhood."

Michael K. Stein, '57 responded, "Yes. There were several upperclassmen in my company who thought that Jews were not soldiers."

Michael served for twenty years on active duty in the Signal Corps. He saw combat in Vietnam and was awarded the Bronze Star Medal, Legion of Merit twice, and a Commendation Medal.

Norman H. Rosen, '59 cited the following experience, "Only once from a member of the class of 1958 who resented my observance of Jewish holy days."

S. Peter Stark, '89 related a story that highlights the fact that, no matter how small the group, Jews in a predominantly Christian environment present a high profile for reasons shown in his response. This is not a matter of anti-Semitism.

> During Beast Barracks, I remember being in a regimental formation on the apron every Sunday morning before religious services. The adjutant would call off each religion one by one to form up in a separate formation per the location of their respective religion. Once all service groups were called out, the main formation went from about 1,000 cadets to about 12 Jewish beanheads scattered throughout the length of the apron. The adjutant then told us to fall out and spectators would see the 12 Jews in the class pinging back to their barracks.

Left unsaid in this response is that the Jewish cadets already had attended religious services the previous Friday night.

An *anonymous responder* wrote that he did not experience a personal anti-Semitic act, but witnessed one. "No, but with the exception of my southern company-mates one used the expression, 'Jew him down.' After a discussion I had with him, there were no more incidents."

Abraham Glass, '44 responded to the question in a separate letter, reprinted below verbatim as received:

> Dear Lewis;
>
> I am the last person you should ask about anti-Semitism. I was raised in a community of 4,000 families. The village contained two Jewish families.

I enjoyed the friendship of six boys and their parents. Anti-Semitism never arose.

During my service, I was a company commander in Camp Fanning, Texas. I received a phone call from the Jewish Chaplain asking if I was an anti-Semite.

I had placed charges against a boy who had stole $18.00 from a camp-mate. The mother of the theft [*sic*] contacted the Chaplain claiming that I was an Anti-Semite. I didn't remember seeing the boy at the Chapel.

At West Point, I lived in barracks with two other cadets. Neither were [*sic*] Jewish. They would ask me about the Jewish religion. Anti-Semitism was not a topic.

In 1941, each Cadet had to have a religious faith. There was [*sic*] 12 Jewish Cadets in the Academy. We met each Sunday in a field-house room. I don't think that the smallness of the room was assigned with bias.

Sincerely,
Abe Glass

Abe Glass served on active duty for twenty-one years in the infantry. He fought in World War II and was awarded the Bronze Star and Purple Heart.

Robert Lewis Kaplan, '53 reported, "2x—2 classmates—1 a roommate who quit after Yearling year & and one from PA."

Herbert I. Stein, '41 reported, " 1 instance during Yearling year by a classmate. Conditions at moment, entering a classroom, did not permit me to slug him."

Robert Erlich, '50 reported, "No overt anti-Semitism, but I could tell that many cadets were anti-Semitic, especially in ranking other cadets in military aptitude."

Duquesne A. Wolf, '46 wrote, "I regret to report that the West Point administration and Corps of Cadets in general permitted anti-Semitism as well as racism during the period that I was a cadet (1943–1946). The following two personal experiences will testify to the above charge:

1. First Sunday at USMA—My complexion was as a "blue-eyed blonde" so that I did *not* fit the stereotype of the appearance of Jewish in the eyes of the Christian cadets. Consequently, on my first Sunday at USMA, I proceeded to Central Area where the Jewish Chapel Squad assembled. Being an "eager beaver," I arrived early and as a result I was the only one at the assembly point. Then two upperclassmen from my company (A-2) approached me and insisted that I was at the wrong location for assembly for Cadet Chapel. Only after I insisted that I was Jewish, did they relent and hurry away.
2. Some 2-1/2 years later, I was asked to advise my cadet Company Commander, and several cadet lieutenants of my cadet company (A-2) regarding their desire to attempt to harass a Jewish 4th Classman (Plebe) in order to force him to resign. I was shocked to learn of this despickable [*sic*] plan, and needless to say I not only advised them against such un-American conduct; but I lectured them on the meaning of Democracy—and that such conduct was unworthy of the noble institution of West Point. The [*sic*] were ashamed of their plan and agreed to treat this Jewish 4th Classman fairly and not single him out for special treatment or hazing. I should add that this Jewish 4th Classman came from a very fine family, and indeed, I had the privilege of meeting his parents who were very worried about their son and his complaints of unfair treatment. I reassured them that I would watch over him to see that no unfair treatment or hazing would occur in the future; and this 4th Classman survived his Plebe year; and I am sure he graduated with honors since he was especially bright and intelligent.

Colonel Wolf served on active duty for twenty-eight years in the infantry, cavalry, and armored corps. He fought in Korea and in Vietnam. He earned a master of science degree in nuclear physics.

Alan D. Sapowith, '47 reported "Some anti-Semitism" from three upperclassmen in his subdivision during his plebe year.

Alvin J. Marrow, '63 reported, "Just some off-color remarks."

Marshall Sanger, '46. Unfortunately, Marshall died in July 2004 without my knowledge of his death and before my questionnaire was mailed in February 2005. His wife, Lila, kindly undertook the task of filling out the questionnaire and mailing it to me. On March 10, 2005 Mrs. Sanger wrote a cover letter to me transmitting the executed questionnaire with two outstanding articles attached: "You and the Army," published in the *Brooklyn Jewish Center Review* (date unknown) and "All of Which We Ask . . . " published in the *Pointer* on December 14, 1945. The *Pointer* is a magazine produced by the cadets for the cadets.

In the first article, Marshall wrote of his experiences in the Army and at West Point. Regarding the latter, he wrote: "As a Plebe I was told that I was no good, that I would never be any good, and that the United States Army could never do a thing with me, yet never once did I ever hear anybody give me the works because of my religion. That holds true for three years of listening to Plebes take it. They always took it, but never did they have to hear anything that might be called unfair."

Both articles are worthwhile reading. This was similar to my own experience during all four years that I was a cadet (1945–1949).

Colonel Sanger served on active duty in the infantry for thirty years. He fought in Korea and Vietnam, earning the Bronze Star Medal, Legion of Merit, and Commendation Medal three times each, the Air Medal, Joint Services Commendation Medal, and the Meritorious Service Medal.

Gill H. Ruderman, '66 responded, "Not really.—See enclosed."

The "enclosed" was part of a chapter about Gill Ruderman from *Duty, Honor, Vietnam: Twelve Men of West Point* by Ivan Prashker. The portion that Gill sent to me was devoted to his cadet years. The chapter opens, "It wasn't hard being a Jew at West Point." Parts of the remainder of the enclosure will appear elsewhere in this book.

Colonel Ruderman retired after more than twenty-six years on active duty in the field artillery. He saw combat during two tours in Vietnam, where he was awarded the Bronze Star Medal for Valor, the Legion of Merit, Purple Heart twice, and the Joint Services Commendation Medal. He has a master's degree in psychology.

Doug L. Lenhoff, '80 was recruited to play football, probably not a man to be easily intimidated. He responded, "Not really, although one of my favorite stories is how my Beast roommate used to stay up late at night. When I asked him why he didn't go to sleep when I did, he said he wanted to see my horns come out at night."

Gregory M. Babitz, '68 related this unfortunate experience: "Yes. I had one roommate that grew up in a private boarding school in the south. He continually made anti-Semitic jokes and comments to me. Despite my protests, he would not stop. When I complained to the upperclassmen, I was the bad guy for wanting a room change. While I and the former roommate remained friends, I could not live with him."

Harold H. Lusky, '60 responded, "Not overtly—However I was approximately 110th out of 550 academically but was 291st out of 550 overall. I was always rated last in my company in the cadet ratings (Co. B-2)—I was not the worst cadet militarily or socially—I was the youngest in my company—not a member of the Protestant or Catholic cliques."

Harold served on active duty in the field artillery for seven and one-half years. He saw combat in Vietnam (MACV) and was awarded the Bronze Star (Vn) and the Army Commendation Medal.

David J. Bucchieri, '67 reported overt anti-Semitism during his plebe year, "Super Jew Poop: usually recited in the Area (of barracks) at the top of my lungs for the amusement of the Gentile cadets." The ditty ran as follows:

> Abie, Ikey, Lukie, Sam
> We're the boys who don't eat ham
> Pennies, pennies pinch 'em tight
> Synagogue, Synagogue, fight, fight, fight.
>
> Look up in the sky
> Faster than a flying gefilte fish
> More powerful than a local rabbi
> Able to leap tall synagogues in a single bound
> It's Super Jew.

David served in the field artillery on active duty for eleven years, including combat in Vietnam. He was awarded the Bronze Star Medal and the Army Commendation Medal.

Note that his is the only report of outrageous "poetry" I have received.

Anonymous response from a member of the Class of '81, "I absolutely NEVER saw any anti-Semitism. As a matter of fact, I think our great institution is one of the fairest, performance based meritocracy [*sic*] in this country."

Jay A. Harris, '80 reported, "No anti-Semitism, but a lot of ignorance from those who were not familiar with the Jewish culture and religion. During my Plebe year I had a roommate from Nebraska. The only Jew in his town was the local banker. He really had no exposure to Jews. We got along fine, but he did admit to me he was looking for horns and a tail!" Jay went on to describe an event that had a most pleasant outcome:

> We met on the balcony of Ike Hall [Eisenhower Hall]. A cadet friend was there with two young ladies. They were from the University of Maryland. Judi had a brother who was a Plebe. Frank was a good friend. He said to me, "Jay, she is one of you." I asked him to explain himself. He said, "She is a 'Juliet-Alpha-Papa'."—military letters for JAP (meaning Jewish American Princess). Before I could say a word, she shouted out, "I am not!" I knew at that moment that this young lady was special. She ended up being my wife. We have been happily married for the past 20 years.

Irwin Steinberg, '50 reported, "Yes—but very minor from certain cadets in upperclasses in my company."

Norman F. Katz, '49, my classmate, reported overt anti-Semitism while a cadet. I was totally unaware of his experience until I received his questionnaire. He stated,

> Yes. As a Plebe in Company K-2 I received many demerits (86 in one month) and was required to face a Regimental Board for possible dismissal. As the upperclass comments were being read out loud, one comment, "This cadet displays poor racial characteristics," caused the board to adjourn. My father called me that night and when he heard what had been said, he prevailed on Congressman Arthur Klein to look into the matter. The next day Congress-

> man Klein had a meeting with the Superintendent, Major General Maxwell Taylor. When the congressman told the Supe my tale, my records were requested. The offending comment was not in the record. Queries to the President of the Board determined that the comment had been pulled as not being appropriate. I was transferred to Company I-2 immediately. I later found that my K-2 roommate had been ordered to not help me in any way as the upperclassmen and the Tactical Officer wanted to get rid of the "Jew". Another example—in Beast Barracks, the only Jewish Plebes in my company were made roommates by fiat. At the time it seemed to be a coincidence to 3 very naïve cadets, but the kind of attention we received made it clear that it was not by happenstance.

Norman's eighty-six demerits exceeded the maximum of twenty allowed for a month and would have required him to walk sixty-six one-hour punishment tours on the Area of Barracks, a large concrete-paved enclosure. He went on to report, "Luckily for me, the President of Chile visited the Academy and requested amnesty. I didn't walk any of the otherwise required 66 tours. At the end of Plebe year, just to be sure that I had that experience, I was given a Plebe tour and walked one hour just before Recognition."

This report is one of a very few reports involving a member of the staff and faculty as one of the perpetrators.

Colonel Norman F. Katz served twenty-nine years on active duty in the Air Force. He served in the Korean and Vietnam wars. He was awarded the Legion of Merit twice, the Bronze Star Medal, the Meritorious Service Medal, and the Air Force Commendation Medal.

Murray B. Blume, '54 reported, "Yes, mildly not seriously."

Herbert Y. Schandler, '52 reported, "No. In fact, fifty years later I find that most of my classmates didn't know or care."

Alan Sheinwald, '87 reported, "Ignorance—not anti-Semitism. Everyone thought my family was in banking or jewelry business."

Ethan Mordechai Orwin, '07, still a cadet when he reported, "No, not really. Many people were ignorant about Judaism, but they were curious rather than intolerant. When one friend was amazed to hear that Jews didn't believe in the divinity of Christ, he exclaimed, 'Come on man, the dude walked on water!'"

Sheldon J. Lustig, '53 emphatically responded, "*NO*."

Aaron Scott Atterman, '04 responded, "No, I did not experience anything I would consider anti-Semitism. Occasionally someone would make an inappropriate comment, but as long as I said something they did not continue. I found that most people were curious about Judaism and more wanted to ask questions and educate themselves then [*sic*] run on ignorance."

Robert B. Rosenkranz, '61 reported, "Very minor; occasional derisive remarks."

Major General Robert B. Rosenkranz served in the field artillery on active duty for thirty-four years. He fought in the Vietnam War and was awarded the Distinguished Service Medal, Bronze Star Medal, Legion of Merit, and the Air Medal.

Edwin M. Joseph, '46 reported, "No. Occasionally some upperclassman during our Plebe year announced privately that they were anti-Semitic but I attributed it to their ignorance before coming to West Point. I was always treated the same as our fellow classmates."

Lieutenant Colonel Edwin M. Joseph served on active duty for twenty-one years in the field artillery. He fought in the Korean War. His awards include the Silver Star, Bronze Star Medal, the Air Medal, Purple Heart, Army Commendation Medal twice, and a Joint Commendation Award.

Howard Prescott, '54 reported, "From an upperclassman in my company. Took him 4 wall (no windows) and broke his nose."

Louis Gross, '54 did not experience an anti-Semitic act, but he reported, "After Graduation ceremony a company mate (from rural Kansas) whom I had coached in academics introduced me to his parents with the statement, 'This is Louis Gross, and he's Jewish.' His mother looked at me intensely and asked her son, 'What's Jewish?' "

Lou Gross is a close friend and colleague in our work in the West Point Jewish Community and at the Academy at large. He is past president of the West Point Jewish Chapel Fund and has donated substantial time and treasure to these projects. An athletic center near Michie Stadium bears his name in consideration for his contribution to this project. The facility houses the gymnastics team and other activities. He has been an active participant in many other capital projects at West Point.

Lawrence G. Michalove, '55 reported emphatically, "None at all!"

Lieutenant Colonel Michalove served on active duty in the Air Force for twenty-two years. He fought in Vietnam and was awarded the Distinguished Flying Cross twice and eight Air Medals.

Gary Bloomberg, '89 reported, "Never anything behind [*sic*] common [*sic*] jokes associated with Jewish stereotypes. Do not think that most cadets knew/cared that I was Jewish."

Edward C. West, '50 reported, "One small (teeny) incident with a Tactical Officer—not worth even talking about."

Colonel West served on active duty in the Corps of Engineers for twenty-two years. He served in Korea, where he was awarded the Bronze Star Medal for Valor, Legion of Merit three times, and the Commendation Medal.

Steven Wade Rotkoff, '77 reported, "My Beast roommate was a Born-Again-Christian and felt it was his obligation to 'save my soul'. It was my first encounter with this ATTITUDE/BELIEF (having grown up in NYC and suburbs). It was not until we came to blows that he quit."

Attached to Steve's questionnaire was a letter to me:

> Dear Mr. Zickel,
>
> Thank you for the opportunity to contribute to your work regarding the experiences of Jewish cadets at West Point. Next under are a random collection of stories based on my experiences both as a cadet and later in the Army. I hope you find them of use. Steve Rotkoff '77
>
> During my Plebe year ('73) the gas crisis was in full bloom. One day at lunch the table com started to rant about how the increased price of gas was making it difficult for him to afford cruising during the weekends and that crisis was the fault of the Jews. He then went into a polemic about how Israel had no valid right to exist and should be pushed into the sea etc. Being a Plebe I was

uncertain how to respond and quite unthinkingly began to sing Hava Nagila. As you can imagine, this got everyone's attention. When asked what I was doing, I said something to the effect that I was Jewish and that I completely disagreed with the table com's assertions. To his credit rather than focus on my singing we engaged in a free and open debate. At the end of the conversation he grudgingly admitted that maybe Israel had the right to exist but that gas prices still sucked!

Also during my Plebe year we were asked to submit candidates for class mottos. Just for laughs I submitted "Bread without leaven . . . 77." It did not win.

As I am sure you will hear from many, Shabbat services during Beast and Plebe year in general were a lifesaver—salami, bagels, lox, herring, it was a smorgasbord of Jewish ethnic food but most importantly it was food! Although we were supposedly the first Beast class without food denial, I lost 33 pounds that summer—who knows what I'd have lost without the local NY JVFW [Jewish Veterans of Foreign Wars]. My memories of services will always be linked to the Bartlett Hall chemistry lab. Whoever arrived first was supposed to move the Bunsen burners and replace them with the portable ark. The visiting rabbi, when we had one, usually used the instructor's lab table at the front of the room as a bema. While services were spiritually comforting and a bit of home, they also [were] what stood between us and the oneg. I'm sure we looked liked wolves on a kill. I know later when I was an upperclassman I noted how ravenously plebes attacked the oneg—I'm sure I did as well, but I was too focused on eating to notice.

In my time as a cadet it was usual to have bus trips to local communities for the High Holy Days. I only participated my plebe and yearling year, both because I did not have the freedom to worship at home (no weekends or passes allowed) and because like all other cadets in that all male environment I was going on trips (religious and otherwise) mostly in "cherchez les femmes."

(I was terrible in French—so odds are this is misspelled!) Shortly after the following High Holy Day season of my yearling year I met my future wife, so I discontinued Jewish religious trips.

Following tradition, Libby and I were married the day after graduation. However, as there was no Jewish chapel we were married in the old chapel in the cemetery. For those who never experienced West Point telling them that you were married in the middle of a cemetery is always good for a raised eyebrow.

What follows are experiences in the Army (post graduation) which were directly related to my being Jewish.

My first unit of assignment I worked for a BN CDR [battalion commander] (LTC [Lieutenant Colonel] Walter Daniel) who was promoted to LT [lieutenant] as a mustang during Vietnam. He had grown up in the hills of West Virginia and after he was commissioned received his college degree mostly by correspondence. He was the best BN CDR I ever served with during my 26 year career and was one of the prime reasons I stayed for a career. One of the things he taught me was that there was a large population in the US that had never encountered Jews (he having been one of them at one time). At one time he seriously believed that Jews had horns based on what his mother taught him, her evidence being Michelangelo's David [*sic*]. He was a backwoods informally educated man who by all rights should have been a bigot but believed truly in judging everyone by the "content of their character". He taught me that people are more than their background and that the Army's underlying philosophy of loyalty to your men, your unit and the mission was a great equalizer that enabled people to become color and ethnicity blind.

Another key character I ran into in this same BN [battalion] was (then) Major Jack Jacobs, a Jewish Medal of Honor recipient and the XO [executive officer] of the BN. Jacobs was from the same part of Brooklyn I had grown up in and we had a similarly sick sense of humor. While he was an experienced and highly decorated combat vet and I was only a LT wet behind the ears, we still became fast friends. In addition to serving together we went to temple together in Monterey (we were assigned to the 7th ID [Infantry Division]) and after he left the BN he asked me to be the best man at his wedding. He is our son's godfather.

In 1990–91 I remembered back to LTC Daniel and seized an opportunity to educate some of my fellow soldiers. I was assigned to the 3ID [3rd Infantry Division] in Würzburg, Germany. In the period leading up to Desert Storm the Rabbis assigned to Europe had been moved to the Mideast. The military had only recently begun Holocaust Remembrance and the Berlin Wall had recently fallen. These coupled, led me to the idea of putting together a trip to Buchenwald in the recently opened East Germany. I convinced the 3ID's EO [executive officer] office to fund buses and got the Division Commander to authorize any soldiers attending the trip the day off. We ended up taking 11 busloads—approximately 500 soldiers. I was able to get the assistance of a local German who was a Jewish historian and we stopped at several historic points on the way. When we got to Buchenwald, based on earlier arrangement, the soldiers were shown an English language film of the liberation of the camp by Patton's Third Army. As I circulated through the group I overheard several soldiers who when viewing the pictures of stacked corpses, and ovens etc. exclaim that they had never heard of the Holocaust and had never been exposed to what it really was.

In 1995 I was assigned to Ft Hood as a battalion commander. I was distressed to find out that despite the fact that Ft Hood is the home of the most soldiers of any post in the world and is remote from any Jewish community it had no assigned Rabbi. At the time the Army had 8 active duty rabbis. They were assigned in a variety of locations many of which had a much larger local Jewish population, while Ft Hood which was the home of at least 100 active duty Jewish families and over 100 retired families made due [*sic*] with a lay leader. I lobbied the Chief of Chaplains and a year later they assigned a newly commissioned Rabbi to Ft Hood.

In typical Army fashion they decided that the chapel my BN sponsored would become the Jewish chapel and I became the Rabbi's mentor into military life. Years later I would return to command the Brigade my earlier BN had been part of and was pleased to discover that the assignment of the Rabbi to Ft Hood had become routine and that the Kosher kitchen for the chapel that I had requisitioned as a BN commander had come to fruition.

The bottom line for me is that being a soldier and being a Jew have been compatible from the beginning. One of [the] things I love about both is that while neither is on the surface about social work and pulling up the less advantaged they both share this strong secondary theme. **Judaism made me a better officer and the army made me a better Jew.**

I hope the material I have provided will be of help to you. Please don't hesitate to contact me if I can help.

Steve Rotkoff

There are interesting and important lessons to be learned from Steve's story. The United States Army must have Jewish officers for the benefit of Jewish soldiers and for the benefit of the ethnic diversity that is an important part of our free society. American soldiers do not fight for the flag, of for a cause. They fight for the soldiers to their right and to their left and for their unit. Therefore they must respect all of these soldiers, regardless of their diverse religions or ethnic origins. Knowledge of Jews, understanding our holidays and some Judaic history is necessary if comfortable relationships are to develop in military units between Jewish and non-Jewish soldiers.

Colonel Steven Wade Rotkoff served on active duty in Army intelligence for twenty-six years. He served in Bosnia, Operation Iraqi Freedom, and Kosovo. He was the deputy combined G-2 [intelligence staff officer] for all ground forces (Combined Forces Land Component Command) during Operation Iraqi Freedom. Prior to that, he commanded the 504th Military Intelligence Brigade at Fort Hood Texas. He was awarded the Legion of Merit three times, the Meritorious Service Medal six times, the Army Commendation Medal, and the Army Achievement Medal.

Justin L. Raphael, '03 reported, "Yes. During Military Intersession my finance instructor warned the class about used car salesmen "jewing us [officers] down." I immediately called her on it and received a full apology and she apologized to the class."

Kevin Price, '97 wrote, "Not really. There was some ignorance and curiosity. A lot of people asked if I experienced any anti-Semitism at West Point or in the Army. The answer is, 'Not really.' I met a lot of people who had never met a Jewish person before, but mostly they were intellectually curious. As is the case with most minorities, once people get to know you, it makes very little difference what religion you are."

Captain Kevin Price served in Kuwait and Afghanistan. He was awarded the Bronze Star Medal, Army Commendation Medal, and Army Achievement Medal.

Herman S. Marman, '60 responded, "Yes. Where are your horns? Where is your tail? Jew Bastard . . . Not institutionally."

Lieutenant Colonel Marman served on active duty in the field artillery for twenty-one years. He served three tours in Vietnam. He was awarded the Bronze Star Medal three times, the Air Medal, the Legion of Merit, and the Commendation Medal twice.

Jeffrey Moss Oettinger, '84 responded, "No—the cadet life style was hard enough; mutual respect for different races, religions, background was the rule."

Major Oettinger was sent to medical school upon graduation from West Point. He served on active duty for eighteen years in the Medical Corps as a physician.

Kenneth I Pressman, '48 responded with some interesting experiences:

> No—but see the following:
>
> 1. During Beast Barracks we had two black Plebes in our company. An upperclassman called us together (less two) and told us that the custom was to not speak to them, but it was voluntary. We discussed, felt that they were putting up with all that we were and voted not to exclude them.

2. We had a hot soccer rivalry with the US Naval Academy. During my senior year, I played only half the game at Annapolis, having injured my ankle earlier in the season. While on the bench I could hear some Middies howling ethnic invectives at our coach, Joe Palone, a wonderful man. For example, "Wop, guinea, paisan," etc. I almost went into the stands. Later on, while I was in the game, one of the Navy players deliberately kneed a teammate in the head. That's all it took. I ran over, slugged him, called him some words. The crowd came on the field. He was thrown out—I wasn't. Quite a stir!!! At our 50th Class reunion those of us from the soccer team had lunch with Joe. Afterwards we were chatting and he said to me, "Ken, you were always my tough guy."—a wonderful man.

Ken Pressman is the brother of my cousin by marriage. He is, indeed, a tough guy.

Ramona Fastow, '05 reported, "Not anti-Semitism, just a profound ignorance of Jewish culture, as well as a very noticeable lack of separation between church and state—West Point is quite a Christian institution." She continued, "Humorous: when I was a new cadet during Beast, one of my squad mates found out that I was Jewish. He said, ' Wow, you're Jewish! Doesn't that mean that you can't eat Pizza?' "

Second Lieutenant Romona Fastow had an outstanding academic and military record as a cadet. She served on the West Point Jewish Community Council, where she was a major force in organizing Hillel and other cadet activities. As president of the council, I witnessed her extensive contributions first hand.

David I. Malkin, '98 responded, "No—In fact I was impressed with the reaction of fellow cadets to my being Jewish. A number of them noted (happily) that I was the first Jew they had ever personally known."

David Persselin, '85 responded, "No. In fact I found non-Jewish cadets to be relatively supportive. When we had separate Kosher tables during Passover, a lot of non-Jewish cadets signed up to sit at them because they were interested in learning more."

Philip W. Ackerman, '58 responded cryptically, "None at all!"

David Niekerk, '78 reported the following experiences regarding anti-Semitism:

> Overall very positive but had two significant events. My Plebe year my squad leader made my life very difficult and tried to haze me out of the Academy saying, "I know what your kind of people are looking for from West Point, an easy two years of free education and then you leave." I had to go before a board of officers as a result of the harassment. One of the officers asked me why I was wearing "red shoes" as an implication being a Jew meant I was "red". The other officer just looked at him and quickly moved the line of questioning on to different topics.

David went on to serve ten years in the Regular Army and then joined the Army Reserve. His parents immigrated to the United States from the Netherlands in 1952 as Dutch Holocaust survivors.

Bradley C. Harrison, '94 reported, "No, but did meet people that had either never met a Jew or were surprised to have Jews at West Point."

Roger Kaplan, '75 wrote, "Minor. Usually comments like 'why are we so Jewish with our funds' from people who were mostly rural and possibly never met anyone Jewish. This occurred while discussing the budget of the Military Affairs Club in 1972. When my table commandant (Class of '72) asked a classmate for his dessert, the table com said, 'You Jew!' When I told him that I was Jewish, he said, 'Sorry about that Kaplan.' "

Eric Billig, '81 wrote, "No, I was approached by Christians who tried to get me to accept Jesus as my Savior and become born again in Christ. On December 12th 2000 I did accept Christ as my Savior and became a Christian."

Joshua Lubarsky, '96 wrote, "Minor—mostly ignorance such as resistance to allowing me to go to services and problems on Sunday mornings during Beast Barracks. There were some cadets who I think held religion against me, but would not/did not say it to my face."

Ronald I. Karp, '72 wrote, "No although there was [*sic*] some comments that I categorized as normal teasing. Since I was the CIC (Cadet in Charge) of the Jewish Chapel Squad, I was sometimes referred to as the 'KOJ' or 'King of the Jews.' "

Avram Isaacson, '96 wrote, "Yes, when I was a Cow (junior year) I was running on Flirtation Walk and noticed that somebody had painted red swastikas on the rocks in several places. I went back to my TAC and TAC NCO (Tactical non-commissioned officer) and reported the incident. It was gone the same day and they made every effort to address it."

Lawrence G. Bronstein, '73 wrote, "Yes, many cadets had never met a Jew before attending West Point. Some came with preconceived hatreds or prejudices. Most did not occur until Yearling Year. Snide or crude remarks sometimes were made in the barracks. Thos [*sic*] soon ended after the offending parties slipped in the shower; never heard another word from them. At least they kept their anti-Semitism quiet."

Lieutenant Colonel Bronstein served on active duty for twenty-three years in the military police. He received the Legion of Merit, the Meritorious Service Medal four times, the Army Commendation Medal, Army Achievement Medal, and the Humanitarian Service Medal.

Mark A. Edelman, '68 wrote:

> There was only one incident that happened to me, other than a few catcalls, as the Jewish Chapel Squad would march to Sunday morning services over the four years I was at West Point.
>
> The incident I remember was in my Plebe year, right after Beast Barracks. I moved into my new company room and I had two roommates. We met for the first time. At that meeting, one of my new roommates said to me, "Hi, my name is Bob Smith (not his real name) and I am from Alabama. And I hate Blacks, Jews and Catholics in that order."
>
> I said, "Bob, we have a problem. I am definitely not Black, but I am Jewish."
>
> Bob was dumbfounded, as he probably thought I was going to say I was a Catholic. He told me that he had never met a Jew be-

fore. He also told me that his father taught him that Jews had horns as well as cash registers in their basements.

Needless to say, Bob needed a little education in 1968 [*sic*]. I showed him my head, no horns!! And we became the best of friends over the next four years.

Adam R. Sasso, '05 reported,

During cadet Basic Training, we would form up after Breakfast on Sunday mornings for church services. The Catholics would form up in one platoon area, the Protestants in another, and all those not going to church would form up in the rear of the formation. One Sunday, my cadet First Sergeant came over to the group not attending church and told us "You're all a bunch of heathens and your blatant lack of religion disgusts me." I was infuriated over the comment but kept it to myself. I vented my frustration to my roommates who told my squad leader what happened. My squad leader consulted the Respect Representative in the company, who said this was a clear violation of the Bedrock Value of Respect. As a result, the cadet First Sergeant had to make a formal apology to the company. I honestly don't think he made this comment out of anti-Semitism, but rather from a lack of understanding of other cultures and religions. This incident had such a powerful impression on me that I knew I wanted to be involved in the Respect Committee. I ran for and was elected to be my company Respect Representative Yearling year, and the following year I was chosen to chair the Committee as the Brigade Respect Captain during Firstie (senior) year. In this capacity I've tried to make others more aware of the many cultures in the Army as well as the nations to which we will deploy.

Second Lieutenant Adam R. Sasso graduated in 2005 and was sent to the Uniformed Services University of Health Sciences Medical School to study medicine. He will serve in the Medical Corps when he becomes a physician.

I left his comments for last because they lead into the discussion in the next portion of this narrative, which addresses the steps taken and being taken at West Point to confront and eliminate discriminatory acts in the Corps of Cadets.

Bedrock Values Programs: Honor and Respect

In 1992 Lieutenant General Robert Foley, then brigadier general, commandant of cadets, and Medal of Honor recipient during the war in Vietnam, observed certain aspects of cadet behavior that he considered unacceptable. He noted the prevalent lack of mutual respect and consideration. Cadets would borrow things from each other without returning them. At the high end of the spectrum he noted extreme gender bias now that women were members of the Corps and had been for twenty years. General Foley knew from experience that soldiers fight for each other in battle—for the soldiers on either side of them—and therefore that it is essential for soldiers to respect one other. These observations prompted him to cause the adoption of the bedrock value "Consideration of Others" as a leadership issue. It was formalized into the "Consideration of Others Program" in 1994. In 1998 it was renamed the "Respect Program." Cadet Captain Sasso became the chair of the Respect Program Advisory Council, the highest-ranking cadet in the Respect Program chain of leadership. The genesis of the program was explained to me by Lieutenant Colonel Dave Jones during a telephone conversation on February 14, 2005.

Dave had witnessed the launching of the program and headed it for several years as the first officer in charge. He explained that the Respect Program was presented together with the Honor Program, long a bedrock value of West Point. Initially, Honor was Bedrock Value Number 1 and Respect was Bedrock Value Number 2. Shortly thereafter it was noted that one could infer from this stated sequence of the two programs that Respect was subordinated to Honor. This was not the intent. Both programs were reidentified as "The Bedrock of West Point is Honor and Respect." He sent me the official literature on the program and its history from which the following information was extracted:

Each year from 1995 through 2002 the program was enhanced with positive improvements and developments sequentially listed below in the order they were added or refined:

Established "Consideration of Others" education teams in companies.

Established new brigade staff positions / published three-volume resource books.

Established special assistant to the commandant for respect (SAR) and equal opportunity advisor position (NCO).

Established the Center for Professional Military Ethics and initiated Respect Program Advisory Council training with the Defense Equal Opportunity Management Institute during graduation week.

Initiated commandant's sensing sessions with focus groups and established "Respect Representative" positions in each regiment.

Introduced computer education program "Saving Sergeant Pabletti" date rape psychodrama; includes lecture by Katie Koestner, nationally recognized anti-date-rape advocate. That year, 2000, the Simon Center for the Professional Military Ethic (SCPME) initiated the Respect Mentorship Program.

Established vice chair for mentorship.

SCPME hired Dr. Murial Bebeau, University of Minnesota, as a visiting scholar to assist in character-development assessment and evaluation.

The Respect Program Advisory Council (RPAC), established in 1998, is charged with the following objectives as the liaison between the Corps of Cadets and the commandant in dealing with issues of cadet character development to ensure that cadets:

Understand and internalize respect for other genders, cultures, and ethnicities.

Leave the Academy better prepared to lead soldiers—they can think critically and resolve issues within their units.

> Are aware of and support the concepts of equal opportunity and non-toleration of discrimination. They recognize that a diverse Army is a strong Army.

All cadets receive fifty hours of values and ethics training in small-group discussion-oriented classes. Respect education included the following:

> *Embracing Diversity:* Cadets are encouraged to embrace diversity through education on biases and cultural observance events. Discrimination based on race, religion, ethnicity, gender, or national origin is prevented.
>
> *Conflict Resolution:* Each of the thirty-two academic year companies has two "respect representatives" to help cadets resolve conflicts and, more importantly, educate cadets on *how* to solve conflicts as future leaders.
>
> *Prevention of Sexual Assault and Harassment:* Cadets are actively informed of resources available and their responsibility to prevent this unacceptable behavior.
>
> *Health Awareness:* Cadets are educated on responsible alcohol use and made aware of resources for substance abuse, STDs, and eating disorders.
>
> *Respect Mentorship:* The Mentorship Program is a six-month reflection under the supervision of a mentor that encourages cadets to identify and address shortcomings in personal adherence to Army Values. The Cadet Honor Committee includes a similar mentorship program. (There are seven listed Army Values in *Army Field Manual 22-100, Leadership*: Loyalty, Duty, Respect, Selfless Service, Honor, Integrity, and Personal Courage.)

The RPAC chair is a brigade-level cadet captain, the position held by Adam Sasso during academic year 2004–05. The "respect captain" has a staff of six cadets: RPAC vice chair, executive officer, vice chair for operations, vice chair for membership, vice chair for information systems, vice chair for health awareness, and vice chair for respect education. The respect captain advises the commandant of cadets, the first captain, and the special assistant to the commandant for respect on all matters within the Corps of Cadets relating to respect and is responsible for respect education in the entire Corps or brigade. The 4,000 cadets in the Corps are divided among four regiments consisting of eight battalions totaling thirty-two companies.

The entire program is set forth in Section 320, Respect Program Advisory Council, of the Regulations of the U.S. Corps of Cadets. Section 319 relates to the Honor Program.

This program is a monumental undertaking for the respect captain and his six staff officers. The program by its objectives and execution, is a proactive step to prevent, or to at least minimize, discriminatory behavior. The program is a credit to the Academy and the Army. The bedrock values of the United States Military Academy are truly Honor and Respect.

Religion at West Point

A very important part of the mission of the United States Military Academy at West Point is to develop outstanding, highly educated leaders with the highest standards of morality, strong values, and in excellent physical condition. A person with these attributes is often referred to as a Renaissance person; sound of mind, body, and spirit. Religion has always been considered a major component of these desired attributes. Hence, attendance at chapel was mandatory at West Point until a young graduate from a prestigious military family sued the government for violating several items in the Bill of Rights of the Constitution by its mandatory chapel attendance policy. The Supreme Court agreed with the plaintiff and found in 1972 compulsory attendance at religious services unconstitutional. Chapel attendance became voluntary, and at the same time it also became illegal to force anyone to declare a religious preference. Such revelations, too, became voluntary. Formerly, placing a soldier's religious preference on his or her dog tags was routine; today the soldier must decide whether or not to do so.

For about the first hundred years at the Academy, the religion practiced in the Cadet Chapel was nonsectarian, at least across the lines of the various Christian Protestant sects. There were a small number of Catholics and few Jews in the Corps. All were required to attend the Cadet Chapel services every Sunday. In perspective, the first Catholics entered West Point about 1810, some eight years after the first Jewish cadet. The first Native American graduated in the Class of 1806. I have no data on other religious groups represented at the Academy during its early years.

Toward the close of the nineteenth century, the Catholic population had grown along with the large Irish migration to the United States. Many of the enlisted soldiers and housemaids on the post were Irish Catholic immigrants. There was a corresponding increase in the Catholic cadet population. Nevertheless, there was no provision for formal Catholic worship. Catholic officers, enlisted men, families, and maids were forced to attend the only chapel on the post; services that were primarily Protestant-based and devoid of Catholic liturgy and ceremony. The Jewish cadets were faced with the same dilemma.

The Cadet Chapel, an impressive Greek Revival edifice, was constructed in 1836. It virtually drips with early American history. The interior walls are adorned with bronze plaques memorializing the generals of the American Revolution, including one for George Washington and one for Benedict Arnold, our first traitor. Arnold's name has been gouged out of his plaque in punishment for his perfidy in his thwarted attempt to sell West Point to the British. On the left interior wall is a plaque donated by the Jewish War Veterans memorializing Joseph Swift and Simon Levy of the Class of 1802, the first class to graduate from West Point.

When the current Cadet Chapel was opened in 1910 (the tall imposing military gothic structure on the hill overlooking the central post), the Old Cadet Chapel was moved stone by stone to a new site where it stands guard over the entrance to the Post Cemetery. It is currently the home of the Lutheran community and houses a columbarium in the basement.

As their community grew, the Catholics felt that the Cadet Chapel program did not meet their spiritual needs, particularly the need for a resident priest to conduct services, counsel members of the community, hear confession, take communion, and officiate at weddings, baptisms, and burials. The Catholics needed a chapel and chaplain of their own. In the Armed Forces of the United States, houses of worship, called "chapels," constructed with federal funds are required by law to be non-sectarian, not to be dedicated to any one religious group or sect. More than one religious group usually uses such a chapel on a rotation basis. However, this type of rotation did not fit the scheduling and use of the single chapel at West Point.

Never had there been a sectarian chapel built on a U.S. military reservation. Therefore, the archdiocese of New York sought help from Congress to authorize the construction of a Catholic Chapel at West Point. Congress passed a law in 1899 authorizing the diocese to construct a chapel "for officers, cadets, soldiers and maids." However, because of the doctrine of the separation of church and state, the U.S. government could fund neither the construction of the chapel nor its maintenance. Nonappropriated funds were required from nongovernmental sources to make the chapel a reality. Those funds had to be raised by the diocese of New York. Eighty years later, the Jewish Chapel was built under the same provisions of the law of 1899, all with donated money.

Chapel attendance was mandatory. Once the Catholic Chapel was built, there were two chapels available. Therefore, when a new cadet entered the Academy, he was asked, "Mister, which chapel do you wish to attend?" He was not asked what his religious preference was. An answer was required on the spot. This posed a dilemma for the Jewish cadets. They found themselves attending what was essentially a Protestant service every Sunday morning. Now that the Catholics were on their own, the nonsectarian services in the Cadet Chapel were becoming less so.

In 1922 Chaplain Clayton E. Wheat wrote a magnificent piece of prose, the Cadet Prayer, believed by cadets and others to be truly nonsectarian in nature. Because it is not specifically Judaic or Christian but adheres to the Judeo-Christian ethic, it is a piece that can be recited by anyone, regardless of particular religious belief, without violating most sectarian precepts or beliefs. Every cadet was exposed to the Cadet Prayer in an information-packed booklet titled *Bugle Notes* given to new cadets upon arrival at the Academy. In former years new cadets were required to memorize the prayer at the start of Cadet Basic Training, often called

Beast Barracks. Despite its poetic beauty and nonsectarian character, it does not truly fulfill the spiritual needs of Jewish cadets. I would expect that this holds true for other religious groups. New cadets are no longer required to memorize the prayer. It is reproduced here in its original form.

> O God our Father, Thou Searcher of men's hearts, help us to draw near to Thee in sincerity and truth. May our religion be filled with gladness and may our worship of Thee be natural.
>
> Strengthen and increase our admiration for honest dealing and clean thinking, and suffer not our hatred of hypocrisy and pretense ever to diminish. Encourage us in our endeavor to live above the common level of life. Make us to choose the harder right instead of the easier wrong, and never to be content with the half truth when the whole can be won. Endow us with courage that is born of loyalty, to all that is noble and worthy, that scorns to compromise with vice and injustice and knows no fear when truth and right are in jeopardy. Guard us against flippancy and irreverence in the sacred things of life. Grant us new ties of friendship with new opportunities of service. Kindle our hearts in fellowship with those of a cheerful countenance, and soften our hearts with sympathy for those who sorrow and suffer. May we find genuine pleasure in clean and wholesome mirth and feel disgust for all coarse-minded humor. Help us, in our work and in our play to keep ourselves physically strong, mentally awake, and morally straight, that we may better maintain the honor of the Corps untarnished and unsullied, and acquit ourselves like men in our effort to realize the ideals of West Point in doing our duty to Thee and to our Country. All of which we ask in the name of the Great Friend and Master of men. Amen.

Over the years, the prayer went through several revisions. I have in my possession two issues of *Bugle Notes*; the one issued to me when I entered the Academy in July 1945, the other given to me by a cadet a few years ago, dated 2000. I became aware that some changes had been made some time in the fifty-five years between the two issues. I raised the question of these changes with the cadet chaplain, Colonel John Cook, and the Protestant chaplain, Major Keith Goode. Both men kindly searched their files and each presented me with a rather extensive sheaf of documents describing the history of the changes and discussions between Chaplain Wheat, the author of the prayer, and members of the Academy staff including the superintendent. The second change was to make the prayer gender-neutral to accommodate the women cadets who entered the Academy in 1976. It was the first revision, but other conceptual changes have some interesting aspects.

In early April 1947 the members of the Chapel Board recommended to Major General Maxwell D. Taylor, the superintendent, that the Cadet Prayer, as beautiful as it was, suffered from two flaws: it was too long, and some of the wording was too juvenile in that it repeated elements of the Boy Scout Oath. With the concurrence of the superintendent and assistance of Cadet Chaplain John B. Walthour, Brigadier General G. R. Higgins, chairman of the Chapel Board and commandant of cadets, wrote to Chaplain Clayton E. Wheat, author of the prayer, requesting his permission to make the changes and seeking his advice in the matter. Chaplain Wheat responded by letter dated April 22, 1947, concurring in certain changes and recommending others. The revision agreed to by all was the elimination of the two penultimate sentences in the prayer beginning with "May we find genuine . . ." and replacing them with

> Help us to maintain the honor of the Corps untarnished and unsullied, and to show forth in our lives the ideals of West Point in doing our duty to Thee and to our Country.

Around 1963 a third issue arose. Since the Jewish cadets were no longer attending services in the Cadet Chapel, as will be related further on, it was suggested that the Cadet Prayer be changed once more to add to the last words "even Jesus Christ, our Lord." On February 1, 1963, the USMA chief of staff sent a memorandum to General Stillwell, then commandant and chairman of the Chapel Board, in which he stated that Major General William C. Westmoreland had discussed the new addition with Cadet Chaplain Speers. The superintendent's views are stated as follows in the chief of staff's memorandum:

> a. He does not look with favor upon including the additional phrase in any published form of the prayer, either now or in the future.
>
> b. He has no objection to including as an appropriate conclusion during recitations of the Cadet Prayer the phrase, "even Jesus Christ our Lord" as has been proposed when the prayer is offered during Protestant worship services in the Cadet Chapel. (The added phrase used during these services does not constitute an official change to the Cadet Prayer. Rather it should be considered an adaptation which is an appropriate conclusion to the prayer when offered during Protestant services.)

The memorandum goes on to state that the Chapel Board accepted the superintendent's recommendation, and that its introduction into the service, since it was not a change to the Cadet Prayer, was at the option of the Cadet Chaplain.

On January 20, 1964, this addition was questioned by Cadet Frederick M. Hinshaw, Jr., Class of 1964, in a letter to Chaplain Theodore C. Speers, then cadet chaplain:

> Dear Dr. Speers:
>
> The reason for my writing this note my [*sic*] appear to be petty to you, but it has been of concern to me for quite a while. Before I discuss what the problem is, I would like to explain that I am *not* deeply religious, and if I did not have to go to Chapel, there is a chance that [*sic*] would elect to sleep later on Sunday mornings. My point is that this matter is not one of religion.
>
> I would like to know your reason for including the words, "Jesus Christ, Our Lord," at the end of the Cadet Prayer. The prayer is written with these words omitted and apparently it was intended to be read without them. I am far from alone in ques-

tioning your motive for including them, because I know there is growing concern about it within my company.

Our feeling, as a consensus, is that the Cadet Prayer was written for the cadets, and as long as cadets attend church to recite it, then it should be read as written. Perhaps we are wrong.

I hope you don't take this note as a violent criticism, because it is not meant to be one. I would, however, appreciate an explanation.

Thank you very much.

Frederick M. Hinshaw, Jr.
Co I-1 USCC
Class of 1964

The chaplain responded two days later. Included in his response was the following:

I inquired from Chaplain Wheat concerning the concluding words of the Prayer and he told me that it was so written for the sake of the Jewish cadets who in those days worshipped with the Corps in our big Cadet Chapel. Out of deference to their tradition the normal ending of a "Jesus Christ our Lord" was omitted. I asked him about the addition of the words "Jesus Christ our Lord" and he replied that that was just what was meant and that was just what should be now in the Prayer.

I had already discussed this with the then Superintendent, General W. C. Westmoreland, and with the Chapel Board, and we informally asked the opinion of some cadets.

The Chapel Board gave its unanimous approval to the addition of the words "Jesus Christ our Lord" and the addition received the approval of General Westmoreland, the Superintendent. We do not consider this to be a change, as was made in 1947 with the omission of a number of words, but the saying out loud what is obviously implied, that "the Great Friend and Master of men" is none other than Jesus Christ our Lord.

Note that Chaplain Speer's response to Cadet Hinshaw omitted the restriction on adding it to the printed version and limiting its use to Protestant services at the option of the cadet chaplain. Apparently there was continued discussion of this addition to the prayer in subsequent years. I found no further documentation on this matter until March 2, 1971, when Major General William A. Knowlton, then superintendent, sent a memorandum to the cadet chaplain again raising the question of adding Jesus Christ to the ending of the prayer. The third and last paragraph of the memorandum stated:

> It is not that I mean to deny Christianity, but I think we have weakened the prayer and turned from something unusual when we specifically identify the Master of Men as Jesus Christ and exclude the possibility of it being just God. I do not mean to start an ecclesiastical battle, but there is an opinion which believes that we have not helped, but rather lessened, the Cadet Prayer when we changed it. How about discussing it with me.

I do not have documentation of the discussion nor of further discourse on this subject until 1977, when Chaplain James D. Ford summarized the history of the matter for the incoming superintendent, Lieutenant General Andrew J. Goodpaster. Ford's summary cited the fact that neither Jews nor Catholics were learning or using the prayer. The record shows that this matter of the addition to the prayer continues to arise periodically from a variety of sources, both civilian and military.

Sunday services for all cadets continued in the two chapels until the mid-1930s. An initiative was taken to change this for Jewish cadets by Merton Singer, Class of 1938 who spearheaded the effort to allow Jewish cadets to have Jewish services. The change from Sunday services in an essentially Christian environment to "stand-alone" Jewish worship was to be gradual over a period of five years. I traced the change from copies of official documents, articles, obituaries, diaries, and discussions with Merton Singer. Many of the documents and articles were given to me by Mrs. Harriet P. Davis, widow of Theodore W. Davis, Class of 1940, and by Merton Singer. Three Jewish cadets were instrumental in launching this change:

Meyer A. Edwards, Jr., Class of 1937
Merton Singer, Class of 1938
Theodore W. Davis, Class of 1940

Included in the Singer papers was a partial chronology of the change titled "Sequence of Development, West Point Jewish Cadet Chapel 1934–1970." He entered West Point in the summer of 1934. In September of that year he approached Chaplain Roscoe S. Foust and requested that provisions be made for High Holy Days services for all Jewish cadets. Chaplain Foust allegedly sent a letter to Singer dated September 29, 1934, offering to discuss the matter. Singer goes on in his chronology to state that Chaplain Foust arranged for Rabbi Bloom of Newburgh to come to West Point to conduct Yom Kippur services that year. Singer initiated the effort to obtain official authorization of formal Jewish worship at West Point.

Rabbi Bloom continued coming to West Point to hold Shabbat services on Saturday afternoons during cadets' free time. However, voluntary attendance became sporadic because of personal conflicts in the lives of the cadets on those afternoons. Regardless of whether they attended Jewish services, the Jewish cadets were required to continue their attendance at the Cadet Chapel on Sunday mornings. In 1936 Rabbi Bloom asked the Jewish Welfare Board (JWB) to provide a rabbi to replace him. The board sent Lieutenant Colonel Benjamin A. Tintner, (Chaplains Corps Reserve). He opted to move services to Wednesday afternoons, when cadet personal conflicts were at a minimum. I suspect that Rabbi Bloom left before a replacement was assigned by the Jewish Welfare Board because of a memorandum written in 1935 and discussed below.

On October 28, 1935, Meyer A. Edwards, Jr., Cadet Private, Co. M. 2nd Class, sent a memorandum to the cadet chaplain requesting that "a Rabbi be allowed to visit West Point and that he be allowed to conduct religious services." He went on to write that the Jewish cadets were "especially desirous that the Rabbi conduct a service some time during the next Jewish Holy Days." He listed the names of fourteen cadets, including himself, in the memorandum.

Chaplain Roscoe Thornton Faust sent a memorandum to the superintendent, Major General William D. Connor, in which he indicated that he "did not believe that there was any reason why such permission would not be given" and offered to take the matter up with the general. I have a copy of his memorandum. Handwritten across its bottom part, and partly illegible, are the words: "Col Hughes Look into [illegible] WDC"

In a paper he wrote on the history of Jewish religious activities at West Point, Theodore W. Davis, Class of 1940, says that the Meyer Edwards memorandum to Chaplain Faust in 1935 was written with the chaplain's recommendation of "hearty approval." General Connor approved the request on November 2, 1935, with the requirement that Jewish cadets continue to attend "regular chapel services" at the Cadet Chapel on Sunday mornings. I have a memorandum to the superintendent USMA dated November 1, 1935, from the commandant of cadets, Lieutenant Colonel Simon Bolivar Buckner, Jr., stating:

> I have no objection to special services for cadets of the Jewish Faith provided they interfere with no military duties and are held in addition to the regular cadet chapel services.
>
> The regular cadet chapel service I consider as a non-sectarian service appropriate for any cadet.
>
> I do consider it objectionable to have Jewish services taking the place of regular cadet chapel services since this will establish a precedent for having separate services for Christian Scientists, Mormons, Celestials, and perhaps of the separate denominations of the Christian faith.
>
> In general, I believe that we should maintain as a principle the fact that cadets should conform to the general routine of the Military Academy rather than attempt to change the general routine to suit their religious or other idiosyncrasies. Those who are unable conscientiously to conform need not come to West Point.

It is likely that this memorandum was the basis for General Connor's position regarding the matter. The commandant wrote strong, if not harsh, words in his memorandum, particularly the last paragraph. They perhaps reflect the conservatism of the military to maintain the status quo in the face of change. Nevertheless, it is plausible to infer that the commandant expected every cadet to accept a prescribed way of worship or not attempt to come to West Point. This was contrary to the mandate that the Academy support the spiritual needs of all cadets. Currently the Academy makes every effort to accommodate the spiritual needs of the diverse members of the Corps of Cadets in lieu of the foregoing philosophy that "one size fits all."

In his paper, Davis acknowledges the appointment of Rabbi Tintner to serve the Jewish cadets. He referred to a meeting between Rabbi Tintner, Chaplain H. Fairfied Butt III, and himself in 1937 to discuss ending compulsory attendance by Jewish cadets at the Cadet Chapel services on Sunday mornings. On August 2, 1937, Chaplain Butt wrote a memorandum to the superintendent recommending that Jewish cadets be relieved of compulsory services at "other chapel formations." Lieutenant Colonel Charles W. Ryder, commandant of cadets, wrote the 1st Indorsement (military spelling) to Chaplain Butts's memorandum approving Jewish services, but stated, "These cadets attending Jewish services must also attend the regular chapel service." This was forwarded to the superintendent, who approved it "as recommended in the lst Indorsement" and sent back to Chaplain Butt through the commandant. Nothing had changed.

However, Rabbi Tintner was encouraged and suggested that the next request come from the Jewish Welfare Board. A letter from Harry L. Glucksman, executive director of the Jewish Welfare Board, dated February 14, 1938, to Brigadier General Jay L. Benedict, the new superintendent:

> In order to carry on a more effective religious program, which would make it possible for all those students, who so desire, to attend Jewish services, we respectfully request that you permit students of the Jewish faith to attend a special Jewish service on Sunday morning and be excused from the regular Chapel service conducted at the same time. I believe that the students of the Catholic faith have this arrangement.

On February 17, 1938, General Benedict responded to the Jewish Welfare Board, stating his "regret that I cannot give you a favorable answer." He cited the lack of facilities for religious denominations other than the Catholics (who had their own chapel); "hence the services of the Cadet Chapel which all other cadets must attend, are as nearly non-sectarian as it is possible to make them." He allowed the continuation of the special Jewish services.

Subsequent to General Benedict's response of February 17, 1938, Rabbi Tintner approached all twenty-seven Jewish cadets seeking their agreeing to compulsory Jewish services every Sunday morning as practiced by the rest of the Corps. He then wrote a three-page letter to the superintendent making the case for such services and relief from attending other compulsory services. He again made reference to the separate Catholic services and the absence of the requirement that Catholic cadets also attend the Cadet Chapel services. The letter was referred to the Chapel Board, consisting of Colonel and Professor Clayton E. Wheat (the author of the Cadet Prayer), Lieutenant Colonel and Professor C. L. Fenton, and Lieutenant Colonel and Commandant of Cadets C. W. Ryder. The board reported back to the superintendent on May 5, 1938, rejecting the proposal on the same grounds as previously stated by others—the nonsectarian nature of Cadet Chapel services and the setting of a precedent for other denominations—and added that there is no "power or authority" to assure the presence of a rabbi every Sunday morning.

In addressing the concern over setting a precedent for other denominations, the Chapel Board wrote the following in the memorandum to the superintendent: "However, it is believed that the Jew has the best claim to a separate service and if a separate service is to be granted to any religious group or sect the Jew should come first."

In the fifth paragraph of that memorandum, the Chapel Board stated that if all prerequisites were met, such as the guarantee of a rabbi each week, the board felt it advisable to create a Jewish Chapel Squad on a temporary basis for one year to test its desirability among the Jewish cadets and to monitor the availability of the rabbi. A permanent squad should not be authorized until after the trial period. On July 11, 1938, the superintendent notified the rabbi that "it has been determined that it would not be advisable at this time to inaugurate such a service as you suggest."

The rabbi was not to be deterred. He went back to the Jewish Welfare Board. Cyrus Adler, chairman of the Army and Navy Committee, wrote General Benedict a letter, dated March 19, 1939, citing its recognition by the War Department "as the agency authorized to provide religious and welfare activities for men of the Jewish faith in the Army" and noting that it had "for some time conducted such activities on behalf of the cadets at West Point." He went on to state that the board recognized its "responsibility for the continuity of the services of a rabbi." The superintendent forwarded this letter to the Chapel Board, which recommended that a trial Jewish Chapel Squad be created for separate Jewish services. Davis wrote in his history paper that the commandant met with Rabbi Tintner and Cadet Davis at 1615 hours on March 21, 1939, in the Mess Hall. The purpose of the meeting was to assure the commandant that all details had been provided for before he recommended positive action to the superintendent.

On March 30, 1939, General Benedict answered Cyrus Adler's letter, informing him that he approved the recommendations of the Chapel Board that a Jewish Chapel Squad be formed for separate Jewish services. Davis recommended that the trial period start promptly and end five months later in September 1939. The first Jewish Chapel Squad was formed officially by Memorandum No. 40, Headquarters, United States Corps of Cadets, West Point, New York, April 7, 1939, effective April 9, 1939. It began operating on Sunday, that date, in the basement of the Cadet Chapel with Cadet R.A. Simon, Class of 1939, designated as the senior cadet. This memorandum was rescinded and replaced by Memorandum No. 157 dated September 5, 1939, Cadet T. W. Davis, Class of 1940, designated as the platoon leader, Cadet James D. Loewus as platoon sergeant, and Cadet Morris C. Shoss to be platoon guide. The platoon was divided into three squads, two of nine cadets each and one with eight cadets; a total of 30 Jewish cadets. The Jewish Chapel Squad has functioned continuously ever since. On Sunday, June 9, 1940, a baccalaureate service was held for Ted Davis and his classmates of the Class of 1940.

The pioneering efforts by these few Jewish cadets, particularly Merton Singer in September 1934—a brave step for a plebe to take right after Beast Barracks—deserves the thanks of all Jewish graduates since, as well as present Jewish cadets and cadets to come. However, Lieutenant Colonel Benjamin A. Tintner, Chaplains Corps Reserve, has been overlooked as the tireless facilitator in launching the Jewish Chapel Squad. He, too, deserves thanks and recognition for a difficult task well executed.

Eventually, before, during (1945–49), and after my cadet days, Jewish services were conducted in the Old Cadet Chapel by either a visiting rabbi or by a cadet. In time, a portable Aron ha-Kodesh (ark) containing Torah scrolls was obtained. It was stored in the chapel and carried into the sanctuary for services. It is now on display in the Alumni Gallery of the Jewish Chapel.

However, despite the recognition and approval by the Academy Command Group of the need for separate Jewish services, those services like the Christian services were required to be conducted on Sunday mornings. In the early 1960s, a new civilian rabbi, Avram Soltes, explained to the superintendent that Sunday morning services had no meaning for Jews because the Sabbath started on Friday night and ran through to sundown on Saturday. The superintendent granted permission to move the weekly Jewish chapel requirement from Sunday morning to Friday night. He agreed for services to be held in a lecture room in Bartlett Hall, an academic building. This was closer to the barracks than the remotely located Old Cadet Chapel. Services continue to be held on Friday nights to this day.

This time change posed special problems for the cadets. Saturdays were busy duty days. There were classes requiring preparation and study. Saturday morning room inspections were the most detailed of the week. They were followed by inspection in ranks, particularly detailed and astutely performed by company tactical officers and upper class cadet officers. Preparation for these inspections was time-consuming. All uniform brass and leather had to be carefully and completely polished. Rifles required thorough cleaning and oiling (no rust or lint tolerated!). Rooms had to be spotless, with desk drawers open to view. If a cadet was having academic difficulties, extra time for study was precious, often requiring staying up illegally after taps. Somehow the Jewish cadets managed. Currently, this is no longer a problem. Saturday classes are no longer held, and Saturday morning inspections are only conducted occasionally. With the pressures of Saturday a thing of the past, Jewish cadets are able to attend Friday night services, which is the heart and soul of the Jewish program at West Point.

Shabbat Worship is Very Special

It is Friday evening and the Rabbi is standing at the small movable Bimah (lectern) in the middle of the Chapel, among the civilian worshippers, military personnel and cadets. Under his Talit (prayer shawl), you see a uniform. Not just an ordinary uniform but rather the Army Combat Uniform (ACU) and well worn combat boots. The cadets know that the standard at the Jewish Chapel is not what you wear, but that you come to worship.

The service begins, but before it does, the Rabbi asks all the female cadets to come forward and say the blessing over the Shabbat candles. One wonders what their children and grandchildren would say years from now if they could see them, these true Jewish American warriors. The Rabbi begins the chanting of the Kabbalat Shabbat services (the Shabbat welcome service) and a peace descends over the Jewish Chapel. The week has been long and hard, and the cadets are far away from home and separated from their loved ones. The Rabbi recites the ancient Hebrew prayers that the cadets may or may not understand. Hearing the Rabbi chant may bring them back to the times they spent in synagogue as children with their parents or it may be the first time they find themselves in a synagogue. In any case, the cadets feel they have come home. Not the home they grew up in but a place where they can nonetheless be who they are and their soul can drink from the fountain of their ancient Jewish heritage.

As the service continues, the Rabbi gives his sermon. The cadets may or may not listen, depending on what their soul needs to heal itself from the past week's tribulations, but when they do, the Rabbi always tries to connect the weekly portion of the Torah to what they are doing or are trying to be – military leaders of character. The purpose of the sermon is to be inspirational, ethical or educational. The sermon, in Hebrew the "drasha", carries the meanings of discourse; inquire, investigate, seek, study, explain and interpret. The sermon at West Point has an added meaning. It is meant to strengthen the cadets spiritually with Jewish values so that one day they can be leaders worthy enough to stand in front of America's sons and daughters and lead them into battle against it's enemies.

The service ends as the whole congregation sings "Adon Olam" (Master of the Universe) and the Rabbi blesses everyone with the ancient blessing of the High Priest. The service is followed by an "Oneg" in the social hall where great food is served. The Oneg is often sponsored by the Jewish War Veterans.

As the cadets leave the service, they think about this pile of concrete and steel called the Jewish Chapel. They may not know its history or who built it, but they realize that without it, they may not have been able to find the strength to go on. They realize that without it, their life at West Point would be all the poorer. They may graduate, but it would be without the pride and understanding of the great contributions Jewish Americans have given to freedom.

Chaplain (Rabbi) Carlos Huerta

The Birth of the West Point Jewish Chapel

The last vestiges of winter at West Point were holding the high ground. Gloom period had not yet yielded to the promise of spring. The work day was drawing to a close as the project manager tried to catch up on his paperwork. He glanced out of the construction trailer window and noticed a cadet staring intently at the cluttered construction site. His curiosity drew him from his work to the cadet. He asked,

"May I help you?"

"I certainly hope so, Sir," she responded. "My fiancé and I are planning to be married in *that building* on graduation day and I am not so sure that it will be ready in time."

"Young lady, you will be married here on that day," he promised her.

And so it came to pass that Lieutenant Christie Bishop, Class of 1984, married Lieutenant Keith Samuels, Class of 1983, in the new Jewish Chapel, the first of what promised to be a long line of weddings and other notable events. Actually the wedding fulfilled the second of two promises. The first was made to Superintendent Lieutenant General Willard Scott that the 1984 baccalaureate services for the graduating Jewish cadets would be held in the new chapel.

More than twenty years earlier, when the newlyweds were toddlers, an idea germinated in the minds of several graduates to build a Jewish Chapel at West Point. Both Merton Singer, Class of 1938, and Robert Granik, Class of 1945, individually recall starting dialogue on this subject as early as that time. Shortly thereafter Rabbi Avram Soltes was appointed Jewish cadet chaplain. He brought creativity, charisma, and a very special brand of enthusiasm to West Point that was to shape and direct Jewish Chapel Squad activities for a generation. During the early years of Rabbi Soltes's tenure as Jewish chaplain, the first seeds were sown for the construction of the Jewish Chapel at West Point. The period was from January 1966 to June 1968, when Major General Donald V. Bennett was superintendent. In an undated signed memorandum, General Bennett wrote: "During this period, I participated in discussions concerning the possible construction of a Jewish Cadet Chapel at West Point. Colonel Merton Singer, Class of 1938, was my basic contact with the Jewish Community within the Corps of Cadets."

The memorandum also cited the general's recommendation to the Department of the Army that "the Chapel be located midway between the Catholic Chapel and the Cadet Chapel in an abandoned quarry site."

The sown seeds began to sprout, but it was a long way to the harvest. In 1967 Rabbi Soltes was summoned by General Bennett, who announced his support for the construction of the Jewish Chapel and notified the rabbi that the site would be in the old, abandoned quarry on Merritt Road. He said he had arranged for the Corps of Engineers to prepare a graphic study of the building.

In the beginning we were seeking a beginning. The only experience from which we could draw was that of our Catholic brothers, who in 1899 sought a suitable house of worship at West Point. At that time, there were approximately twenty Catholic cadets in the Corps. As mentioned earlier, the Catholics were required to raise the funds to build their Most Holy Trinity Chapel with nonappropriated funds raised by private sources under a law passed by Congress for that specific purpose. The same law governed the funding of the Jewish Chapel.

This endeavor promised to be laden with complexities, the extent of which proved to have been somewhat underestimated, because of our enthusiasm and optimism. The interests and requirements of the Department of the Army and the USMA had to be dealt with, and at the same time it was necessary to conduct a dignified and effective fund-raising campaign. Simultaneously, the design and construction of the chapel had to be kept in concert with the fund-raising campaign for budgetary purposes and with the requirements governing architecture and construction at West Point. This required a lean, responsive, and knowledgeable organization.

In April 1968, the West Point Jewish Cadet Chapel Fund, Inc. was founded and presided over by Merton Singer. The articles of incorporation of the fund were signed on October 9, followed by a letter of support from the superintendent, Major General S. W. Koster, to the Supreme Court of the State of New York on November 29. Most of the members of the original committee were graduates of West Point in civil life. There were also a number of nongraduates, one of whom was to become the driving force behind the program. All were active businessmen, professionals, elected officials, and clergymen. All carried substantial workloads and responsibilities of their own. Gradually, this group boiled down to a few who were willing and able to devote a substantial amount of time and unwavering commitment to the task at hand. Singer moved to Texas, vacating the chairmanship of the Fund in September 1970.

Our first watershed meeting was held on September 30, 1974, in New York City at the office of Saul Horowitz, Jr., Class of 1946, president of HRH Construction Company, to explore fund-raising strategies and to begin tailoring our organization. Saul was our leader. He replaced Mert Singer as president of the Fund. His quiet strength and sound judgment provided us with the direction needed to achieve our objective. Less than a year later, Saul was returning to New York from New Orleans, where in his role as president of the Associated General Contractors of America he had been chairing the organization's national convention. His return flight crashed at John F. Kennedy Airport. We lost a dear friend and leader; a devastating loss to all of us.

Herbert M. Ames, the only nongraduate in the active group, firmly picked up the reins of leadership and accomplished the objective. One cannot adequately describe his executive abilities, objectivity, determination, drive, and sound judgment. We owe him a debt of gratitude for his selflessness and complete dedication to the project. He possessed the ability to assign responsibility along with the required level of authority to exercise it, while lending moral support at just the right time. Herb generously shared the limelight with others, always understating his own role.

The organization created consisted of officers and trustees backed by a Committee of Overseers and a National Advisory Committee. The Committee of Overseers was made up of national leaders of industry, business, and government, and Academy graduates. The National Advisory Committee consisted of seventeen United States senators, forty-eight congressional representatives, eighteen general officers, an admiral, and fifteen officers and executives of national, secular, and religious organizations. An ad hoc committee selected from the officers and trustees was designated as the operational organ, with specific assigned responsibilities for each member. The committee consisted of Herb Ames, Alvin E. Orlian, Class of 1943, Robert Granik, Stanley Love, Class of 1946, Harold Gottesman, Class of 1950, Jerome Waldor, Class of 1950, Alan Lichtenberg, Class of 1951, Louis Gross, Class of 1954, Herbert Lichtenberg, Class of 1955 and myself, Class of 1949. Though all of us were responsible for fund-raising, three specific operational tasks were assigned: Alan Lichtenberg was appointed treasurer, Bob Granik was designated corporate counsel, and I was appointed engineering and construction manager. I was elected vice president in order to be able to sign contracts and purchase orders on behalf of the Fund. The balance of the committee provided advisory backup in addition to their fund-raising efforts. Herb Ames provided direct liaison with the USMA command group and with the Department of the Army.

At the outset of operations we were all aware of the old saying about the camel being a horse designed by a committee. We took this admonition seriously. Every effort was made to avoid decisions by committee where decisions by the responsible individual were appropriate and proper. Each member, therefore, functioned with substantial autonomy, but each was sensitive to matters that deserved, if not required, committee approval. Without rigid operating rules, we all had a sense of the limits of our autonomy. Working relationships were quite comfortable, conflicts virtually nonexistent.

A remarkable characteristic of the ad hoc committee and the board of trustees was their responsiveness to calls to convene, even on short notice. In the sixteen years from the founding of the Jewish Chapel Fund in 1968 to the opening of the chapel in 1984, it was never necessary to cancel a meeting for lack of a comfortable quorum. Some members traveled from areas far beyond New York City to attend the meetings, always at their own expense. (We agreed early on that the fund would never be called upon to pay for travel, lodging, or food for any of us.).

By 1974 it became necessary to simultaneously initiate a number of key actions. Preliminary design of the building was a requirement to establish firmer fund-raising goals. Fund-raising had to be accelerated in order to meet the requirement of the United States government that the Chapel Fund demonstrate to the United States Military Academy acceptable evidence of its fiscal ability to construct the chapel prior to breaking ground. The creation of another Dick's Folly overlooking the Hudson River was not an option.* A proffer (formal offering) had to be made to the Secretary of the Army as a prerequisite to obtaining a license and right of entry to construct the accepted chapel on the designated site. It was up to the Academy to approve the design of the facility.

---

* Dick's Folly is an abandoned half-finished castle across the river from West Point. It was started by a Mr. Dick for his mistress. When she left him during the castle's construction, Dick walked away from the project, leaving it in its unfinished state. Hence the name.

Because of the importance of the project and its visual prominence from its high position on the ridge overlooking the Plain at a point between the Cadet Chapel and the Catholic Chapel, it deserved, and we therefore selected, an architect of the highest repute to design it, Max Abramovitz of Harrison and Abramovitz. The firm and the architect had a long-established national reputation for their work on such projects as the United Nations Building, part of Lincoln Center for the Performing Arts, and several outstanding religious buildings.

The style and configuration of the building were closely coordinated with the Academy superintendent and his staff. One crisp Hudson Valley day, members of the ad hoc committee met with the superintendent, Major General Sidney B. Berry, Class of 1948. Part of the meeting was held on the Plain, from which we observed a vertical crane boom rising over the ridge line from the designated site for the chapel. A red flag flew from the tip of the boom. General Berry explained that the elevation of the flag was tangent to an imaginary line drawn from the top of the Cadet Chapel to the top of the spire of the Catholic Chapel. The top of the Jewish Chapel was not to exceed that elevation. I could understand the logic behind this caveat, but for some reason it struck me as a bit funny. I recall thinking that the determination of that elevation limit above the mean sea level datum would be an excellent problem for a plebe class in land surveying. We actually built the chapel to an elevation four feet below the limit line to provide a better proportional relationship to the length and width of the sanctuary. I accompanied the architect on a predesign visit to the Cadet Chapel, where we established its proportions of length to width to height of the high-roof portion of the nave. Max Abramovitz decided to keep the same proportions for the Jewish Chapel, thus resulting in the lowering of the top of its roof. These dimensional and spatial relationships contributed greatly to the magnificence of the finished building. The architect received design approval from the Academy planning board.

Max had selected an outstanding group of consulting engineers to design the structure, mechanical, and electrical systems. About that time, in my personal practice as a forensic engineer, I was selected to investigate a distressed shopping center sold by a major bank to a large Wall

Street brokerage firm. The buyer had engaged a structural engineering firm to perform a pre-purchase inspection. Unfortunately, the inspecting engineer had overlooked the distress that had placed the facility in a state of impending collapse. Coincidentally, that same structural engineering firm was selected by Max Abramovitz to design the structural elements of the chapel. The principal engineer called Max, offered to withdraw from our project when he discovered that I was managing it for the fund. When Max asked me for my opinion. I responded that I was perfectly comfortable to have the engineer remain on our project based on the firm's excellent reputation. As serious as the oversight was during the pre-purchase inspection, I did not feel that it was indicative of their usual performance. Unfortunately, the engineer elected to withdraw from the chapel project.

On May 27, 1976, the secretary of the army signed the right of entry at a ceremony held in his office. It was attended by Herb Ames, Rabbi Soltes, Al Orlian, Bob Granik, Bernie Abrams, Class of 1947, Congressman John M. Murphy, Class of 1950, Bob Peltz, Class of 1950, Alan Lichtenberg, Eugene Marder, Class of 1949, Herb Lichtenberg, Lieutenant Colonel Herbert S. Kennigsberg, Colonel William Hammill, Cadet Elliot Rosner, Class of 1976, and me. This was an important milestone along the road to fruition.

One year later, Secretary of the Army Alexander, Lieutenant General Andrew Goodpaster (superintendent USMA designee), Herb Ames, and members of the fund met with President Jimmy Carter at the White House to discuss the project with him. At the close of the meeting, President Carter signed a proclamation supporting the construction of the Jewish Chapel. President Ronald Reagan added his support when he took office.

In 1981, another momentous event occurred which was to this project what a booster rocket is to a missile launch. Marty Silverman, president of North American Leasing Corporation, pledged $1 million to the Chapel Fund. He also pledged himself to the program and provided us with the wizardry we needed to raise the required funds. He committed himself to the project in many ways and became an active member of the ad hoc committee. His story is an illustration of the American Dream personified.

Marty, son of an immigrant from Poland who settled in upstate New York, worked his way through Albany Law School, from which he graduated in 1936. In World War II he fought as an infantry soldier in Patton's Third Army, where he rose from the rank of private to captain. He was highly decorated and left the Army as a major after serving as an attorney in the Nuremburg war crimes trials. He volunteered to assist in the prosecution and trial of the German troops responsible for the infamous Malmedy Massacre. When he returned home, he and his wife, Dorothy, started a business that grew to be one of the largest leasing companies in the United States. Later he was to play an even more important role in the chapel project.

Fund-raising from other sources continued. Committee members established local fund-raising groups led by local graduates in major cities throughout the country. Fund-raising events were held from time to time. The most colorful of these took place at the Red Parrot Night Club in New York City on May 2, 1982. The West Point Glee Club, the Hell Cats (a rousing fife-and-drum corps made up of members of the West Point Band; all enlisted men auditioned before they are accepted), and the cadet Color Guard who march in every parade at West Point, all added an impressive dimension to the occasion. The event was well covered by the media. One method of raising funds was to offer the opportunity to memorialize the donors or someone of their choosing on plaques erected in the chapel and formally dedicated. It was a slow, often agonizing, undertaking. Time had become a serious factor, as it brought inflation with it and the resulting need for additional donations. Each year of delay increased the cost of construction.

That same year, 1982, the committee took steps to select and to enter into a contract with a construction management firm. There was considerable discussion as to the size of the companies under consideration. There was some concern over the possibility that a large firm might consider the project so small, that it would not assign its best personnel or provide the attention it deserved. When Tishman Realty and Construction Company was suggested, some members of the committee were skeptical, myself most especially, because of its size and its massive projects, ranging in cost from double-digit to triple-digit millions of dollars. These fears were somewhat dispelled when we discovered that the president of the parent company was James R. Endler, Class of 1956, a former Corps of Engineers officer. Furthermore, he planned to assign Robert Segal, Class of 1953, a retired colonel of the Corps of Engineers, as the field project manager. Bob had just completed the construction of Epcot Center in Florida. Tishman became a more palatable choice and I withdrew my objection.

Our design-construct team was complete. It brought some interesting military history with it. In addition to the military backgrounds of Endler, Segal, and myself, Max Abramovitz also had a unique military engineering past. During World War II, Max had built airfields in China for General Claire Chennault and his Flying Tigers. He went on to serve as a civil engineering officer in the Air Force, rising to the rank of lieutenant colonel. To these men, the Jewish Chapel meant much more than just one more project to build.

Abramovitz, the Tishman organization, and I commenced working together. Though cost was a factor, quality was given priority. The chapel was not to be designed as if it were a depreciable commercial real estate investment. I established this as the criterion, and stated it firmly, at the first conference of the design-construct team when the Tishman estimators suggested certain cost-reducing changes that would have seriously compromised quality. I stressed that the chapel would have to last for over 100 years. We proceeded accordingly.

As 1982 drew to a close, we realized that we were finally on the verge of commencing construction. Two major interfering issues remained to be resolved: We still had not raised all the funds necessary to meet the criteria set for "proof of financial ability to perform," and the funding for the construction of off-site utilities remained up in the air. It was a necessity to make construction a reality in the eyes of prospective donors. We therefore requested and proposed that construction be commenced using the money on hand without full funding. Marty Silverman came to our rescue a second time. He personally guaranteed the United States government that all funds necessary for the completion of the chapel would be available. This met the "fiscal ability" criterion. One remaining obstacle blocked breaking ground: the funding of off-site utilities required to serve the building.

The site for the chapel designated by the Academy officials was on the west side of Merritt Road near its intersection with Delafield Road. We discovered that the only utilities on Merritt Road were electricity for the street lighting and water. There was no telephone accessibility, gas, sewerage, or steam line available on the road. The nearest location of the missing utilities was down at the foot of a steep slope from the east side of Merritt Road to Stoneylonesome Road (formerly Mills Road) behind Arvin Gymnasium. We estimated the cost of extending these utilities up the slope to Merritt Road to be approximately $500,000. This posed a serious dilemma. We could not proceed with construction without the missing utilities and questioned whether it was our responsibility or that of the Army to extend them within reach of the site.

Herb Ames and I felt that providing reasonable access to off-site utilities was the obligation of the government, particularly for a not-for-profit project. Furthermore, once the utilities were brought up to Merritt Road, it would benefit the government by opening up the area to further development. We sought help from the superintendent, Lieutenant General Willard Scott. Though he agreed with our position, he advised us that it could take from five to seven years to fund the utilities via normal budgetary channels and procedures. This delay would have two negative effects on the project: donors would lose interest and rising costs would complicate fund-raising. There was no alternative and no one to turn to short of a donor willing to bear the cost of this added expense.

We received help from an unexpected source. Carl Goldstein, an associate of Herb Lichtenberg, offered to present the issue to Congressman Joseph A. Addabbo, chairman of the House Appropriations Defense Sub-Committee. However, Addabbo had the reputation of being "unfriendly" toward the Army. We had to risk his possible animosity, so we accepted Carl's kind offer. He and Herb Lichtenberg visited the congressman in the late summer of 1982. He assured them that he would look into it. On September 30 of that year Herb Ames and Congressman Benjamin A.

Gilman, in whose congressional district West Point is situated, met with William Clark, principal deputy assistant of the secretary of the army, to discuss the utility issue. The matter reached the desk of the deputy chief of staff for personnel, Major General N. Norman Schwarzkopf, for study. The general wrote a memorandum for the secretary, dated November 1, 1982, suggesting "acquiescence by the Department of the Army." He went on to state that "The Army is presently without legal authority to pay for bringing the utility lines to the site in the opinion of the General Counsel. The letter expresses this opinion and indicates that legislation is necessary to authorize this expenditure."

On November 18, 1982, Secretary of the Army John O. Marsh, Jr. wrote to Congressman Addabbo explaining that Congress would have to legislate for the utility funds to be provided.

On December 20, 1982, on short notice, Herb Ames convened the committee at the Lichtenberg drapery showroom. Controlling his excitement, he announced that the release of the funds for the off-site utilities was imminent. If the president signed the MX Missile bill on the following day, the Army would have the funds. Congressman Addabbo had appended the funding of the utilities to the bill. One of our in-house comics labeled this "kosher pork"! To be perfectly fair about it, none of us were aware of the congressman's strategy to bring this to fruition. He has since died. He ultimately demonstrated his friendship toward the Army, at least toward West Point, for which we are most grateful.

With the likelihood of the bill being signed into law, we discussed the possibility of having a ground-breaking ceremony on December 28. Herb called the superintendent, Lieutenant General Willard Scott, to determine whether he agreed to such short notice for such a momentous event. The general agreed and offered the full cooperation of his Public Information Office and other departments. We prepared a guest mailing list and wrote the text of the invitation telegram. We arranged for the Hotel Thayer to provide a luncheon for the attendees. Key post personnel and services were contacted to prepare for the ceremony. Everything was in place waiting for a "go." The funds were released the next day. The telegrams were time-dated 0231 23 December 1982. On December 28, over

150 people attended the ground-breaking ceremony on that gray, cold rainy day. We mobilized construction forces as the New Year turned. The first daily report issued from the field was dated January 10, 1983. Work had commenced!

As construction moved forward at a deliberate pace, the Corps of Engineers contracted to extend the off-site utilities up to Merritt Road. Our construction activities were punctuated from time to time by the unforeseen events so common to construction projects. The architect and I were summoned to the office of the chief of engineers in Washington to agree to design the building for seismic loading. We negotiated a reasonable seismic standard and returned to modify our structural design. This change added to the project cost. Rock excavation was expected, but not to the depth it had to be carried. The abandoned quarry had been backfilled with large boulders and blasted rock. Soil borings showed rock at a relatively shallow depth, but each boring hit a large boulder, not bedrock as reported. Approximately 2,700 truckloads of blasted rock and large boulders had to be excavated and hauled off-site for disposal off-Post. We finally hit bedrock and were able to socket the superstructure into it to comply with the seismic requirement.

Thus the first $1 million was spent bringing the building out of the ground. The second $1 million was spent on the concrete superstructure, thanks in part to the seismic loading requirement. Dimensional control of the superstructure concrete formwork was an engineering feat in itself as the two long parallel walls of the sanctuary crept upward to their height of 60 feet. Formwork carpentry approached the precision of cabinet work to assure that the steel roof trusses would fit at the top of the massive U-shaped structure and that the interior walls, designed to expose concrete, were uniform and visually pleasing.

I made periodic visits to the site to review the status and quality of the work, and to attempt to prevent delays caused by slow decision-making that would slow down construction. Bob Segal's foresight and managerial skills minimized crises from delays and errors. In addition to my visits, the post engineer's project manager and the area engineer (a subdivision of the New York District Engineer) visited the site regularly. The construction staff consisted of Segal, his assistant, a job superintendent, some common labor, and a secretary. This field overhead cost approximately $30,000 per month.

At the end of each month, Tishman's accounting office in New York rendered the month's construction bills to me for review and approval. Once I approved the submittal, I forwarded the bills to Alan Lichtenberg for disbursement of funds and sent an information copy to Herb Ames. I maintained constant communication with Segal in the field and the accounting office in New York. A single bound copy of all construction bills each month had the bulk of a fair-sized telephone book. The monthly disbursement for construction averaged more than $350,000.

Over the course of construction, we entered into contract with forty individual contractors and vendors in addition to Tishman Construction Company, the architect, and a number of special consultants. Each required separate bookkeeping and disbursements totaling over $7 million.

Once construction fell into its routine, the committee turned its attention to interior decoration, furnishings, and works of art. Herb Ames wisely suggested that we engage an "artist in residence" of high repute to render judgments on the acceptability of all donated artifacts and that no one would be permitted to bypass his judgment, regardless of marital relationships, friendships, or the size of his or her donation.

Sidney Simon, a noted sculptor and painter, was selected for this position. His works are and have been exhibited in the Metropolitan Museum, the Museum of Modern Art, the Whitney Museum, and Cornell University Medical Center (all in New York City) and the American embassy in Paris. At the start of World War II, Simon was selected by President Franklin Roosevelt to organize and create a corps of artists to "paint the war." Many of their paintings hang in the corridors of the Pentagon. A representative collection was loaned to the new Jewish Chapel and was exhibited in the Alumni Gallery. As a member of General Douglas MacArthur's staff, Simon designed the five-star pentagonal array for the newly created rank of general of the army. His personal creations are prime focal points of interest in the chapel. He designed the ark containing the scrolls which is reflected outside on the facade as the tablets of the Ten Commandments, the Eternal Light hanging over the altar, and the mezuzahs on all the doorposts, each containing a scroll with the words, in keeping with the mandate in Deuteronomy 6, that the declaration of the existence of only one God, "Hear, O Israel, the Lord our God, the Lord is One," be written "on the doorposts of thy house and upon thy gates."

The curtain within the ark, mandated for the original Temple of antiquity to separate the scrolls from all else, is a particularly noteworthy work of art. This multihued Tree of Life was conceived by Simon to be dyed and woven in such a manner as to cause the colors to blend into subtle gradations of hue. It required an artist with exceptional skill in fiber technology and dying techniques to properly execute his concept. By chance Simon learned of Paula Renee, who had developed techniques for controlling colors through the use of microwave and convection ovens. She translated his creation into cloth. Each element of the curtain is symbolic of biblical events and history. It is related to our American heritage through the use of appliqués sewn to the base material depicting the tree.

The curtain was completed in June 1985 and received an Award of Excellence from the International Juried Art Competition in Harrison, New York. It was placed on exhibit at the Long Point Gallery in Provincetown, Massachusetts, the following month and was stolen. It was valued at $25,000. A media campaign and the offer of a reward resulted in its anonymous return six weeks later. It was finally installed in the chapel in October 1985.

High on each sidewall of the sanctuary, Max Abramovitz designed and located five "eyebrow" windows after experimenting with a variety of natural lighting effects on a variety of scale models.. These are glazed in clear glass. Each window symbolizes one of the Ten Commandments. Each commandment was expressed in artistic symbolism by Philip Ratner, an artist and sculptor of renown. His work is on display in the White House, the United States Supreme Court, the Library of Congress, the Statue of Liberty, and Ellis Island. He translated his designs into the clear glass panels using a flexible diamond-tipped grinding tool. The same technique is employed in etching Steuben glass.

Sidney Simon screened a large number of art works donated to the chapel. One of the most generous gifts of art was donated by Mr. Bernard M. Bloomfield of Philadelphia. He brought thirty-four pieces of antique silverware and pewter Judaica which had been collected over many years from sources throughout the world dating as far back as the seventeenth century. He also donated an original copy of the first English translation of the Bible from Hebrew ever printed in America. These items are displayed a few at a time in museum cases in the Chapel Gallery, cadet lounge, and library. The chapel is laden with beautiful works of art by artists such as Agam, Moshe Novak, and Chaim Gross.

The architect began selecting interior furnishings, from pews to lounge furniture, during the construction activities. Furniture was required for the rabbi's study, two administrative offices, two classrooms, the library, a conference room, anteroom, gallery, and bride's room. The physical layout of the building is designed to draw visitors through it before reaching the sanctuary. In keeping with tradition, the sanctuary faces east in the direction of Jerusalem, as in all synagogues. This requirement governed the floor plan. The main entrance to the building is located in a courtyard at the north end of the complex. One enters in a westerly direction into the Donors Hall, a comfortable, spacious, rectangular sky-lit area. The route of travel then turns southerly into the Alumni Gallery, a long wide hall with many works of art and artifacts, as well as the Alumni Wall display containing the names of every known Jewish graduate from 1802 through to the present. The gallery passes an open landscaped atrium donated in memory of Saul Horowitz by his family. Across the court to the east is the library. Continuing southward through the gallery one enters the semi-hexagonal anteroom to the sanctuary. The cadet lounge or social hall lies farther to the south. The sanctuary is adjacent to and east of the anteroom. One enters beneath the choir loft and steps into the rear of the seating area with its soaring 54-foot-high ceiling. The interior walls of the sanctuary are exposed bush-hammered concrete. This hand-worked process uses a bush hammer (a device that looks like a meat tenderizer) to remove the surface cement matrix from the concrete, exposing the coarse aggregate, thus producing a textured, nonglare surface. The high "eyebrow" windows are trimmed in limestone. The starkness of the stone and concrete is softened by the wood-stripped barrel-vaulted ceiling, wood pews, and the wood altar area. Scarlet pew cushions, a wine-colored drape on the bima, and the American flag on the altar add spots of color into the gray concrete. When the ark doors are opened, the Tree of Life curtain adds color to the surroundings and becomes the visual focal point.

Tragically, Rabbi Soltes died in May 1983, just thirteen months before the chapel was completed. Like Moses, he was allowed to see the Promised Land but destined not to enter it. Be thou at peace.

The question arose as to a replacement for our lost friend and religious leader. We sought another civilian rabbi. At the time, all West Point clergymen were civilians. The superintendent agreed, but the chief of chaplains of the Army insisted on a uniformed chaplain. In time, all chaplains at West Point were uniformed. Chaplain (Major) Mark Abramowitz arrived at West Point in September 1983. His first official duty was to officiate at the luncheon at the Thayer Hotel held just prior to the cornerstone-laying program and ceremony. Rabbi Abramowitz occupied the "house" and made it a "home." In his four years at West Point he touched the lives of Jewish cadets from the classes of 1984 through 1990 as their spiritual leader, teacher, and counselor. Chaplain (Lieutenant Colonel) Abramowitz left West Point in July 1987 to join the faculty of the Chaplains School. Well done.

Chaplain (Major) Kenneth Leinwand was sent to us to replace him. His effective style of conducting services included strumming a guitar. The cadets were fond of him. He currently holds the rank of colonel and recently was the chief chaplain of U.S. Army Europe.

On May 3, 1985, one year after the chapel was completed, the Eastern New York Chapter of the American Concrete Institute selected the Jewish Chapel for its annual award for the best architectural use of concrete. The following year, on June 9, 1986, at a ceremony at the Department of Defense, William Howard Taft IV, deputy secretary of defense, awarded architect Max Abramovitz the department's 1986 Award for Design Excellence for his creation of the West Point Jewish Chapel. I attended this function, basking in Max's great achievement. The secretary stated that the chapel was the most outstanding permanent building in the world owned by the Department of Defense.

On September 23, 1986, the West Point Jewish Chapel Fund formally transferred the "building, fixtures, furniture, and grounds" to the United

States government as a gift at a ceremony on the chapel grounds. Lieutenant General Dave R. Palmer, superintendent, accepted the gift on behalf of Army Secretary John D. Marsh, Jr. The Army initially refused to accept ownership because the chapel is a sectarian facility. It eventually offered to accept it if we could find one sectarian chapel anywhere in the world owned by the Department of the Army. We found a Catholic chapel at Fort Leavenworth, Kansas, belonging to the Army and maintained by it.

And so our work was done, the culmination of a generation of effort that followed more than a generation of effort started by a brave plebe, Merton Singer, who in 1934 convinced the cadet chaplain that Jewish cadets needed Jewish services. In the course of creating the chapel, three of our members made their "Last Roll Call," while the remainder of us watched each other age. Since then the numbers of the original group have dwindled down from twenty-three to eight; of the ad hoc committee from twelve to four as of this writing.

Jewish Religious Activities at West Point, 1984–2005

The West Point Jewish Chapel Fund continued to function after the chapel opened and still does. Some members thought that we could walk away from involvement upon the completion of the building program, but it soon became apparent that we would need to be involved forever more. However, all continued to participate. Additional members were added to the board of trustees. The ad hoc committee was disbanded, though those of us with specialty positions on the committee continued to do our work as needed. The board met as a group twice a year, and continues to do so to this day. Our objectives are to support chapel activities with funds and personal participation in chapel programs. We assist the rabbi in every way possible. Eventually, Herb Ames stepped down from the presidency and was replaced by Lou Gross. When Alan Lichtenberg became ill, his brother, Herbert, assumed the responsibilities of treasurer. I continued to watch over the physical condition of the building and eventually managed several more projects at the chapel, as will be described later.

The requirement established by the chief of chaplains at the Department of the Army to eventually replace all civilian chaplains with uniformed chaplains gradually resulted in almost all chaplains at West Point meeting that criterion. The death of Rabbi Soltes occurred when this change became policy at the Department of the Army. The Jewish chaplaincy at West Point, therefore, was the first to be affected by the change. The fund was interested in another civilian chaplain to assure longevity of assignment. Uniformed chaplains are rotated every few years, as are all military officers. The one advantage of civilian chaplains is obvious; they stay in office for years on end, assuring continuity of operations and activities. The superintendent, Lieutenant General Willard Scott, supported our preference, but the chief of chaplains was adamant. He sent Chaplain (Major) Mark Abramowitz to replace Rabbi Soltes. Though our request had been denied, we were very fortunate to have him, as I mentioned in the preceding chapter, but he was transferred in time to another assignment and a new chaplain was assigned. In the sixteen years from Rabbi Abramowitz's assignment in 1983 to 1999, we had six uniformed Jewish chaplains, none of whom had any experience with the Academy, its traditions, and its cadets prior to their assignment to West Point. By the time they became fully familiar with these Academy characteristics so different from the greater Army, they were moved into new assignments elsewhere. Turnover of this kind does not bode well for the unity and continuity of any congregation.

The change to uniformed chaplains was done on an attrition basis; as a civilian chaplain left, he was replaced in accordance with the new policy. In time, the cadet chaplain, the head of the Academy chaplaincy, became an officer with the rank of full colonel. The Jewish chaplain is a subordinate of the cadet chaplain, as are all other chaplains on the post. Chaplain (Colonel) Scott McChrystal was the first to be assigned to that position. He arrived during the tour of the fifth rabbi after Rabbi Abramowitz's arrival in 1983. Chaplain McChrystal was a major force in support of the development of the Jewish community. Herb Lichtenberg, Lou Gross, and I consider him a close friend. He retired in the summer of 2005. We were sorry to see him leave.

Several of the uniformed chaplains currently assigned to West Point are graduates of the Academy who turned to theology as their military career choice. One of them was Chaplain McChrystal's replacement, Chaplain (Lieutenant Colonel) John J. Cook III, Class of 1979. Chaplain Cook was designated a Distinguished Graduate and was the Cadet First Captain of his class. This is a relatively new turn of events in the Army chaplaincy, though I do recall that a graduate of the Class of 1946 received permission from the Department of the Army to enter a Catholic seminary upon graduation, his first step toward priesthood.

These gentlemen offer the advantage of their attachment to West Point and their understanding of the pressures of cadet life and Academy traditions. I recall one or two Jewish cadets who expressed some interest in becoming rabbis in the Army chaplaincy, but I am unaware of any of them following through on this. The Army is likely to enthusiastically endorse this concept because of the chronic shortage of Jewish chaplains.

Despite the change from mandatory to voluntary chapel attendance, the chaplaincy at West Point is a large, vibrant organization. A wide spectrum of denominational diversity is represented in the Corps of Cadets and among the other military and civilian personnel at West Point. They are served by five operating chapels on the post—the Cadet Chapel, Catholic Chapel, Jewish Chapel, Old Cadet Chapel, and the Post Chapel. There is a growing sectarian diversity at West Point, a reflection of the American population as it goes through an ethnic metamorphosis. This has created a need for additional facilities for worship and related activities, as I will discuss later.

Now that religious activities at West Point are voluntary, there is the question of how many Jewish cadets have not come forward to identify themselves. When new cadets arrive to commence their basic cadet training, they are given the opportunity to fill out a card indicating their religious preference, if they care to declare one. A second opportunity is presented to them at the class orientation during the first week of training. Those who choose not to identify themselves as Jews do so for a variety of reasons. Some may be concerned about the possibility of being subjected to anti-Semitism that could complicate their lives as cadets. Others may feel that to be labeled as Jewish could interfere with career advancement after graduation. Still others feel that they do not relate to the active practice of Judaism, in some cases because they come from secular homes. Since it is against the law to force anyone to reveal their religious affiliation, we can only consider those cadets who identify themselves as Jews as being the verified strength of the Jewish Chapel Squad.

I discussed this issue with Chaplain McChrystal, who told me that reluctance to come forward is common in virtually every denomination represented in the Corps of Cadets. He believed that probably 20 to 50 percent of all denominations do not come forward to declare an affiliation. This estimate was somewhat borne out by the rabbi, who advised that he receives many telephone inquiries from parents of new cadets to find out whether their sons or daughters have come forward to identify themselves as Jews and to avail themselves of all the chapel offers. Usually many of them have not. We make no attempt to contact them. This matter rightfully belongs to be resolved exclusively between the cadets and their parents.

In 2005, I attended the orientation of the new cadets and met with the entire group of twenty-four Jews who had come forward when the brigade chaplain, Father Edson Wood, directed them to meet with their respective chaplains. Rabbi Huerta, Lou Gross, and I were present at that gathering. The Jewish plebes asked us questions that probably reflected some of the reasons why others did not identify themselves. In addition to the reasons listed above, some where concerned that they could not read Hebrew and would feel "out of place." Some stated that they had never attended a Jewish service. There were some who believed that if they participated in chapel activities, they would be required to adhere to a high level of religious practice. These were minor trepidations, but apparently enough to keep others away. We minimized or assuaged these fears and antipathies by conveying to the new cadets that they should look upon the chapel as their "home away from home" and assuring them that we were not trying to impose any level of religiosity that they had no interest in achieving.

At the first Friday night service after their arrival, I usually address the cadets again. Our expressed recognition of their fears and attention to their needs makes them aware that at the Jewish chapel there is a community and support system for them. In my address I emphasize that I am always available to any cadet who is in need of someone with whom to talk. The rabbi certainly makes it clear that he is there for them; no strings attached. Our major concern lies with those new cadets who make snap decisions to leave West Point without the benefit of counseling or discussion with someone. A number of cadets who approached me during their first week of cadet basic training to express their intent to leave and changed their minds after counseling graduated successfully four years later. Attending their graduation gives me special pleasure.

We find that a number of non-Jewish cadets attend our Friday night services. Over many years we have hosted Jehovah's Witnesses and Seventh-Day Adventists. Lately, some Muslims have joined the group. They attend the Jewish Chaplain's Night held in mid-week and occasionally Friday night services. At the moment, a Muslim cadet is the director of the Jewish Chapel Choir while he continues to practice Islam. Other non-Jews also attend from time to time.

At the end of each academic year, when we plan for the baccalaureate service held prior to Graduation Day, we often have difficulty in sorting out the Jewish cadets from the non-Jewish cadets who have been attending services. Recently, a Christian cadet who attended our services for four years insisted on participating in the Jewish baccalaureate service, sitting on the bima with his Jewish classmates. He was, of course, welcome to do so.

It is clear that the attendees, Jews and non-Jews, are often attracted to our services because we provide Oneg Shabbat food after services for all to enjoy. The other two attractions are the warm familial atmosphere and the charisma of the rabbi.

Lou Gross, Herb Lichtenberg, and I constantly sought, and continued to seek, new ways of increasing cadet attendance at the chapel. In 1997 Lou noticed that the Christian groups had advisory committees that work with their respective chaplains to, among other things, help catalyze cadet attendance. He suggested that we organize a Jewish Community Council made up of the rabbi, lay leaders, military officers, cadets, Department of the Army civilians, volunteers, members of the Jewish War

Veterans, and any "old grads" interested in helping. I was appointed president of the council, and scheduled meetings one night a month during each academic year. Initially, the council made some strides toward increasing cadet participation in the Jewish community, but not enough to meet the degree of growth we sought.

The following year, an outstanding cadet from the Class of 2000 sat on the council. Scott Paul Handler eventually rose to the rank of cadet captain on the brigade staff and was designated a Distinguished Graduate (the top 10 percent of his class). Upon graduation, he and one classmate were awarded an East-West Center Fellowship "for two years of graduate study dealing with the Asia-Pacific Region" (out of a hundred such grants, only thirty-four are awarded to Americans). Scott had been an exchange student at the Air Force Academy for a semester and was active in the Air Force Jewish Community during his visit. Scott explained that Air Force had opened a Hillel chapter that catalyzed the Jewish cadets into greater attendance at chapel activities. He suggested that we do the same. The Community Council approved his suggestion. It was forwarded to my colleagues on the board of trustees of the West Point Jewish Chapel Fund for approval and funding. President Louis Gross obtained the approval of the fund and contacted his classmate Ben Breslauer for an entrée to the Hillel organization. Ben's great-uncle from Idaho, Yovir Montefiore Marks, Class of 1908, was related to the Sorif family. The Sorif Foundation supports the Hillel program, particularly in small schools that lack resources to staff and house a Hillel chapter. Hillel showed great interest in a West Point chapter. In short order we were into the program with the full approval of the superintendent and the commandant of cadets.

There were ancillary reasons for my interest in bringing a Hillel chapter to West Point. I wanted to create an environment of social interaction between the cadets and Jewish civilian students. My hidden agenda was to try to alleviate a problem faced by young Jewish soldiers—finding a Jewish spouse. Mixing with their peers through Hillel activities could be a start in that direction. The second reason for my interest in the program was to introduce the Jewish civilian students to the military in the hope that their experience would dispel any stereotypical thinking and attitudes toward professional soldiers, particularly the concept of Jews at West Point and as members of the military profession. The Hillel events have been highly successful in increasing cadet involvement in community activities and in changing some civilian student attitudes toward the military.

The first Hillel event at the chapel was planned and managed by the "older" generations sitting on the Community Council. We invited students from Queens College to participate. After the event, I asked the cadets for their frank evaluation. Once they realized that their unvarnished opinions were truly sought, they respectfully admitted that they had not liked the party. In frank terms, we had bombed! My response, with neither rancor nor hesitation, was that we should try having the cadets plan and arrange the next event. We promised to provide the funds but reserved the right to veto anything not adhering to official Academy policy and practice. This change produced many enjoyable events and continues to do so.

In true military planning style, the cadets organized themselves into a "general staff" (S-1, -2, -3, and -4) under the leadership of the appointed CIC, Cadet in Charge of the Jewish Cadets. They began writing military operations orders for each event, following the standard Five-Paragraph Field Order used for all military missions throughout the Army. I was astounded when I received the first order. I had never directed or requested them to follow this format and procedure, though I felt certain that their lay leader, Major Elizabeth Robbins, Class of 1992, had prompted it. After the conclusion of the event, they submitted an after-action report, also to my surprise. This was an excellent training vehicle and has remained in practice since the first event. It is also a team-building exercise, in consonance with Academy training.

In the midst of our developing these chapel activities, our new chaplain, Major Carlos Huerta, reported for duty. Rabbi Huerta is an outstanding man in every respect—physically, intellectually, spiritually, militarily, and personally. He stands over six feet in height and has the build of a defensive lineman; he is an imposing figure. He has a winning smile and maintains a warm, pleasant, jocular demeanor that makes him easily approachable; an important characteristic in a chaplain dealing with cadets.

He expresses his delight with a resounding "HOOAHH," the battle cry of today's soldier. His demeanor generates the familial atmosphere contagious to all in the West Point community as well as in the Jewish community. He rarely wears a dress uniform. He prefers wearing BDUs, the battle dress uniform.

Rabbi Huerta is truly a mud-boot soldier, an officer who is soldier-oriented, an American patriot, and an observant Jew in every respect. He originally was a field artillery officer in the Army Reserve. He is airborne-qualified and proudly wears the wings of a paratrooper with many jumps to his credit. Academically, the rabbi is highly accomplished. He holds a doctoral degree in mathematics and a master's degree in physics in addition to his theological degrees. Currently he is taking courses in Middle Eastern studies leading to another graduate degree and also devotes time to the study of the Koran. He has all of the attributes one would want in a Jewish chaplain. He is a role model for the cadets and is someone who relates well to them.

Before he came to us, Rabbi Huerta was teaching at a yeshiva in Jerusalem. He had a commission in the Army Reserve and agreed to be called to active duty as a chaplain at West Point. He proved to be all we sought in the way of a chaplain and more. Everyone at West Point, from the superintendent down to the cadets, warmed to him; the cadets in particular revere him.

When the post-9/11 war in Iraq began, Rabbi Huerta volunteered to deploy with the 101st Airborne Division. He joined them at their home station, Fort Campbell, Kentucky, and flew to Iraq with them. He left his wife with eight children, one of whom was a toddler, to await his return to West Point. We "sweated him out" with his family until his safe return ten months later. While he was in Iraq, he was selected as Rabbi of the Year by the Rabbinical Council. I attended the award ceremony with his wife, Merle, who gave a moving acceptance speech in his absence, including reading letters she had received from him. Shortly thereafter, he was selected by the *Forward* as one of the fifty outstanding Jews in America, along with such notables as Senator Dianne Feinstein, Abraham Foxman, and Deputy Secretary of Defense Paul Wolfowitz.

Rabbi Huerta's advanced academic degrees in mathematics and physics have not gone unnoticed by the dean of the Academic Board. The rabbi teaches mathematics for the Department of Mathematics and Hebrew (an elective subject) for the Department of Foreign Languages. He also tutors cadets in mathematics and physics. Prior to his tour in Iraq, he functioned as the battalion chaplain for the 1st Battalion of the 1st Regiment at West Point. This battalion of the National Guard provides security at the Academy, particularly at the four gates, the entrance points to the West Point central post. Often, during inclement weather at night, the rabbi could be found walking the posts with the soldiers on guard duty. He was ordered to return to Iraq in the fall of 2005 to provide Rosh Hashanah, Yom Kippur, and Succot services for some of the more than 1,000 Jewish soldiers on duty there. He stayed until mid-November.

Rabbi Huerta is an outstanding leader, truly a soldier, and an ideal mentor for the cadets. His sermons are down to earth. He masterfully weaves the Academy motto, "Duty, Honor, Country," into the parsha of the week and into the halacha. The cadets take to him like iron to a magnet. We are blessed to have him and have taken steps to keep him at West Point, if staying can be in consonance with his career objectives. The rabbi's participation on the Community Council has been a welcome addition.

When I learned of the rabbi's forthcoming deployment to Iraq with the 101st Airborne Division, I immediately thought in terms of finding a substitute. At the next meeting of the Jewish Community Council, I brought up the subject. The lay leader of the cadets, Major Elizabeth Robbins, Class of 1992, and the cadets at the conference table, virtually in unison, as if on cue, asserted, "We can handle it! We don't need a substitute." The response was astounding and quite gratifying. I learned early in my life to accept when competent individuals make such an offer. There were, however, three areas where a substitute rabbi was essential: conducting the baccalaureate services, counseling new cadets during Cadet Basic Training, and for the High Holy Days services.

Our first choice for conducting baccalaureate services was Chaplain (Colonel) Kenneth Leinwand, who at the time was the chief of chaplains for US Army Europe (USAREUR) and the 7th Corps. In that assignment he was responsible for the spiritual well-being of 60,000 troops and

130,000 civilians stationed throughout the continent. He had served as the Jewish chaplain at West Point from July 1987 to June 1990 in the grade of major. He is an ideal military chaplain. The cadets were fond of him during his tenure, particularly for his use of a guitar during services. The Department of the Army and the commanding general of USAREUR cooperated and granted him temporary duty for the 2003 baccalaureate. We were most thankful to have him back. The service was on a Thursday night; he flew back to Europe three days later.

Our next problem was to find a rabbi for the summer, particularly for the new cadets in basic cadet training. Chaplain (Captain) Bruce Bublick, U.S. Air Force Reserve, stepped into the gap to undertake this responsibility. We needed a rabbi to be available to counsel the new cadets in addition to conducting Shabbat services and to be available for Chaplain's Time on Wednesday nights. Though our cadets and lay leader could have adequately run the Friday night services and Chaplain's Time, we all agreed that the new cadets needed the professional ministrations of a rabbi. Rabbi Bublick also agreed to conduct High Holy Days services. Sadly, he was also called upon to conduct a military funeral, his first, for First Lieutenant David Bernstein, Class of 2001, who was killed in action in Iraq. David's funeral was well attended by the Jewish community, several of his Army comrades-in-arms, and members of the Command Group.

Rabbi Bublick has proven to be a highly reliable friend of the West Point Jewish community. We and the U.S. Army chaplaincy owe him a vote of thanks for his fine work and willingness to fill the void whenever asked. He volunteered to become the chaplain at Camp Buckner during the summer of 2005. This is a satellite installation of West Point located on the military reservation and used for summer field training for second-year cadets. On occasion he displays his loyalty to the Air Force. Prior to an Army–Air Force football game, he sent the following message via e-mail:

From the Book of Numbers, Chapter 37
And thus sayest Moses to the Lord,

"Behold, I lifted mine eyes and saw before me a man of God. And this man of God had a fine form, and he appeareth to me as a mule. Yes, a mule; the strongest and most loyal of all of your creatures. And this man of God appearing as a mule was adorned in the finest accoutrements, colored in black, gold, and grey.

"I looked to the heavens for a scant moment, and when my eyes returned . . . Behold! The man of God no longer resembled a mule. The colors were turned to blue and silver. I saw large, majestic wings boldly extended as the man of God soared to the skies in the form of a falcon bird.

"The falcon bird flew up the banks of the majestic river but soon returned. He devoured all of the remaining mules saying beware of a falcon dressed in mule's clothing."

GO AIR FORCE
BEAT ARMY

Note that the Book of Numbers has only thirty-six chapters. This thirty-seventh chapter was Rabbi Bublick's invention for this purpose. We appreciated his sense of loyalty to his service, but most of all his sense of humor.

Lay leaders in the Army perform their religious function in addition to their official duties. At West Point a lay leader is usually called the OIC, officer in charge. We usually have an OIC for the entire Jewish cadet population and a second OIC for the Jewish Chapel Choir. A cadet is also designated to be in charge of the Jewish cadet population and another for the choir. They are titled CIC. The OICs and CICs work closely with the rabbi while staying in close touch with their charges. These are demanding positions. The quality of the chapel activities and the performance of the cadets are in the hands of these leaders. The current OIC and her predecessor are unique in that, because no other officers are available, they found themselves in charge of both the cadet population and the choir.

I shall introduce the reader to Major Elizabeth Robbins, Class of 1992, the predecessor of the current OIC. Her official position was associate professor of social sciences; her branch, Corps of Engineers, her rank when she became OIC was captain. Major Robbins is an outstanding officer who handled her duties calmly and efficiently, particularly during the added load caused by the rabbi's deployment to Iraq. Her excellent leadership skills were demonstrated by the manner in which she disciplined the cadets by applying just the right amount of authority without stifling their enthusiasm. Under her leadership, the Jewish community thrived despite Rabbi Huerta's absence. Friday night services went on as scheduled. Hillel programs continued as planned, the choir did well and continued its program of visiting Jewish communities around the country. As is the case with all uniformed personnel, Major Robbins was transferred to the Pentagon. We were sorry to see her leave.

However, good fortune smiled down upon us once more. Captain Susan Schwartz, U.S. Naval Reserve, Retired, stepped into both jobs skillfully. For readers who are not familiar with comparative military ranks, a Navy captain is equivalent to a full colonel in the Army. Captain Schwartz has been doing an excellent job despite her unusually high combined workload of teaching and being a "double OIC." Her official position is assistant professor, Department of Electrical Engineering and Computer Science. Her extensive teaching duties combined with the Jewish cadet activities and those of the choir have become an awesome task. Captain Schwartz has accompanied the choir on many of its visits to congregations around the country. One of these trips was to sing at the White House during a Chanukah party hosted by President George W. Bush on December 6, 2005.

As of this writing I have had the pleasure of working with ten classes of Jewish cadets and have found them to be an outstanding group of young men and women. Jewish women began attending West Point with the first class of women admitted in 1976. They are a credit to the Corps and to American Jewry.

Earlier in this chapter, I wrote about the questions asked of me by the new cadets who arrived in July 2005. Jewish cadets come from a wide range of religious practice, from Orthodox families across the full spectrum to secular families. Some come from families where only one parent is Jewish. The program at the chapel is geared to accommodate all cadets of every background. Our more observant cadets try to keep kosher. We keep the kitchen well stocked with kosher foods. When training in the field, kosher field rations are supplied by the Army to those who want them. They are a version of the MRE's (Meals, Ready to Eat) used Army-wide as field rations in training and in combat.

From time to time a cadet will ask to be prepared for Bar Mitzvah. The first of these events occurred three years before the chapel became a reality. Lyle Jay Kellman, Class of 1982, became a Bar Mitzvah, with Rabbi Soltes as officiant, on February 20, 1981. The first Bat Mitzvah was Sherri Langston, Class of 1989. Rabbi Leinwand officiated. Two others had their Bar Mitzvah ceremony together several years ago. The Chapel Fund purchased their taleisim. It was my honor to present them. The attendees included roommates, classmates, athletic teammates, professors and their families, as well as the families of the two cadets. It was remarkable to witness the participation and support of the large non-Jewish group. It personified the alumni slogan, "Grip Hands!"

The rabbi prepares the cadets to conduct services for their troops when a Jewish chaplain is unavailable. We have some cadets who can lead services with the speed, fluency, and agility of a chazan (cantor); others have never before been in a synagogue. Virtually every Jewish holiday is celebrated one way or another. The academic and tactical departments, the superintendent, the commandant, and the dean are all very supportive of these events within the limitations of military requirements. The Chanukah celebration includes traditional foods and the lighting of the large stainless steel menorah mounted on the hill overlooking the parking area next to the chapel. Succot is celebrated by erecting a succah in the chapel garden. It is occupied and used by the cadets in accordance with tradition. Passover Seders are held in the chapel social hall for cadets and their families. Passover food is available in the Cadet Mess Hall for cadets who are observant. In the past, primarily before the chapel opened, we held public Seders in the Cadet Mess Hall or at the Hotel Thayer. The superintendent and staff were always invited. On occasion, 300 or more people attended. Members of the Academic Department, non-Jewish friends of Jewish cadets from the Corps, families, and visitors from many different religious groups were part of the celebration.

The first public Seder was hosted by Israel Orlian, father of Alvin E. Orlian, Class of June 1943, in 1941 with twelve Jewish cadets, the superintendent, Major General Francis B. Wilby, the commandant, Colonel

Phillip E. Gallagher, and others in attendance. I recall Seders at the Hotel Thayer during my years at the Academy, 1945 to 1949. Major General Maxwell Taylor, the superintendent, attended some of them.

All of these religious celebrations involve traditional foods, and all of them are strictly kosher. This portion of the story would not be complete without recognizing the incredible contribution of the Jewish War Veterans and their spouses in providing food for most of the Oneg Shabbats, the Seders for the cadets, and other events at the chapel. This activity is efficiently orchestrated by Lieutenant Colonel (Retired) Walter Stern and his wife, Anita. Both of these wonderful representatives of the "Greatest Generation" sit on the West Point Jewish Community Council. Colonel Stern is the National West Point Chapel liaison officer, and Mrs. Stern is the West Point co-chair for the Jewish War Veterans of America. They assign each oneg to one of the JWV posts in the Greater New York area. This was initiated by Past National Commander Edwin Goldwasser in 1971. Mrs. Stern recalled frying potato latkes (pancakes) on the Bunsen burners in the chemistry laboratory for Chanukah parties circa 1980 before the chapel opened.

All the volunteers do an outstanding job of providing food and moral support for our cadets. They look upon the cadets as their grandchildren. They are an essential part of the fabric of the West Point Jewish Community. At each baccalaureate service prior to Graduation Day, they present items of Judaica to each member of the graduating class. Their participation in chapel programs is one of the magnets attracting cadets to chapel activities. They are truly team-builders. We shall always be grateful for their important contribution to Jewish life at West Point. Many of the JWV members attend Friday night services and other functions.

There are a number of other recurring events of interest within the West Point Jewish community. In May of each year, the members of MACHAL—the organization of Americans who volunteered to fight for the new State of Israel in the War of 1948—hold a memorial service in the chapel and at the West Point gravesite of David "Mickey" Marcus, Class of 1924, brigadier, supreme commander, Jewish Forces, Jerusalem Area. Prime Minister David Ben-Gurion reminded Marcus upon appointing him brigadier that he was the first *aluf* (general) of a Jewish Army in 2,000 years. The Academy provides a color guard, bugler, and firing party for this event. It is most poignant to observe these old veterans proudly draw their aged bodies to attention as they perform at these ceremonies.

Each year we arrange to hold one or more plebe retreats. Very often these are held at the home of some hospitable plebe parents. The idea behind this event is team-building among classmates. This year, the Chapel Fund decided to treat them to a weekend at a Jewish hotel in the Catskill Mountains. Virtually everyone we worked with to arrange the weekend was either a mother or grandmother anxious for their young daughters and granddaughters to meet the cadets, though we made it clear that there were also women cadets coming to the retreat. A number of Muslim cadets signed up for the retreat, but cancelled because, unfortunately, their imam was injured in an automobile accident and they wanted to visit him. A glowing after-action report was forthcoming after the weekend.

The cadets initiated an annual event they aptly named the "Jewish Warrior Weekend." They invite students from colleges and universities throughout the Greater New York Metropolitan area, upstate New York, and New England to visit West Point for a football weekend. Added to the civilian group are cadets and midshipmen from the Air Force, Naval, and Coast Guard academies.

The visiting students are integrated into cadet life by being housed in cadet barracks, each student the guest of a cadet. They eat with the cadets and attend Friday night services followed by the typical Oneg Shabbat. Saturday morning services are available for those interested in attending. We obtain a block of football tickets for those who wish to attend the game on Saturday afternoon. There is a party in the chapel on Saturday night and a barbeque, also at the chapel, on Sunday afternoon in the Social Hall and chapel garden. Before the civilian students depart, our cadets ask them for comments on their experience at West Point during the weekend. The responses generally reflect a new learning experience, enjoyment, awe, respect for the military, and personal gratitude. Most of the students who respond indicate that they find West Point, the cadets, and our Jewish community a pleasant surprise.

In 2005, we were fortunate to host three young Israeli officers, a captain and two second lieutenants. They enjoyed a visit with the superintendent, attended a few classes with their cadet hosts, a football game, and other festivities. A highlight of their interaction with the cadets was their individual presentations of their experiences of ethically challenging combat situations.

There are usually two or three Hillel events per semester. There have been many repeat visits by college groups. Some of the visiting Hillel chapters are from Cornell University, University of Connecticut, Columbia University, Barnard College, Queens College, and Hofstra University. We keep the programming flexible to accommodate all variations of religious practice.

Every summer Hillel holds its International Student Leaders Assembly at Camp Moshava in Honesdale, Pennsylvania. This is a week-long event devoted to exchanging ideas and training student leaders. Several of our cadets attend part of this assembly with Mr. and Mrs. Louis Gross. The cadets are warmly received and are always a major attraction. Both male and female cadets attend in uniform.

Our reciprocal Hillel events at other colleges and universities are made by the Jewish Chapel Choir. They also visit a number of civilian congregations each year, where they perform for Shabbat services. They are housed by members of the host congregations. The choir is a very important chapel activity. There are several other choral groups at West Point. Ours is small but attracts non-Jewish cadets, often with amusing consequences when the rabbi of a host congregation attempts to award aliyas to non-Jewish members of the Jewish Chapel Choir.

The Alumni Gallery

Anyone who has had the experience of presiding over an organization, particularly a religious congregation, knows that every such group has some proactive members who resolutely prod the president to institute changes or to launch projects. During my presidency, I found that the West Point Jewish Community Council was no exception. My fellow alumni, by nature, are hard-driving when they feel that their ideas are worthy of implementation. Furthermore, they have access to graduates willing to back their ideas and to a command level well above me, the superintendent, whom they will contact without compunction, if they feel that their ideas are falling on deaf ears. Consequently, it is in my best interest and that of the organization to consider all suggestions seriously and to respond to the authors with facts and cogent reasons if the suggestion is to be rejected. More than three-quarters of a century of life's experiences have taught me to listen and carefully consider all the suggestions submitted by the membership. So when I received an e-mail message with a project proposal from William L. Schwartz, Class of 1959, I assured him that it would receive serious consideration.

Bill's first e-mail was sent to about twenty Jewish graduates and to Chaplain (Lieutenant Colonel) Richard White (then the Jewish chaplain) on June 20, 1999. He urged that we establish a "Memorialization Project" which would display the name of every Jewish graduate on some wall of the chapel. Rabbi White forwarded his message to me. In addition to assuring Bill that his suggestion would be carefully considered, I also informed him that all proposed wall "memorials" at West Point required an approval by a special committee. I emphasized that such approvals or disapprovals were out of my control.

His suggestion presented an excellent solution to the problem of selecting an appropriate display for the Chapel Gallery depicting some aspect of Jewish American military history. The reader may recall that the configuration of the chapel floor plan purposely was designed to require visitors to walk through the gallery to reach the sanctuary. My reaction to Bill's suggestion, therefore, was enthusiastic.

Bill's proposal was presented to the Community Council. It was received with a variety of responses ranging from negative to positive. Those against the project eventually realized that the display could be a unifying bond between the Jewish cadets and the Long Gray Line, and that they could look forward to seeing their names on the wall along with several hundred years of Jewish alumni. As a result, most of the initial opponents soon became supporters. Of equal or possibly greater value, the display would be an effective teaching tool for the thousands of visitors to the chapel each year, particularly the Jewish visitors.

It was also apparent that this was to be a research undertaking of enormous magnitude. Fortunately, we were blessed with two outstanding scholars and researchers sitting on the Community Council, Ms. Elaine McConnell and Lieutenant Colonel (Retired) Harry Garten. They comprised the research group. Elaine is a professional librarian and archivist who is a member of the staff of the Cadet Library and volunteers to help in many chapel and post activities. Harry has been a tireless volunteer at the chapel and supporter of West Point. Every summer, conditions permitting, he escorts a contingent of cadets from West Point and the Air Force Academy and midshipmen from the Naval Academy to Israel for several weeks. He also sits on the selection board that interviews candidates for those trips. Professionally, Harry is an attorney. The third person on the planning team was Colonel (Retired) Irwin "Buzz" Solomon. Buzz is an active college professor. He developed a variety of concepts on how and where to use the data in addition to the graphic wall display. My job was to design the actual wall display.

The next step was to obtain ratification of the project by the West Point Jewish Chapel Fund, presided over by Lou Gross. This would be our sole source of funding the project. The fund appropriated $100,000 and selected Colonel (Retired) David Peter Gleichenhaus, Class of 1961, as chairman of the Memorialization Committee. Pete lives on the West Coast, as does Bill Schwartz, the author of the project.

Now we needed the design and official approval. "Memorialization" was a misnomer, because the wall would contain the names of all graduates from 1802 to the present, the majority of whom are still living. It became "The Jewish Graduates Project" and the gallery was renamed "The Alumni Gallery."

Before submitting graphics to the Academy Monument Committee for approval, I discussed the project with Lieutenant Colonel John Luther, director of Academy advancement. The director is a member of the superintendent's staff and is the link between alumni and the superintendent. He later assured me that the superintendent's response was positive and to proceed with the design.

I sought the advice and guidance of Douglas Logan of George Logan & Son of Cold Spring, New York. The Logans have been providing bronze plaques and monuments to West Point for several generations. My concept was for a series of identical bronze plaques, each to accommodate two columns of brass nameplates of forty names each; a total of eighty names per plaque. Each plaque was to be two feet wide and four feet, three inches high. The brass nameplates were to be mounted by sliding them into vertical tracks on both sides of each of the two nameplate panels on each plaque. The line of plaques was to be mounted on the west wall of the gallery following a plaque containing the title of the display. I sought a line from the Torah that would appropriately describe the display for inclusion on the title plaque. We tried several, none of which did credit to the display.

When I posed the question to my wife, Dr. Yael N. Zickel, an Israeli sabra with an excellent biblical education, she recommended a quotation from King David's elegy to King Saul and his two sons, Jonathan and Malchisua. All three were killed by the army of King Achish in the Battle of Mount Gilboa between Israel and the Philistines. The following is the last stanza of King David's poem in the Second Book of Samuel:

> From the blood of the slain, from the fat of the mighty,
> The bow of Jonathan turned not back
> And the Sword of Saul returned not empty,
> And in their death they were not divided,
> They were swifter than eagles, they were stronger than lions.

The title plaque was accepted by acclamation as follows:

ALUMNI GALLERY
1802 TO PRESENT
(star of David)
" . . . SWIFTER THAN EAGLES . . . STRONGER THAN LIONS"
Samuel II, 1.23

The project graphics and explanation were submitted to the Monument Committee and were approved without changes.

Meanwhile our researchers, Elaine and Harry, were laboring over the archives and other sources, looking for graduates who were unquestionably Jewish. In other words, who were Jewish by parentage or by recognized conversion, Jewish by upbringing if only one parent was Jewish, participated in Jewish activities at the Academy, and (for those still living) agreed to have their names on the wall. Those who came from secular homes without religious experience in childhood were and are included if they identified themselves as Jews.

We composed a letter that was sent to all living graduates describing the project and giving them the opportunity to respond in the event they preferred not to have their names included in the display. Three alumni asked to be omitted from the display. We were careful not to include those who had converted to another religion. One early nineteenth-century graduate listed in the Register of Graduates had a list of six descendants, the last of whom graduated in 1946. Somewhere along the line there was a conversion in the family. Our researchers were able to identify those who were Jews.

By graduation in 2005, we had 823 verified names plus an additional seventy in classes through 2009 who are still cadets. We believe that there are between 5 and 10 percent more whom we have not been able to identify, particularly from the nineteenth century.

The Logan Company manufactured the plaques and nameplates. We ordered several additional plaques for future classes. It became painfully apparent that the paneling on the gallery wall was too light to support the cohort of ten plaques to be initially erected. It was necessary to remove the paneling and install two rows of structural strips within the wall to support the heavy load. The paneling was then replaced and the ten plaques mounted with the title plaque. Once the bronze plaques were on the wall, the tedious job of installing the nameplates was undertaken by Elaine McConnell and Charlene Mulyca, then administrator of the Chapel Fund.

The project was completed in time for the baccalaureate service for the Bicentennial Class of 2002. Pete Gleichenhaus and I had the privilege and the attendant joy of dedicating the Alumni Gallery at the service. The names of the Class of 2002, soon to graduate, were ceremoniously unveiled after the service. The reaction of the cadets and their families was proof enough that Bill Schwartz's idea and our efforts were worthwhile.

This ceremony is now an annual tradition at the Jewish Chapel. It has become a milestone for the new cadets to anticipate. When I address them at their first Friday night service after entering the Academy, I draw their attention to the display and emphasize that their names will be added when they graduate and become part of the Long Gray Line—a worthwhile goal!

The reaction of the public to the display, particularly the Jewish public, is one of surprise, even disbelief. The chapel receives close to 8,000 visitors each year. All of them walk past the wall. It is most enjoyable to witness old grads coming through searching for their names and proudly showing them to their grandchildren. Occasionally, they discover that the name of a Jewish grad is missing, or come upon the name of a classmate who was not Jewish, but for some reason, perhaps because of attending Jewish services, was picked up by our researchers from Jewish Chapel Squad rosters. We are currently planning some means of marking the nameplates of those killed in action.

The Three Amigos

Louis Gross, Class of 1954, and Herbert S. Lichtenberg, Class of 1955, entered the Academy after I graduated. I first met them when I joined the board of directors of the West Point Jewish Chapel Fund in 1969. Though my involvement in the project continued for several more years, the demands on my time diminished. That changed in the next decade as I found myself heavily engaged in the planning and construction of new projects at West Point.

It began when the Association of Graduates (AOG) contracted with me to manage the development of the Rupert Johnson Memorial Stadium at Doubleday Field and for the restoration of Quarters 101, the oldest building on the reservation and the home of the commandant of cadets. During that same period, my classmates asked me to renovate and expand the Class of 1949 Lodge near Delafield Pond. I undertook that project and all the others, except for the two AOG projects, on a pro bono basis.

Lou Gross became president of the West Point Jewish Chapel Fund in 1994. Shortly afterward, he appointed me president of the West Point Jewish Community Council. Lou and Herb Lichtenberg had been close friends for many years and participated in many charitable activities together. They are generous, gracious men, always considerate of others.

The tailgate barbecues hosted by Lou and Herb at all home football games are one of the social highlights of the season. They have diligently hosted those tailgates for approximately a quarter of a century. These incredible barbecues have been and continue to be held on the covered patio of Holleder Hall next to Michie Stadium. A cohort of braziers and cooks broil over 300 pounds of meats, poultry, and sausage. Beer, soft drinks of all types, snacks, and desserts round out the menu of these sumptuous feasts. While Herb mingles with the crowd and keeps an eye on the cooking crew, Lou roams about with a camera draped around his neck. He photographs guests singly and in groups. He pins all the photographs on a tack board which he places on display at the following tailgate for all to see. They are for the taking by those in the photos.

The tailgates are major undertakings. As many as 400 people attend on a given day. Lou and Herb begin working a day or two in advance of the game day buying and storing the food. On the day of the game, they pack the perishables in coolers, load up one or two cars, and drive to West Point from their homes in Long Island early in the morning. They do all of the heavy physical hauling of these loads until the cooking crew arrives to relieve them. They have faithfully hosted these events year after year, to the complete enjoyment of the officers, cadets, and soldiers and their families of the West Point community.

Herb was the major donor among his 1955 classmates for the construction of the Lichtenberg Tennis Center. This project was managed by the Association of Graduates and the U.S. Army Corps of Engineers. The center houses a large indoor tennis facility with ten courts, locker and shower rooms, a conference room, and administrative offices. It filled a major need at the Academy.

The three of us, Lou, Herb, and I, began working as a team after Lou assumed the presidency of the Fund. We focused on the two activities that needed the most outside support—the Academy chaplaincy and the Directorate of Intercollegiate Athletics.

We were introduced to the first of these needs as our work with the rabbi and religious activities at the Jewish Chapel brought us into close contact with Chaplain (Colonel) Scott McChrystal, the new cadet chaplain. In the course of our discussions with him, we learned of the needs of the chaplaincy, including major facility problems.

The most urgent problem at the time was the structural failure of the floor of the Chapel of the Most Holy Trinity, the Catholic chapel. I examined the floor and found it in imminent danger of collapse.

We agreed to undertake the replacement project. We engaged an engineering firm to perform a detailed study of the problem and to recommend a replacement system. Upon review of the report, we authorized the engineering firm to design the restoration and prepare working drawings and specifications. Upon approval of the documents by the director of housing and public works, we engaged a contractor do perform the work. All of this was accomplished with donated funds.

When we demolished the existing concrete floor, we discovered that the four columns supporting the transept roof had lost most of their foundations. The loss of the foundations placed the transept roof in jeopardy. The columns required substantial underpinning and reinforcement. Demolition commenced on July 5. The chapel had to be ready for a wedding on Labor Day. The project was completed on time and on budget within that narrow window of time.

Lieutenant General Daniel Christman, superintendent, visited the construction regularly. During one of his visits in the summer he remarked that the temperature in the chapel was unbearably hot. We offered to examine the feasibility of installing central air-conditioning. An engineering study found it feasible. We authorized the firm to prepare plans and specifications for approval by the Army and ultimately for construction. We now have the approved plans in hand and, with the efforts of the Association of Graduates and the director of Academy advancement, we sought the $1 million needed for construction.

This project defined the roles to be played by each of us in future projects. Herb seeks the donors and generates project ideas (though he likes to say that he is only the chauffeur, and that all of the work is done by Lou and me!). In reality, all three of us are involved in the business aspects of each project, such as contracts and the selection of the vendors.

Lou and I are both professional engineers. His areas of specialty are mechanical and electrical engineering; mine are in civil, structural, forensic engineering, and construction management. Therefore, I also deal with the contractors, engineers, and architects during design and construction on technical matters. This has proven to be a productive three-way working relationship. As our volume of work increased, someone began referring to us as the Three Amigos which they found easier to say than "Lou, Lew, and Herb." This appellation became our identification.

The cadet chaplain brought to our attention that there are religious groups at the Academy that do not have places of their own in which to worship. We agreed to renovate and adapt Building 147 as a Cadet Ecumenical Center. This building lies between Eisenhower Hall and what was then office of the Directorate of Intercollegiate Athletics. It was built in the nineteenth century as the Post bakery. In later years it was converted into two sets of quarters. Coincidentally, these quarters were occupied by two of my classmates, Jack Hammack and Ted Boland, when they were stationed at West Point.

The building consists of two stories and a basement. The two floors have essential identical configurations. Each has a combination dining and living room area extending the full length of the building except for a small kitchen at one end. This combined area made an ideal assembly hall. In addition, each floor has two rooms converted to offices and a bath. The scope of work included air-conditioning, a new electrical and lighting system, new kitchens and baths, a new roof, interior and exterior painting, a new entrance, new carpeting, and new landscaping.

At about the same time that Building 147 was being developed, Lou's classmate Ben Breslauer donated a substantial sum of money toward the creation of a large formal garden along the south side and rear of the Jewish Chapel to honor his great-uncle, Youir Montefiore Marks of the Class of 1908.

The garden, a masterpiece of horticulture, rises several levels above the elevation of the chapel floor via a circular handicap ramp that wraps around a large circular lawn. It contains thousands of plantings among hundreds of plant species from special grasses to flowers to shrubbery to trees. The outdoor furniture consists of sofa-size benches and tables with large umbrellas and seating strategically placed.

The garden provides an ideal ambience for relaxing, studying, or meditating. The latest addition is a bubbling fountain in bronze with a flight of doves hovering over a bird bath placed in the center of the large circular lawn. This was presented by Harold Gottesman, Class of 1950, shortly before his death. I found this a very enjoyable project to manage. It provides an elegant finishing touch to the Jewish Chapel.

The Old Cadet Chapel, an historic landmark monument erected in 1836, is virtually a museum of the American Revolution and early American military history. It was the place of worship for Jewish cadets during the 1940s and 1950s. It is currently the chapel for the Lutheran community.

This historical gem was deteriorating. Water intrusion, in particular, was destroying the wood trim and plaster around the windows. The pews were nicked, scratched, and broken in places. The carpeting was abraded and seedy looking. The Amigos teamed up with the Directorate of Public Works (DPW) to restore it to good condition. We undertook the removal and restoration of all pews and the refinishing of wood floors. The DPW painted the interior, installed new carpeting, repaired the exterior, and restored the window shutters. We found a serviceable pipe organ at Vassar University that was being replaced by a larger instrument. We obtained the organ and arranged for its installation on the balcony of the Old Cadet Chapel.

One day I noticed severe deterioration of the stone façade and exterior stairways of the cathedral-like Cadet Chapel. The deterioration, particularly on the rear stairway and the run of stairs down to the cadet barracks, had advanced to the point where these components posed a major hazard to anyone using them. The plaza and front entrance steps were also deteriorating. We brought this to the attention of the director of public works, who scheduled the project and eventually let a construction contract for their repair. Chaplain McChrystal requested that I examine the work during construction and consult with the contractor on the details.

The sound system at the Cadet Chapel was inadequate. A sophisticated new system was needed that could provide uniformly audible sound throughout the cavernous nave. Lou led this project. We purchased and installed the system with donated funds.

Currently, we are attempting to improve the level of comfort within the chapel during the warm months of the year. Lou has been experimenting with forced ventilation schemes. Recently, I envisioned a means of air-conditioning the chapel with a central system that would require a professional feasibility study and a source of donated funds to install it.

The director of intercollegiate athletics revealed that many of the needs of his directorate could not be funded with appropriated funds. Others that were federally fundable could not be approved by the budgeting authorities. These limitations severely stunted the growth of Army athletics, which must compete with well-funded civilian colleges and universities. One of the needed facilities was for intercollegiate gymnastics. Lou and Herb funded the facility, and I managed the design and construction. It is a steel industrial-style building of approximately 23,000 square feet with a two-story core along the full length of its centerline. One half of the building is devoted to gymnastics, the other to basketball practice courts. Named the Lou Gross Sports Center, it is located across the parking lot from the Lichtenberg Tennis Center.

The Academy must compete to hire the best coaches for each intercollegiate sport. In the process of improving the coaching staff, the director of intercollegiate athletics found that it was necessary to offer certain perquisites along with attractive pay packages to compete for coaches on the open market. Comfortable housing is a major attraction for candidates, but federal law prohibits the use of appropriated funds for this purpose. Donated money was needed.

The Three Amigos agreed to take on this project. The site selected for the housing was Worth Place off Washington Road across from Keller Hospital. Worth Place is a cul-de-sac street. The "pouch" of the cul-de-sac had been the site of the helipad for the medevac helicopters that served the hospital. The Non-Commissioned Officers Club was located east of the helipad before it was demolished some years ago.

The houses are all identical colonials with attached garages. Each is approximately 3,600 square feet with full stand-up attics and full or partial basements, depending on site conditions. The cost per house was $420,000 just for construction. The infrastructure—streets, drainage, sewerage paving, curbing, lighting. and sidewalks—was built and paid for by the Army. As of this writing, six houses are up and occupied, and three more are under construction.

Jewish donors provided most of the funds for the work described above and none of the funds came from the assets of the West Point Jewish Chapel Fund.

We also turned our attention to the Jewish Chapel, which is now approaching its twenty-fifth year. Repairs, upgrades, and other improvements are clearly needed. Even though the maintenance of the building is the responsibility of the Army, federal funds are often lacking at the moment of need. We are reluctant to let the building deteriorate or to delay improvements that will enhance the chapel's use or, if left undone, will truncate the cadet programs. At such times we take over and perform the work with donated funds.

Among other things, we demolished and replaced the handicap ramp from the parking area using granite pavers in lieu of the old concrete surface. DPW replaced the bronze railing along the ramp to meet the current standards of the American Disabilities Act. They also expanded the parking area to at least triple its capacity. We expanded the shelf space in the chapel library extending it to the ceiling along all walls. The objective was to create a center for Jewish history and learning. Currently, we are planning a total replacement of the kitchen appliances, cabinets, and flooring, not only to replace worn-out facilities, but also to adapt the kitchen to meet the requirements of its current use. The two sets of main entrance doors were worn and required refinishing. The stairs from Merritt Road to and including the entry plaza need reworking and repair. Mortar and calking have disappeared from many of the joints in the stonework. This work is in the planning stage. We hope that the DPW will obtains funds to do the repairs. If not, we will raise funds to do it ourselves.

In 2005, before he finished his tour of duty at West Point, Chaplain Scott McChrystal nominated the Three Amigos for the Order of Aaron and Hur—the highest award given to civilians by the Army's chief of chaplains. The award is given to those who have "emulated the ancient example of Aaron and Hur and have upheld the honor of the Chaplaincy of the United States of America reinforcing the spiritual objectives of their ministry."

The order was established in 1974 by the Army chief of chaplains. It is metaphorical of Exodus 17:8–13, which recounts the story of the Israelite warriors under the command of Joshua who were battling the forces of the fierce tribe of Amalek. God promised Moses that as long as he kept his arms extended over his head, the Israelites would prevail. If Moses dropped his arms, the fortunes of battle would turn in favor of the Amalekites. Moses obeyed God's warning and the Israelites were winning the battle. However, his arms began to tire and, as he lowered his arms, the Amalekites began crushing the Israelite army. Aaron and Hur rushed to Moses' side, placed a rock for him to sit on, and together each held up one of his arms until the sun set. This act enabled Joshua and his troops to defeat the Amalekites. Those awarded the order have been "holding up the arms of the Chaplaincy."

On January 19, 2006, Chaplain (Major General) David Hicks, the Army chief of chaplains, presented the award to each of the Three Amigos at the National Prayer Breakfast at the West Point Club. Approximately 500 military and civilian members of the command and some members of their families were in attendance. Chaplain (Colonel) John Cook, the current cadet chaplain, announced that only one other person had been awarded the Order of Aaron and Hur since its creation in 1974. Though it is rooted in Judaic history, adherents of all religions are eligible to receive this award.

Later that year Herb was designated a distinguished grad by the AOG. Past designatees have been General Westy Gail, H. Norman Schwarzkopf, and those astronauts who are grads. For the year 2007 my class nominated me for the distinguished graduate award.

As I write this story it is the month of February 2006. Herb Lichtenberg is approaching his seventy-third birthday, Lou Gross recently celebrated his seventy-sixth birthday, and I am about to celebrate my eightieth birthday. Many more projects will need management and funding. The Jewish Community Council will continue to need proactive alumni support. But we three Amigos recognize that Father Time is watching us, and that it is time to pass the torch to younger alumni to continue the march. We have begun our search.

PART 2

MY STORY

Philip Roth, in his book *Portnoy's Complaint*, described in accurate detail the neighborhood where I spent the first decade of my life—the enclave of lower-middle-class Jews in the Weequahic section of Newark, New Jersey. Very few non-Jews crossed my path during those early years of my life. It was toward the end of this decade that I became interested in attending West Point.

We owned our two-family home at 119 Schley Street. It is now under the entrance ramp to Interstate Highway 78. The late Roaring Twenties, the first two years of my life, rapidly slid into the deep depression of the thirties. In short order our home was lost to the mortgage company. I recall sitting in the car while my father fought with the lender unsuccessfully to keep it. We became tenants. Somehow, our tenant had become our landlord. My young life seemed unaffected by the change in ownership. That endless wait in the car and my fathers sad face are my unpleasant memory of the loss.

My birth beat Charles Lindbergh's historic flight to Paris by almost two months, but I almost did not live until his departure date. I have been told that an intern at the hospital where I was born found me in the nursery close to death from malnutrition. Therefore, when my brother Bob arrived three years later, the birth took place at home. Mother had lost all trust in hospitals because of my near-death experience. We almost lost Bob in 1933 from the lethal one-two punch of asthma and pneumonia. His recovery was miraculous in the absence of antibiotics and other modern medical marvels.

We were a religiously observant family. Mother kept a strictly kosher home. She baked challah for every Shabbat and every holy day. Friday night dinners were elegant occasions: candles, white tablecloth, Kiddush over the wine, blessings over the challah followed by the usual chicken dinner. Holidays were major family events usually involving a gathering of the clan—all the aunts, uncles, and cousins, more than forty in all, who lived within driving range of the Weequahic enclave.

My father prayed daily and studied the intellectual aspects of Judaism in the precious little time available to him from his struggle to support us. For the longest time, he held two jobs. Dad had the enviable talent of absorbing and retaining vast quantities of information. He had the intellectual curiosity that drove him to continuously add to his reservoir of knowledge. He enjoyed "holding court" with our extended family to share this knowledge. Everyone hung on to his every word, but in time my brother and I realized that no one in his engrossed audience understood a single word of his discourses.

Passover Seders were extended-family extravaganzas. Mother's six sisters and one sister-in-law pooled their resources and wonderful culinary talents to turn out banquets that clearly displayed those talents. Dad always officiated at the Seders. He countenanced no levity during the ceremonial portions of the Seder. However, between the antics of us young children and the comedic support of a few devilish and slightly irreligious uncles, Dad usually had his hands full keeping order at the vast table. Nevertheless, these were joyous events, and once the ceremonial portion of the Seder ended, levity ruled. Some of my aunts and uncles could have been successful stand-up comedians; at least we children were convinced of that.

We belonged to a small, poor synagogue a few blocks from home. The rabbi and his wife ran a Hebrew school. The synagogue and school were located in a ramshackle, grungy house. I began Hebrew school in this warren when I was seven years old. I was fascinated as I learned to read and write the Hebrew alphabet. My religious schooling was to improve three years later when we moved away from Newark. Public schooling in Newark was quite good. Bragaw Avenue Elementary School was a short walk from home. The student body was virtually 100 percent Jewish, as were most of the teachers. The school closed for all the major Jewish holidays.

These were the days of the street vendors with their horse-drawn wagons. Milk was delivered to the house. Virtually every family refrigerated their perishables in an ice box requiring the daily delivery of ice. Mr.

Prisbel, the vegetable man, hawked his wares from a ramshackle truck. He would sing out "Toms, pots" for tomatoes and potatoes, and other abbreviated names of vegetables I've long since forgotten. Mr. Prisbel had a short, stubbly beard that never got longer or shorter, a phenomenon that fascinated me. The cutlery man came by occasionally to sharpen knives and scissors.

In the cold of winter the "sweet potato man" with his rolling oven baked them on the street and served them with a big glob of butter; all for a few cents each. In the summer we could always look forward to the bells of the Good Humor ice cream truck. Other delicacies notwithstanding, there was the delicious charlotte rousse, a thin wafer of cake topped with a swirl of whipped cream, all ensconced in a cardboard cylinder. It was the ultimate treat.

The neighborhood crawled with kids. We managed to have a wonderful time without the planned schedules of twenty-first-century youngsters and the ubiquitous soccer moms who haul them from activity to activity. We used our imaginations and limited resources to entertain ourselves. One of our favorite pastimes was to make elastic guns out of wooden clothespins, small pieces of lumber, and large rubber bands cut from the inner tubes of tires. We rigged them in such a way that we could "fire" a rubber band about ten feet. We fought friendly battles with these homemade weapons. Trash can covers were used as shields. I do not recall any of us being injured from this dangerous activity. My first experience in combat was "fighting" these skirmishes.

Dad was a test pilot during World War I. He talked about a Colonel White from the Army Air Service who taught him to fly before his eighteenth birthday. His most hazardous assignment was to test fire a machine gun through the whirling propeller arc, a new technology that cost many shot-off props and dead-stick landings before they worked out the synchronization. All of this took place at the Standard Aircraft Company in Elizabeth, New Jersey, where the venerable Curtiss JN-4, the Jenny, was manufactured. Mother worked in the plant as a bookkeeper. She was a beautiful young woman who was invited to take a screen test by the movie industry. My grandmother vetoed this. Instead she married my father.

Dad was admitted to Cooper Union after the war and graduated in 1923 with a degree in mechanical engineering. His first job was with Walter Chrysler, where he participated in the design of the first Chrysler automobile. Unfortunately, he elected not to move to Detroit with the company. His mother convinced him that "the West was not for a Jewish boy!" He was not to obtain another position in engineering until the commencement of World War II.

My parents were born at the dawn of the age of the twentieth-century quantum leaps in science and engineering. They witnessed the birth of flight and lived to see the walk on the moon and beyond. Dad was fascinated with science and engineering, absorbing new developments as they emerged. His enthusiasm for engineering was the one identifiable academic influence he had on my career interests; I was also fascinated with engineering and looked forward to studying it.

Both of my parents were born in the United States. Mother's family was the first to arrive in the United States. Her father (my namesake) arrived in 1886 before the Statue of Liberty was erected; my paternal grandparents immigrated a few years later. Dad was raised on the Lower East Side; Mother in Hell's Kitchen, an all-Irish neighborhood. Both were staunch American patriots, proud of their citizenship and of their Jewish heritage.

A major source of pride for my father was that he was born on June 14, Flag Day. He planted the seeds of American patriotism in our hearts, along with a strong sense of values and ethics. One way he accomplished this was to take us on modest automobile excursions to historic sites such as Valley Forge, Fort McHenry in Baltimore harbor where Francis Scott Key wrote our National Anthem, Independence Hall and Betsy Ross's house in Philadelphia, and George Washington's Mount Vernon home. The highlight for me of these family roadtrips was West Point.

These trips were the first learning sojourn into American history for my brother and me. We were fascinated and looked upon our country's history with awe and upon its players as true heroes. To this day we both have a strong interest in the history of this nation.

On occasion, we traveled to Washington, D.C., to celebrate the High Holy Days, with my mother's brother and his family. Dad took advantage of these trips to introduce my brother and me to the capital and its points of interest. In 1934, during one of these visits he drove my us to Washington National Airport, and chartered a light aircraft and pilot for a flight over the city. One can imagine the awed reaction of our neighbors in Newark who gathered around to listen to a seven-year-old kid describe his flight. It was a unique event for anyone, much less a child, to fly in 1934!

Never once, despite all of these historic visits, did my father ever prompt me, urge, or suggest that I should consider trying for an appointment to West Point or to seek a career in the Army. On the other hand, neither he nor my mother discouraged my aspiration. Both parents fully supported the goal I set for myself at the age of nine years. Though they may have considered it a childhood fantasy, they realized as time went on that this was anything but a kid's yearning. They were always ready to help me, but only if I asked.

As I look back into the early part of my childhood, I realize that there were other influences that reinforced my desire to serve my country. Among them were the radio shows that we religiously listened to in the late afternoon and early evening. These were "hero" shows where the good guys were easily discernable from and overcame the bad guys: Tom Mix, Jack Armstrong the all-American Boy, Don Winslow of the Navy, Superman, and the grand master of them all, the Lone Ranger. Some years ago I listened to a tribute to this hero and heard that many an American soldier invading a foreign shore relieved his tension with the Ranger's famous cry to his horse, "Hi-yo Silver, away!" These shows, as simplistic as they may have been, were dramas of good over evil. These characters were icons and the mentors of my generation.

It was in this Jewish American environment that my desire to attend West Point and to serve my country strengthened. This flame was fanned by the growing anti-Semitism in the United States and the world: information about genocide of 6 million Jews by Adolf Hitler and his Third Reich began leaking out of Europe, and the constant haranguing and ranting of our domestic anti-Semites and demagogues, such as Father Coughlin and Gerald L. K. Smith on the talk-radio circuit. Even one of my heroes, Charles Lindbergh, joined them, to my deep disappointment.

Their diatribes infuriated me. The accusation that Jews do not and cannot fight plus other lies stoked my resolve to pursue a military career. I knew then as I know now that America and her ideals are worth defending.

In 1937 we moved to Montclair, a lovely New Jersey suburb. This was at the urging of my brother's physician. Bob continued to suffer from chronic asthma and extensive allergies. Supposedly, the air in Montclair was cleaner because the town was at a higher elevation than Newark. I am not sure that the air was cleaner, but Bob and I experienced the move as a breath of cultural fresh air and an adventure. The Montclair school system was excellent. I left Newark halfway through the fifth grade. When I entered the Montclair school, I was required to start at the beginning of the fifth grade. At the end of that year, I was promoted to the seventh grade, skipping the sixth. The experience of meeting and befriending all of those non-Jews, including African-Americans, was fascinating if not exhilarating for both of us. We thrived in our new surroundings.

My parents joined Temple Shomrei Emunah in Montclair, a Conservative congregation led by Rabbi Irving Lehrman. He was an outstanding man who had a way with young people that endeared him to them. In addition to his rabbinical abilities, teaching and speaking skills, he had been an accomplished college baseball player. We admired him for that above all else. He prepared both Bob and me for Bar Mitzvah. Bob proved to be quite the Hebrew scholar and for a while we thought he was going to become a rabbi. Instead he studied medicine and became a highly respected orthopedic surgeon. My wife, Yael, claims that it is no accident that both Bob and I ended up with knives in our hands; him with a scalpel, me with a bayonet!

All through our childhood, the extended family was the center of our social life. I am sure that the universal lack of money had much to do with this. My maternal grandmother aptly filled the role of family matriarch with quiet dignity. Collectively we were known as the Lowenstein family. The seven sisters and three brothers and their spouses and children comprised the "clan."

The Lowensteins constituted a warm social circle with a minimum of conflict. They gathered almost every Saturday night for the men to play penny-ante poker, the women to trade recipes and gossip, and the children to do whatever we could get away with. I enjoyed the warmth and mirth of these gatherings. The adults bonded to a point where all agreed to a "Lowenstein family plot" at a local cemetery. As we got older, the cousins did the same thing at the same cemetery. I was excluded. They were convinced that I would be buried in Arlington. But I was a member of the Lowenstein Cousins Club, the new generation of the extended family.

The greatest contribution of the extended family to me was its genuine interest in my accomplishments and its encouragement in whatever we did or planned to do. Somehow or other a representative group would attend every major event in our young lives. I always felt that I had a cheering section. It nurtured my feeling of self-confidence.

Meanwhile, my attraction to the military continued to grow. In my preteen years I would occasionally round up young kids walking by my house, whether or not I knew them. I would convince them to form a squad and allow me to march them up and down the street in front of our house. This was my first venture into leadership, much to the amusement of my parents and neighbors.

When I was about eight years old, an older cousin gave me his copy of the Manual of the Boy Scouts of America. He and his father had outstanding records in scouting. He was an Eagle Scout and Explorer; his dad had earned the highest award in scouting, the Silver Buffalo. I devoured the contents of the manual and swelled with pride when, at the age of twelve, I was inducted into local Troop 4, Montclair. This was a Lord Baden-Powell troop led by Howard van Vleck, a patrician from one of Montclair's most prestigious families. He was a superb role model for the members of our troop. It was 1939.

I reveled in the survival skills taught to us in the Scouts. Camping, regardless of the weather, provided me with some of my happiest days. The program could not have been more suited to me if it had been tailored for me. The morality, attention to duty, the requirement to help others, and the wealth of other skills became part of me. Scouting was to end sooner than I expected. War clouds had been gathering, and the storm erupted on September 1, 1939. World War II had started.

Two years and three months later, Pearl Harbor was bombed and our lives were destined to change forever. At fourteen, I was too young to go to war. My parents had been married five years before I was born. It angered me not to be able to join America's growing fighting forces. Why had my parents waited so long to start a family? I am sure that they were relieved not to have a son of draft age, but I never received an answer to my question.

In time, part of my frustration was relieved when the Civil Air Patrol, an official auxiliary of the U.S. Army Air Corps, advertised that it was organizing a Cadet Corps of high school students from the surrounding counties. It was to meet weekly at the Montclair State Teachers College. It was 1942. I was a fifteen-year-old high school junior and wasted no time in joining the Cadet Corps along with hundreds of other boys.

We went through a training program consisting of a multitude of aviation subjects, such as aerial navigation, radio transmission, Morse code, basic aeronautics, military tradition, and close-order drill. One evening, standing in ranks with the entire corps, First Lieutenant Tublitz of the Senior Patrol approached me and ordered me to report to Captain Noble, the senior squadron commander of Squadron 221-1. I wondered what I had done wrong to warrant this attention. The captain informed me that I had been selected to become the corps commander. I was flabbergasted. This was a real opportunity to lead. I took it.

My initial act was to create a cadet staff and organize the corps into smaller units, each with its own commander and chain of command. As we began to take shape, the Air Corps decided to add a women's corps equal to and alongside the male unit. The high school girls turned out in droves. The Air Corps assigned a Women's Army Corps (WAC) lieutenant to assist me in training this new group. The CAP Cadet Corps was soon seen as the "in" group to join. Before long I found myself commanding a small battalion of cadets. We assisted the Senior Squadron on certain of their missions. The Air Corps provided us with five light aircraft, Taylorcraft L2-Ms complete with Air Corps markings and olive-drab paint. The real plum for the cadets was to be chosen for a flight with a senior member of the patrol.

Two moments of unexpected celebrity came out of my CAP activities. I was invited to be the featured guest on the NBC *Margaret Arlen Show*, a coast-to-coast morning radio show that was a forerunner of the current *Today* television show. Her announcer was Harry Marble, a well-known name in many American homes. I still have the script autographed by Miss Arlen and Mr. Marble amongst my memorabilia.

The second event occurred while at summer field training at Mitchell Field, Long Island. One Sunday morning, while preparing to return home at the end of the training period, I was told to climb aboard a B-24 bomber that was to fly out over the Atlantic. While flying, I was to be interviewed by the host of the weekly radio show *We, the People Speak*. This was another coast-to-coast broadcast aired every Sunday afternoon.

We broadcast from the flight deck of the massive four-engine bomber. Before taking off I managed to telephone my parents, who immediately notified the "clan" of this unexpected event. After the broadcast, the pilot gave me the opportunity to take the controls and turn the plane back toward Mitchell. It was one big "WOW" for me! These were heady experiences for a sixteen-year-old high school kid.

The time to begin my effort to obtain an appointment to West Point was rapidly approaching. The procedure for a civilian to seek an appointment during the 1940s began with writing a letter to one's congressman and to both senators requesting to be placed on their list of interested candidates. Notices would eventually be sent to those on the list announcing when and where the next competitive examination would be given. Each legislator was permitted to have a number of appointments in the Corps of Cadets. The number of openings available each year depended on how many of the permitted number were at the Academy at that time. Appointments could be made with or without the results of the competitive examination. The decision belonged solely to the legislator. The most even-handed way to appoint was on the basis of the competitive examination grades, the highest being the principal appointee followed by the first and second alternates. The names of these three would be sent to the Academy for entrance examinations and further evaluations.

Legislators who appointed without the use of the competitive examination score often used the appointment as a political favor. Preparation for the examination was a major undertaking requiring intense study. Therefore, the method of selecting an appointee became a major concern to me. My parents had no political connections. I needed to know how my congressman would select the principal appointee. Although I planned to take the examination for the open senatorial appointment, I never believed that I could prevail at the state-wide level. Therefore, I limited my query to my congressman. I decided to call him and request a person-to-person meeting with him. He agreed and invited me to visit him at his home in Livingston, New Jersey, on October 10, 1944.

My father drove me to the congressman's palatial mansion, sited a long way back from the street. I learned from the congressman later that his son flew a light aircraft for the Army and would occasionally come home to visit in his aircraft and would land it on the front lawn of the house. The scene was overwhelming. I felt a rising tide of discouragement but insisted on going up to the house alone. Dad stayed in the car, and I hiked up to the front door.

Congressman Robert W. Keane answered the door himself. I found myself face-to-face with a tall, imposing, distinguished man with a mustache. I felt like a sapling in front of a giant California redwood. We shook hands. He asked what I cared to discuss. I came right to the point, looked into his eyes, and said, "Sir, I am planning an intense course of study in preparation for the competitive exams to West Point. Before I invest the time and effort, I would like to know if you plan to appoint the candidate with the highest grade."

He drew himself up, smiled down at me, and replied, "Young man, you have my word of honor that the man with the highest score will receive my appointment."

We shook hands, I thanked him and turned to leave. He stopped me and asked, "How did you get here today?" I explained that my father had driven me and was waiting at the curb. He reacted, "My goodness, please ask him to come in." I hiked back to the street. This time we drove up to the door. We spent a pleasant hour with the congressman and left.

This event was an exhausting experience for a seventeen-year-old. I felt as if I had climbed up Mount Olympus and negotiated with Zeus!

Encouraged by my discussion with the congressman, I plunged into my studies with fervor and zest. I crammed each day, committing a vast compendium of facts to memory. I devised systems for study by rote, such as the study of American history. Rather than start with the Founding Fathers and proceed chronologically, I broke history down to a series of major subjects, such as the evolution of the Constitution and its amendments, the development of and changes to the monetary system, landmark legal decisions, wars, and so on. I committed this breakdown to memory. English literature posed a unique organizational problem. I resolved this by designing timeline charts of both English and American literary works and authors, including famous extracts from works of note. This part of the examination exceeded the scope of the high school level of literature. I committed the chart to memory. Mathematics, algebra, and geometry were not a problem. Vocabulary, however, required more memorizing.

Dad rigorously tested me every night after dinner. By the time the examination date rolled around, my mind was literally stuffed with information. It was obvious to me that when the examination was over, all of that crammed information was going to fly right out of my head. The location of the examination was the main post office in Newark. I vividly recall stepping onto the elevator to the examination room, turning and seeing the expression of anticipation on my father's face as the elevator doors closed.

The wait for the results of the examination was agonizing. Our postman, Mr. Pitts, participated in the nail-biting. Whenever an official federal envelope arrived for me, he would wait for me to open it. It finally did. I was Congressman Keane's principal appointee! Much to my surprise, a response from Senator Hawkes also arrived. Much to my astonishment, I was his second alternate appointee. I could not believe that my score was the third highest in the state-wide contest. Subsequently, I received letters from Senator Hawkes advising that I had been elevated to his principal appointee and asking whose appointment I would accept.

I accepted the senator's appointment, relinquishing the congressman's appointment to a local boy.

The initial notification from Congressman Keane arrived on March 1, 1945, twenty-four days before my eighteenth birthday. I realized what that look of anticipation on my father's face meant as the elevator doors closed at the post office; I was on the threshold of draft age. Since winning the appointment was an unknown, I had already made a contingency plan if I failed to make it. I had no desire to become a draftee; I wanted to enlist. At that point in the war, the only available service open to an enlistee was the Navy, but solely as a rear gunner on a torpedo bomber. The draft was then providing manpower to all of the services. I obtained the application, filled it out, and hid it in my desk. It stayed there.

The next step in the process of becoming a cadet belonged to the U.S. Army and the United States Military Academy. I was required to take a physical examination, another written examination, and an interview by a board of officers. The last two posed no problem for me. The interview seemed to be a test of my demeanor, composure, and ability to articulate. I was asked to describe in detail how I had traveled from my Montclair home to Governor's Island in New York harbor where the interview was held.

The physical examination took two days. I could not have imagined how detailed and thorough the process was. After all of the prodding, poking, peering, and testing, the results finally arrived. Much to my chagrin and disappointment, I was disqualified because of a large mole on my left wrist and eight diopters of exophoria in my right eye. It was already April, and the reporting date at West Point was July 2. What to do? There was not much time to correct these defects, if they were correctable.

I had been bloodied, but refused to quit. I told my parents that I was willing to have the mole removed surgically and would discuss the eye problem with Dr. Emanuel Goffman, an ophthalmologist and one of my staunchest supporters. He was an Army Reserve officer with an illustrious record. Dr. Goffman first examined my eyes to verify the Army's diagnosis. I, indeed, measured eight diopters of exophoria, a tendency for the eye to turn outward. He arranged for me to visit Dr. Kerne, an ophthalmologist specializing in eye therapy to correct certain deficiencies, including muscle problems like exophoria. This was a new development in ophthalmology. She started me on a rigorous exercise program.

Meanwhile we contacted Dr. Alexander Zimany at the Skin and Cancer Hospital in New York City where plastic surgery was performed on April 12, 1945, eighty-one days before my reporting date. The first thing I heard as the anesthetic wore off was that President Franklin Roosevelt had just died. The operation was a success, and I began my recuperation. I was scheduled for reexamination by the Army in late May.

Before the reexamination, Dr. Kerne warned me that the examining doctor was likely to accuse me of cheating on the eye exam. She instructed me to persuade him to call her if this occurred.

The results of the surgery were accepted. But as warned, Captain Kimmelman of the Army Medical Corps accused me of cheating on the eye exam. He refused to accept the results and refused to call Dr. Kerne. I was livid. My journey to this point had been too long and arduous to accept his snap judgment. I demanded to speak with his superior officer. He ushered me in to speak with Major Stack, also a physician. He was a tall, slender, distinguished-looking officer with a no-nonsense but laid-back demeanor. I later learned that in keeping with his patrician-like appearance, he rode his horse in Central Park each morning before coming to work. The following dialogue took place:

Major S: "What's the problem?"

Capt. K: "He's cheating on his eye reexam."

LLZ: "I am not. My doctor warned that I would be accused of this. I've been through intensive therapy that corrected the condition."

Capt. K: "Let him go to VMI or the Citadel. I'm not signing off on this."

LLZ: "VMI is not an option. I have struggled to get this far. I *will* go to West Point."

Major S: "Sign the damned thing and let him go."

Capt. K: "No sir. You sign it, if you wish."

Major S: "Son, I will sign this under one condition; that you come to visit me when you graduate."

LLZ: "Thank you, sir. I promise." (And I did.)

I made it! Indeed, the pen is mightier than the sword!

It was time to mentally prepare myself for the upcoming "trial by fire." Long before trying for an appointment to West Point, I had learned about the rigors of the plebe system. I was well aware of what awaited me. Most incoming cadets were not aware of the details of the system. The initial shock was much more severe for them than for those of us who knew something about it.

The medical saga that miraculously opened the gates of West Point for me had its price. The healing process from the April 12 surgery was slow. It was far from complete on July 2 when I reported for duty. During the eighty-one-day period of recuperation I was unable to exercise. I was essentially sedentary the entire time. My arm and upper-body strength diminished while my weight increased. The transplanted skin on my wrist was fragile, and the six-inch by six-inch donor site on my abdomen was still raw. Though psychologically ready for the ordeal, I was a long way from being physically ready to undertake it. It was in this condition that I was "greeted" by First Classman Benjamin Lester Landis, Jr., Class of 1946, with a loud bellow trumpeted a few inches from my face, "Drop that bag, Mister! Pick it up! Drop it! Stand tall! Suck in that gut! Pull your chin in! Shoulders back!" Beast Barracks was underway—the twig was being bent.

Plebe Year

When I entered the Academy, I could not have been in worse physical condition. The surgical wounds on my left wrist and abdomen had not yet fully healed. I was also about twenty pounds overweight. After Beast Barracks, I had lost forty pounds and was sent to the hospital for nourishment. (Plebes in those years were frequently kept from eating.) My body strength diminished with the weight loss. I was ordered to report to my cadet company commander to explain this failure. When I displayed my wounds and explained the weight gain and loss of strength, my treatment by the upperclassmen eased a bit. However, physical weakness and excessive weight gain were not seen as soldierly qualities!

Both of my roommates in Beast Barracks disappeared within the first ten days of training. One had psychological problems and was hospitalized for psychiatric treatment. I never saw him again. My second roommate resigned and went home. The loss of roommates created a difficult situation for me. I was in virtual isolation. We were limited to conferring only on official business when out of our rooms. The absence of someone with whom I could talk, compare notes, relax, and form a friendship had a tough effect. Most lacking was the availability of someone to awaken me and help me with my equipment if I overslept. And indeed that happened!

We were scheduled for a night march at an unpublished time between taps and reveille. I stayed up too late preparing my equipment. I awakened terrified, hearing the command "Close march!" I looked out into the assembly area to see my company climbing the hill to the Cadet Chapel. There was no question; I was in real trouble. Oversleeping a formation or missing it for any reason was a major offense.

I grabbed my equipment (rifle, full field pack, etc.) and raced out across the area in the general direction I saw my unit marching. Then I heard that dreaded command, "You, man. Halt!" I froze and was confronted by an upperclassman. He surprised me with his humane reaction when I explained how this had happened. He told me where the companies were rendezvouing and said he would slip me into my unit.

Unfortunately, my unit moved out before we got there. The upperclassman slipped me into another company and told me not to speak to anyone. I marched off with them. To this day I vividly recall the first rest halt. I was lying on my back staring at the stars. I recall thinking I would have preferred to have been sitting on one of those stars.

When I arrived at our bivouac area at Round Pond, I again heard "You, man. Halt!" This time it was my cadet company commander. He was incensed. The field exercise was a competition between companies, and he was honor-bound to report absences. When he called the roll at the barracks, someone had answered "Here" when my name was called. At the break in the march they discovered that I was missing and sent out a search party looking for me, to no avail.

This issue dogged me all through plebe year until Recognition Day the following June. The meanest upperclassman congratulated me on surviving! Most important, not one upperclassman or officer throughout my plebe year ever made an anti-Semitic comment about my performance.

The Fourth Class (Plebe) System

The purpose of the discussion in this section is to explain the details of the plebe system as I experienced and knew it during my four years as a cadet, with the subsequent changes to the system woven into the explanation to assist the lay reader in understanding the stories submitted by the Jewish graduates in or with their questionnaires (see chap. 3). It may also be of interest to graduates who have not followed these changes through the years.

Until 1961 cadets were assigned to companies in each regiment according to height to create uniformity for parades. The tall cadets were called "Flankers"; the short cadets were called "Runts." I was a Runt.

Unfortunately for me the shorter the cadet, the more severely was the plebe system applied; the taller the cadet, the more lenient. The gradation seemed to uniformly follow the change in the height of the cadets. We Runts were accused by the Flankers of having a Napoleonic complex; hence our austere approach to the plebe system. Regardless of labels, there was no doubt that it was more difficult to be a plebe in a Runt company than in a Flanker company. The system today since "height integration," is considerably different from the system under which I lived in 1945 to 1946.

The word "plebe" is derived from the Latin word *pleb* which was the title of the lowest-level citizen in the Roman social hierarchy. The dictionary describes the pleb as a coarse, vulgar common person, a meaning still conveyed by the English word "plebeian." The plebe's status, similarly, is at the lowest level of the social and military hierarchy of the Corps of Cadets. With respect to the refinements of demeanor and behavior of the upperclassmen, the plebe is considered coarse and common; in essence, raw material.

Before the reader criticizes this as elitism, bear in mind that every upperclassman started out as a plebe. Also bear in mind that virtually every incoming plebe class consisted then as now of a high percentage of valedictorians, star athletes, Eagle scouts, high achievers, and others with outstanding accomplishments. Some came and come from wealthy families, some from poor families. Some were and are children of general officers, some of enlisted soldiers.

The plebe system, by design or otherwise, was and continues to be a great leveler. It is designed to instill a humility to these high achievers. I shall never forget the response from a classmate when an upperclassman asked him where he was from (a usual question asked of plebes). His answer was, "Sir, do you want my winter address or summer address?" Also, I shall never forget the wrath that descended upon him for his "aristocratic" answer.

The new cadet entering Beast Barracks (cadet basic training) does not attain plebe status until he or she successfully completes the two-month period of basic and is officially, by ceremony, accepted as a member of the Corps. This occurs now, as it did in 1945, just before the commencement of the academic year. In 1945 the life of the plebe was more spartan, austere, restricted, and treatment was more harsh and severe than it is currently. At the time it seemed as if the system was trying to drive cadets out of the Academy. Of the 985 new cadets who entered with me only 574 graduated in June 1949.

Beast Barracks in 1945 was initiated with shock action from the moment the receiving upperclassman walked up to the new cadet and yelled "Drop that bag!" until the commencement of academics at the end of basic, at which point it diminished somewhat, but continued through the entire freshman year. The program was designed to rattle the first-year cadet, thus testing and increasing his ability to function efficiently under extreme stress. The stress was continuously inflicted from reveille until taps by confrontations for the merest of transgressions; small as a thread of lint on the black braid of the uniform dress coat, the slightest impropriety during meals, or failing to accurately recite a bit of trivia required to be memorized. The contorted faces of upperclassmen and their high-decibel admonishments generally crushed the hapless delinquent plebe.

In contrast, a few years ago Lieutenant General Daniel Christman, then superintendent, related an incident where he chanced upon an upperclassman screaming at a plebe. He quietly beckoned to the upperclassman to come to him. In modulated tones he asked the cadet if he felt intimidated by a general's attention. The upperclassman admitted that he did. The general asked, "Am I screaming at you?" Answer: "No, Sir." The general responded, "Point made." This is typical of the changes in the treatment of plebes that has slowly developed in the sixty-plus years from 1945 to the present. Here are other examples of the changes:

The "brace," the extreme posture required of plebes to maintain outside their rooms and classrooms, consisting of chins pulled in, shoulders pulled back, and abdomens pulled in, was relaxed in two steps. The Class of 1972 was the last class to brace through the entire year. The Class of 1973 was the last class to brace through Beast Barracks.

Meals, under the old system, were marathons of harassment. We sat ten cadets to a table. Three or four plebes sat at one end. The six or seven other chairs were taken by upperclassmen. The table commandant sat at the head of the table. Waiters brought food and beverages to the table. One plebe, designated the "gunner," received the food, announced it, and passed each platter to the head of the table. The other two plebes were responsible for the beverages. The "water corporal" handled the cold beverages, the "coffee corporal" the hot beverages. They announced their respective beverages, filled the cups or glasses, and distributed them.

If an upperclassman desired a refill, he would knock his glass or cup (once for a glass, twice for a cup). The responsible plebe would raise both hands to catch the glass or cup and shout, "Glass, please!" The upperclassman would toss it down the table to him. Heaven help the plebe who dropped it! Throwing glasses and cups was illegal, but many upperclassmen took the chance of not getting caught.

If the table com wanted to know how much milk remained in the pitcher, he would ask, "How is the cow?" The water corporal would recite: "Sir, she walks, she talks, she's full of chalk. The lacteal fluid extracted from the female of the bovine species is highly prolific to the *n*th degree" (*n* being the number of glasses of milk remaining in the pitcher).

If a plebe committed some infraction of recitation or rules of etiquette, the table com would command, "Sit up!" The plebe would drop all eating utensils, cease eating, and would sit at rigid attention until told to resume eating. This routine was partly responsible for my losing forty pounds in six weeks.

The Class of 1979 was the last to be exposed to the "Sit up" command for the whole year. Subsequent classes would be relieved of this only after Christmas break. Based on a leadership decision the Class of 1983 was the last class not to automatically "fall out" after Christmas break. Subsequent classes were allowed to sit at ease all year.

An upperclassman never touched a plebe. If he wanted to adjust an item of uniform or equipment on the plebe, he would ask, "Mister, may I touch you?" However, the upperclassmen were experts in causing the plebe to inflict pain and discomfort on himself. Coercion without applying physical force was the *de rigueur* of the system.

The plebe was in social isolation all year except for interaction with his classmates, in the classroom, and on the athletic field. Plebes did not initiate conversation unless they needed to ask a question. The escape valve for this isolation was the interaction with his roommates. I can attest to the importance of that. As mentioned, one of my misfortunes during Beast Barracks was that both of my roommates left the Academy within a week or two of entering. My resulting isolation was akin to solitary confinement, adding greatly to the stress and tensions of those early months.

We were required to perform certain personal services for upperclassmen. Dry cleaning, laundry, and mail were delivered to each cadet company orderly room. Designated plebes were required to deliver these items to the upperclassmen. I recall being punished by an upperclassman who claimed that I was carrying freshly pressed uniforms in a careless manner. I did not agree with his assessment, but there was no court of appeals for the lowly plebe!

In the winter, some upperclassmen would shut off the heat in their rooms and open a window before retiring. A plebe was tasked with arising before reveille to turn on the radiators and close the windows, so that the occupants of the room would not have to face the cold upon arising. The last class of plebes required to deliver the mail was the Class of 1983.

Plebe punishments were usually within the confines of the upperclassman's room. These "visits" by the plebes were euphemistically referred to as "calls." They usually were scheduled late in the afternoon before the supper formation at 6:15 p.m. The plebe would report in "as ordered" and would be directed to a particular location in the room. The punishments included being kept at rigid attention (in a brace) for an hour or more, push-ups to exhaustion ("Hit the floor for forty-four" was a common command), and exercises using a rifle as a weight and holding it steady in a number of extremely stressful positions for extended periods of time. During these activities, the "host" would constantly (and loudly) harass the plebe with commands to "Pull in your chin!" "Shoulders back!" "Suck up your gut!" all punctuated with denigrating remarks.

The hallmark of "punitive success" was perspiration flowing down the plebe's face in copious quantities. Some cadets had the good fortune of being able to activate their sweat glands on command, to the early satisfaction of their tormentor. I was not so fortunate. I can recall a workout so extreme that I was unable to pick up the water pitcher at supper.

As I stated above, all of this transpired without the upperclassman laying a hand on us. These calls became a contest of will, with the plebe avoiding folding under the pressure and pain. This treatment also required the plebe to develop a sense of humor. In all fairness, I must say that no matter how severe any of my transgressions were, never once did any upperclassman make an anti-Semitic remark to me.

The end of plebe year was marked by a traditional ceremony called Recognition. This took place after the Graduation Parade in June. The plebes lined up, and the upperclassmen walked down the line shaking their hands. This act elevated the status of the plebe to that of upperclassman. As with other plebe-related traditions, Recognition also went through changes to the point of its elimination in 2003.

The Class of 2004 was the first to be promoted to private first class in lieu of Recognition.

In 1945, Plebes were not permitted weekend leaves, Christmas leave, or spring break leave. With the exception of being transported to and from a few football games in New York City and to the Army-Navy game, plebes were confined to the Academy for their full first year. This too changed.

The Class of 1967 was the last class to spend Christmas at West Point during plebe year. In the 1980s weekend leave was introduced, and the Class of 2002 was the first class to go on spring break.

Old grads, defined here as those of us who graduated before any of the austere aspects of the plebe system were relaxed, are proud of having survived the crucible of the old system. Some old grads are critical of the relaxed plebe policies. They are fond of lamenting, "The Corps has!" The unabridged saying is, "The Corps has gone to hell!" I am personally of the belief that today's young graduate, male or female, is as fine an officer as has ever donned the Army green adorned with the gold bars of a second lieutenant.

On a lighter note, let me recount the reaction of my parents to the plebe system when they observed one small incident involving their beloved son. The academic year had just begun. My parents came up to West Point to spend a Sunday with me. The parents of George Chamberlin, my classmate, rode up with them. Both families spent a pleasant day that included dinner at the Thayer Hotel and a bit of sight-seeing. George and I, as all plebes were required, had to be in ranks for supper formation before the upperclassmen. Both sets of parents were standing approximately fifty feet from the formation. They spotted us just as a few upperclassmen descended upon us to apply the usual harassment. From the pained expressions on their faces, I knew that this was a distressing scene for them to witness. The remainder of this story came from my mother:

"As we drove home all of us were silent with our thoughts. Suddenly, both fathers began to cry. Your father, in true talmudic fashion, turned to Mr. Chamberlin and posed the question, 'Why are we crying? Where else, to what better place, can one send his son to become a man?' We mothers began to laugh."

This assuaged their emotions, but George and I felt anything but assuaged.

The Elusive Young Man

Friday nights were usually hectic. There were classes on Saturday mornings and Saturday inspections in rooms and in ranks after a full-Corps parade. All required careful preparation. All personal equipment, furniture, lockers, uniforms, weapons, shoes, and brass breastplates, buckles, and hat adornments would receive close scrutiny by the inspecting tactical officers. For the lay reader to better understand this workload, I must elaborate on some of the items that were work-intensive to prepare.

Uniforms were required to be spotless, pressed, and free of clinging lint or other foreign matter. Shoes were required to be "spit-shined," a process involving adding layer after layer of polish on the capped toes of the shoes using water and ultimately shaving lotion as a hardening compound; all done with two fingers wrapped in a soft-cloth handkerchief applied in circular strokes. New shoes required hours of polishing to cover all the pores in the leather. (My father was fond of reminding me that I could have a career shining shoes if I ever left the Army.)

If the uniform of the day included the heavily starched white trousers, it was necessary to either don the trousers before the shoes or to cover the toes with socks before pulling on the trousers. The former was difficult, so the sock method prevailed. During early September 1945, one of my classmates kept stripping the shine off the toes of his shoes as he donned the white trousers. An upperclassman explained the "sock trick" to him. This hapless plebe walked into ranks with the socks flapping off the ends of his shoes like webbed feet. He eventually resigned.

The brass breastplate (worn across the intersection of our white shoulder belts) and the waist plate (the belt buckle that connected the ends of our white waist belts) were the worst items to prepare because they were so susceptible to damage and very time consuming to repair. Every nick, gouge, and scratch needed to be polished out using an impregnated cloth, jeweler's rouge, or anything else that could create an unblemished mirror-like finish. God help the cadet who nicked these brass items with his rifle in the course of performing the manual of arms! Repairs could absorb hours of the cadet's time.

One day my roommate's father visited our room and observed us laboring over this cursed brass. He was a tool and die designer, and true to his profession he came up with an automated way of performing this boring task. He shipped a rather large electric motor to us with a set of buffing heads on spindles. We were eager to try out what promised to be our salvation: a labor-saving device. My roommate, with full faith in his father's mechanism, took his best breastplate and slowly moved it against the whirling buffing head. (We all kept a lesser plate for daily use that would have been more prudent to use in this test.) What followed was tragedy and comedy all rolled into one. The whirling buffing head snatched the breastplate from his hand and sent it flying around the room, bouncing it off the ceiling and walls, and, adding insult to injury, it ricocheted off the cast iron radiator. My roommate watched in horror, the rest of us were spellbound and then burst out laughing. I still laugh when I recall the incident. So much for technology; we returned to the polishing cloths.

Our M-1 rifles were required to be free of rust, dust, dirt, lint, and excessive oil. The wood stocks had to be free of scratches and nicks. The rifle, in order to be cleaned properly, required field-stripping, meticulous cleaning of the receiver, barrel, trigger housing, and base plate. The bore had to glisten. From time to time the stock had to be scraped and polished with linseed oil.

Wall lockers had to be displayed open. All items not on hangers had to be folded to an exact size and stacked. Stacks had to be perfectly vertical when checked against a stretched string at each corner. Desk drawers were displayed open with all contents neatly arranged. Desk tops had to be polished, clean, and free of paper.

All common-area items were the responsibility of the room orderly, a weekly rotating duty among roommates. These items included the gun rack, bookcase, shoe-shining and cleaning materials storage, waste paper baskets, floors, and so on. The name of the room orderly was posted in a designated location so that the inspecting officer would know who to report if any of the common-area items were not up to standards.

The preparation for classes was added to the workload described above. This could be particularly daunting for the cadet who struggled with his academics. Most of us spent the hours from call to quarters at 7:15 p.m. until taps at 10:15 p.m. studying. If we could not prepare for inspection before taps, we would arise after taps to complete the work. This was not authorized without permission for "late lights," a privilege granted only under special conditions. The cadet barracks were inspected after taps by tactical officers as they saw fit. We never knew in advance when one of them would appear. Those caught out of bed would be subject to report.

One Friday night during my plebe year, I was faced with a substantial workload to be accomplished before taps. I had to prepare for a mathematics exam scheduled for the following morning and also for the usual Saturday inspection. In addition, I was room orderly that week. I spent the time before taps studying and decided to prepare for inspection afterward.

Shortly after the post-taps inspection by the cadet subdivision inspector, who had to verify the presence of all cadets in the sixteen rooms in his subdivision, I slipped out of bed to begin my chores. Taps meant "lights out," so I had to use the hallway lighting to do my work. I removed the top drawer from my desk and dumped the contents on the hallway floor. As I began sorting out the items for replacement, I heard the click, click of leather heels on the hall floor below. Leather heels meant that the wearer was an officer. Cadets wore rubber heels. This was an accommodation by the Tactical Department to give cadets a chance to survive a moonlight visit. It was clear that an inspecting officer was on his way. Just as I swung up into my upper bunk, I heard the officer trip over my desk drawer as he entered the room. My two roommates were sound asleep. My name card was on my desk. He knew who the culprit was. He walked over to me and shined his flashlight in my face. I did not move. He left.

I jumped out of bed and finished preparing all of my personal equipment. Common-area work was next. I was cleaning and rearranging the shoeshine box when I again heard the ominous sound of hard heels on concrete. Once again I vaulted into bed. I heard him trip over the shoeshine box and enter the room. I peeked and saw him flash his light on the room orderly's name plate. I also recognized Lieutenant Colonel

Robert Sears, Class of 1939, my company tactical officer! He again tried to trick me into opening my eyes. He flashed his light in my face, turned away, spun around, and tried once more. I never budged. He left. I finished working and went to sleep.

Colonel Sears was an outstanding officer. He was a short, wiry gymnast who became intercollegiate champion on the parallel bars when he was a cadet. He knew me as a new member of the plebe gymnastics team. Colonel Sears had been an Army Air Force pilot in the European Theater during World War II. He was shot down over Germany, taken prisoner, and held in a stalag, a POW camp for fliers. He negotiated a deal with his captors. If they increased the food rations for the prisoners, he would entertain the Luftwaffe officers with gymnastic shows at the officers club. They accepted his offer.

Back to my story. The morning after our Friday night cat-and-mouse game, Colonel Sears came charging into my room to inspect. My roommates and I leaped to rigid attention. He walked around the room, moved up close to my face, and asked, "Tired, Mr. Zickel?" "No, Sir!" I replied. He turned away, whirled around again almost nose-to-nose, "Are you sure?" "Yes, Sir!" I answered. He backed off a few feet, wagged a finger at me, and said, "Mr. Zickel, you are a very elusive young man!" He turned on his heel and left the room. Though the circumstantial evidence was flawless, he never reported me for being out of bed after taps.

There are many humorous stories about interactions between cadets and tactical officers. Two are worthy of telling here.

An upperclassman living across the hall from my room got out of bed one night after taps to brush his teeth. In the midst of this operation a tactical officer came running up the stairs and entered his room. He barely made it into bed, but the officer saw the last movements of his flight from discovery. He went over to the cadet's bed, raised the end of the blanket to see if he was wearing pajamas (the required sleeping attire). The cadet jumped up on all fours, whirled, and stared into the flashlight with his mouth full of toothpaste foam. The officer screamed, dropped his flashlight, and bolted out of the room. I have no recollection of the outcome of this encounter except that it became the element of humor for many days thereafter!

Cadets were expert in hiding contraband in their rooms. Usually the contraband was perishable food. One cadet was more daring. He kept a parrot in his room and would hide it in his laundry bag during room inspections. The tactical officers were usually graduates and knew many of these tricks from their cadet days. One morning a tactical officer was concentrating on contraband hidden in laundry bags. As he went from room to room, he punched each bag with his hand, seeking hard objects. He eventually injured his hand on some hidden metallic object. He went back to his office to arm himself with a riding crop and continued his vetting of laundry bags. The last bag he was to strike that morning answered his blow of the riding crop with an ear-shattering shriek. He found the parrot! Here again, I have no recollection of the outcome of this act of "animal cruelty" or of the punishment heaped upon the head of the parrot's owner. This story, too, became a source of humor in the Corps.

Outside the Box

Plebe year was history. The joys of summer leave beckoned, and I was ready. I looked forward to renewing old acquaintances and having fun with high school friends, visits with family members, and, in general, having a good time. Instead, I found myself bored by the lack of enjoyable activity. Friends were gone; it was a social desert. I vowed that I would not repeat this the following summer. One way or another, I would find my way to "faraway places with strange-sounding names." It was a wonderful idea except for the fact that I lacked the funds to do this. I pondered the question as I returned to duty.

It finally dawned on me that I had finished my first year of Spanish language study, with a second year coming up. If I could come up with a link between a trip to Latin America and enhanced language studies, perhaps I could conjure up the support of the Academic Department for such a trip. My excitement was short-lived as I realized that this was too ambitious an objective. It would require a minor miracle to pull off. Then a light flashed on in my mind. One of our Spanish instructors was Capitán Esperon de el Ejército Mexicano; Captain Esperon of the Mexican Army.

I made an appointment to meet with him. The following dialogue ensued:

Z: "Sir, where is the Colegio Militar?" (the Mexican Military Academy)
E: "In Mexico City. Why do you ask?"
Z: "I would like to visit the Colegio next summer."
E: "That's an excellent idea!"

After I explained my financial dilemma, I asked if the Mexican consulate or embassy had an aircraft for trips between New York or Washington and Mexico City, and, if so, would they be willing to take me. He said that he would look into it.

Some time later, he advised that the consulate in New York had a twin-engine Lockheed Lodestar with limited seating. It flew from Brownsville, Texas, to Mexico City every Thursday. I was welcome to join them on a space-available basis. In my youthful exuberance I believed that I could hitch a ride to Brownsville on a U.S Army aircraft. Then I realized that if the Lodestar was full, I would have to wait a week for the next flight, if it had space available. This was unacceptable. The risk was too great, the time limitations of leave being what they were.

Disappointed, I let the matter drop and tried to think of other options for travel anywhere. Sometime later there was a notice in the *Daily Bulletin* advising that President Alemán of Mexico and his son were to visit West Point. Plan B began to gel. I returned to Captain Esperon and asked if he knew President Alemán. "But of course! We are old friends." he replied. I then suggested, "Why don't you inform the president that you have a number of Spanish-language students who would like to visit Colegio Militar? He will invite us and the United States would then have to provide transportation!"

The captain was as excited as I was at the prospect of the trip becoming a reality and agreed to do it. I mentioned to some of my classmates that this trip was a possibility. Two of my closest friends, John Mione and Tom Crawford, expressed their desire to join me. Neither studied Spanish.

The big day arrived. After the usual parade and tour of the Academy, the president was escorted to the Academic Board Room with Major General Maxwell Taylor (superintendent), the commandant of cadets, and the dean. Captain Esperon was with the group. During a lull in the conversation, the captain turned to the president and informed him that he had "a number" of cadets who would like to visit Colegio Militar. The president responded enthusiastically, "But, of course! They shall come as guests of the Mexican government! How many cadets?" The captain and I had never addressed this, so he pulled a number out of the air, "Sixteen."

General Taylor immediately responded as I had expected: "We shall provide transportation, of course." This was first down and goal to go! Two matters remained to be resolved. The sixteen cadets had to be selected, and General Taylor was a bit incensed because he had not been advised about the plans to arrange for this trip in advance of the president's arrival, nor had the concept gone through an evaluation by the dean. Colonel Greene, head of the Department of Foreign Languages, asked a more ominous question, "Who is behind all this?" Captain Esperon had no choice, he had to turn me in.

I found myself standing at attention in front of Colonel Greene while he excoriated me about bypassing the chain of command, and about the embarrassment I had caused for the superintendent and for him. I was so delighted with the result of my effort that the tongue-lashing was painless. What astounded me was that I was never formally punished for this violation of military protocol. Then came the body blow.

In true Academy style, they selected the sixteen cadets in order of merit in Spanish studies. I was not among them, and my two friends certainly did not qualify. I am not sure how it happened, but somehow my friends and I were included as unofficial guests on the trip. Touchdown!

The Department of State sent emissaries to West Point to educate those going on the trip about Mexico, its customs, its sensitivities, our required deportment during certain activities, and our general behavior while in the country. We were primed for the trip.

The day arrived. We found ourselves in the plush-lined cabin of a twin-engine C-47 aircraft complete with galley and a crew of servers. We were traveling in style. As we entered the traffic pattern of the municipal airport of Mexico City, we were astounded to see the Corps of Cadets of the Colegio Militar in their sharp red-and-black uniforms lined up on the tarmac. Red carpets had been rolled out to receive us. This was a long way from 119 Schley Street in Newark. The official party deplaned first. They went through the pomp and circumstance of the formal reception. We hangers-on watched from the aircraft.

The Mexican Army provided the three of us with a sedan and driver that took us to the Waldorf Hotel in downtown Mexico City. We were checked into the bridal suite while our classmates were billeted in the austere cadet barracks at the Colegio. The Army kept a sedan and driver outside the hotel around the clock for the entire time we were there. It was to take us wherever we desired to go. We were better off than our classmates in the official group. Was this heaven, or what?

Despite our unofficial status, we were included in all official activities and ceremonies. These included formal balls and bullfights. The remainder of the time we were on our own to enjoy the pleasures of that exciting city. We took full advantage of our unbelievable good fortune. Wherever the three of us went, the public recognized the uniforms from photographs of our arrival in the newspapers and of ceremonies and activities featuring cadets. We constantly heard, "*Mira, mira, los cadetes de West Point*." This was often followed up with invitations for coffee or something stronger.

With constant access to our ever-ready transportation, we managed to visit many of the wonderful places within comfortable driving distance of our hotel; the pyramids, Taxco (the silver town), the Floating Gardens. The three compadres visited a movie set to watch the filming of *Adventures of Casanova* starring Lucille Bremer and Arturo de Córdova. They were warm, friendly, and graciously posed with us for photographs that are still among my memorabilia.

If we went wandering about at night, Mexican cadets accompanied us as unofficial bodyguards. My escort was José Sifuentes, well over six feet tall and fullback on the Colegio football team. He was perfect for the job. He called me "Luisito," little Lewis. Standing next to him, this was a perfect description of me. My Spanish improved considerably on this trip; others in the group developed a remarkable fluency after a few drinks. One evening we joined the official party at the lavish El Patio nightclub. One of my classmates was taken by a beautiful hat-check girl. He began "making time" with her. The more he drank, the more fluent his Spanish became and the more she was falling for his line. We had to forcibly extract him from a deepening situation.

One day the three of us went into Sanborn's, a popular restaurant, for lunch. All the tables were taken. We noticed a beautiful young woman sitting alone at a table for four. She caught our eye and beckoned to us. Our hopes soared with our fantasies as we sat down. We enjoyed the lunch but were disappointed to discover that she was the pregnant wife of an American embassy officer. At least we had a table.

The time came to say "*Adios amigos.*" We shook hands and hoped that our paths would cross again. We really became close with some of the Mexican cadets. Some of our classmates had such a great time that they literally had to be helped onto the airplane for the trip home. As we took off and circled the airport, the Corps of Cadets was standing at attention saluting us.

Shortly after our return to West Point, we heard that the Department of State reported that we had done more to enhance friendly relations between the United States and Mexico than President Truman's visit. Subsequently we reciprocated and brought our hosts to West Point. We could not begin to entertain them as lavishly as they had entertained us.

Annual trips to foreign countries by our cadets began to be taken after our trip to Mexico. I have no means of determining whether our trip influenced these activities, which are still the norm to this day. To the best of my knowledge, our trip was the first of its kind.

My involvement in making it a reality in the manner I did taught me a lesson. One can operate "outside the box" on occasion in a structured organization such as the Army. There is obviously an attendant risk that must be carefully evaluated. The downside result must be weighed against the result of the unauthorized action planned. On a few occasions, I applied this successfully during the Korean War.

Football Rally

Taps had just sounded. My roommates and I were settling down for the night. Suddenly, the calm was shattered by the raucous alert horn blaring from the guard room. A familiar voice intoned, "Attention all cadets. Attention all cadets. Brush your teeth with Pepsodent and beat Notre Dame!" Join me on the Plain for a party."

Joe Eggers, my roommate, announced, "That was Bob Hope. Let's go!"

The Corps poured out of the barracks through the sally ports. We found an enormous bonfire and Hope on a wooden instructor's platform. He was sporting articles of Cadet uniforms. He was definitely in his element, doing what he did best—entertaining the troops. Though I cannot recall one of his superb one-liners, we enjoyed an evening of laughter and pregame camaraderie.

The Picnic

After the pressures of Plebe Year subsided and our well-deserved leave revitalized us, the Class of 1949 commenced its Yearling Year ("sophomore" to the civilian world). Part of that summer of 1946 was spent in tactical training at Camp Buckner, located on Lake Popolopen on the West Point reservation. We were billeted in barracks at the camp, a bucolic spot. Current classes continue to train there during their second summer at the Academy. We trained hard and played hard at "Popolo."

Soon after my arrival at the camp I received a letter from home in which my mother lamented the fact that I would miss the annual picnic of the Lowenstein Cousins' Club. It was to be held at the usual place, Echo Lake Park in Mountainside, New Jersey. This was a highlight event every summer for this wonderful family. I hated to miss it.

It crossed my mind that we might be able to have the picnic at Popolo. I wrote back suggesting that they consider having it at Camp Buckner on the "beautiful shores of Lake Popolopen." I explained that there were cabins and picnic sites around the lake built by the Army. If they were interested, I needed a complete list of everyone coming for submittal to the authorities, who would decide whether to issue a permit. The response and list came by return mail. It was a unanimous decision to accept the invitation.

The officer in charge was incredulous when he saw the size of the attendee list. After I convinced him that these were all family members, he said, "Mr. Zickel, I will approve this, but you must bring these vehicles onto the post in convoy. Have them line up outside the gate on the shoulder of the road and wait for you. You will draw a jeep from the motor pool, meet them outside the gate, have them turn on their headlights and follow you through the gate to the parking area. If you need food, contact the mess officer." I did not press the food issue. I knew that the Lowenstein "girls" would do their culinary thing much better than the Buckner mess ever could imagine.

I sent the instructions to Mother, who distributed them by telephone. (We often joked that if there ever were a Lowenstein family crest, it would consist of a coffee pot and a telephone. Telephonic communications were a big thing in the family, and they were world-class coffee drinkers!). D-Day arrived bright and sunny. I drove the jeep out the gate and found a long line of cars parked on the shoulder. I "trooped the line," directing them to turn on their headlights, and proceeded toward the gate. An MP was on duty.

He stopped the column, "What's this? A funeral?" "No," I replied, "It's a family picnic. Here's my pass." "This is all your family?" Astounded, but convinced, he let us enter the camp. As we wove our way through the camp to the parking area, my classmates stared in disbelief. "What's Zickel up to now?"

The day was a complete success. Only a few of us are still alive, and fifty-nine years later we continue to reminisce about the lovely day on Popolo. And, oh yes, the Lowenstein "girls" excelled once more!

Roadside Service

In 1939 or 1940 my father purchased a 1938 Buick Roadmaster from one of his clients, a wealthy dowager from New York City. This car, configured for a chauffeur with a roll-up window to isolate the rear compartment, had been driven for less than 3,000 miles. It was big, heavy (almost two and a half tons), luxurious, and beautiful.

Seven years later the "tank," as I named it, faithfully transported my parents to and from West Point many times during those first three, almost four, cadet years, when we were not allowed to leave the Post. The proximity of home to the Academy was a gift to both my parents and me. They took full advantage of our geographical good fortune and visited me frequently. We shared this positional advantage with my classmates who were not conveniently close to their homes. A visit usually included lunch at the Hotel Thayer, several automobile circuits around the Post, visits to points of interest, a snack at Grant Hall, updates on my travails, and news from home.

Occasionally they brought someone with them who had never been to West Point, giving Dad and me the opportunity to perform as tour guides. Dad was incredibly knowledgeable about the Academy. I had provided him with a copy of *Bugle Notes*, the "Plebe Bible," packed with historical facts and traditions of the institution that he had committed to memory. Occasionally I bantered with him, telling him that he was a better plebe than I was.

During one of these visits, my classmate and friend Jack Hayne joined us. I cannot recall how that came to pass nor whether his "one and only," Pearl, was with us. Pearl was a wonderful young woman who visited Jack as often as possible. She and Jack were married after graduation, and today she remains a wonderful young woman.

We were driving near the Cadet Chapel as the tank suffered a flat tire. Jack insisted on changing the tire, a task he performed with great skill and efficiency. A wave of guilt swept over me. He was doing all of the work and I was a mere observer. I felt that I had to do something to even the workload. I dropped to the ground and commenced doing push-ups. Though the constraints of my choker collar and other restrictive uniform components made this very uncomfortable, I managed to keep it up until the jack was removed from under the car. My guilt was assuaged!

First Class Year finally rolled around and we were eager to take advantage of our new privileges—two in particular: weekend leaves and the purchase of a new car in the spring. The proximity of home in Montclair, New Jersey, enabled my parents to pick me up for weekend leave and return me to barracks on Sunday evenings. It was mandatory that we sign in not later than 6:00 p.m.

At that time, 1948–49, there were no superhighways or high-speed parkways between Montclair and West Point. All of the roads in that direction were two lanes wide and peppered with traffic lights. Dad was still driving the 1938 Roadmaster, which was not in the best of condition ten years later. He believed that he could keep it running by living up to his "service mantra": "Points, plugs, and condenser and frequent oil changes." The "tank" finally rebelled. It broke down late one Sunday afternoon on our way to West Point. There were no telephones in sight. Cell phones and OnStar were almost a half-century away. We had to wait for a police car to chance upon us.

The clock was ticking and I had visions of being late ("No excuse, Mister. You should have left earlier," I could already hear those words). A New Jersey state trooper finally showed up. We explained the time dilemma. The trooper said, "Hop in son. We'll get you there on time." He radioed for a tow truck, I said my goodbyes, hopped into the police cruiser, and off we went—siren wailing and lights flashing!

It then crossed my mind that this was a New Jersey trooper. What would happen when we arrived at the state line? He answered my question, yet unasked, by contacting the New York State Police. They kindly agreed to have someone meet us at the state line. Sure enough, there he was waiting for me with his whirly light flashing. I profusely thanked the Jersey trooper, switched cars, and again, with lights flashing and siren wailing, we virtually flew through Thayer Gate and raced into the area of barracks right up to the steps to the stoop close to my company orderly room.

The cadet in charge of quarters was waiting on the stoop, sign-in book in hand, as I raced up the steps. I looked at the clock to record the time. It was one minute to six. I turned to thank the trooper, but he had left. God bless those two guys!

The spring of 1949 finally rolled around. Graduation was just a few months off, and it was time to purchase a new car, the ultimate privilege! I was most fortunate to have Dad as my adviser. He had considerable experience in the automotive world as a designer and an automotive parts salesman. We finally concluded that a small 1949 Buick Super Sedanette would be the optimum choice. The First National Bank of Scranton, Pennsylvania, had been financing automobiles for cadets and officers for many years and was eagerly waiting to add the Class of 1949 to its list of customers. I purchased the new car from Broadway Buick in Newburgh, New York. The price was $2,381 delivered. I financed $1,781; Dad loaned me the balance. I had a new car! Broadway Buick is still in business. It is now owned by my classmate Joe Steffey, an All-American lineman from the famous Army team of the forties.

The big day arrived to pick up the car. Mother, Dad, and brother Bob all joined me to take possession. Dad was still driving the tank. He insisted on being my pace car on the trip home. Mother and Bob rode with me. Automobiles of that vintage required a break-in period at speeds between forty and fifty miles per hour for the first few thousand miles. Our two-car convoy moved out at the breakneck speed of forty miles per hour. My "crew" in the new car dutifully following the tank began to get itchy as we plodded along. Mother, who had a bit of the devil in her personality, urged me to pass Dad. As we drifted by at the wild speed of forty-five miles per hour, he became enraged. I can still see his anger flashing between the cars fifty-six years later.

The gun-metal blue Buick was my pride and joy. I named it the "Blue Bitch." It proved to be the perfect vehicle for a new second lieutenant whose first assignment was Fort Riley, Kansas, followed by Fort Benning, Georgia. My excitement and joy over my new car were soon to be dampened by a freak accident.

While on leave at home in Montclair, I was waiting at a traffic light on the right-hand side of an electric trolley car pointed in the same direction as my car. Before the light changed, the trolley operator turned to the left into the trolley barn on the opposite side of the street. As he entered the turn, his rear platform swung into my lane, struck the left rear side of my vehicle, and raked it all the way to the front headlight. I was boxed in by cars to my right and could not move. I sat horrified as I watched my beloved car sliced open like a sardine tin. To exacerbate the situation, I had to leave for Fort Riley in a few days.

The local Buick dealer estimated the damage for insurance purposes. Instead of going to the insurer, I had a better idea. The trolley car was owned and operated by Public Service Gas and Electric Company with its home office in Newark, New Jersey. I wasted no time in finding and meeting with their company adjuster. He began to waffle over the issue. I cut him short and advised that I was under Army orders to report to Fort Riley and had to leave shortly. If he refused to pay for the damage, I threatened to turn the matter over to the judge advocate general. I had no idea whether I could implement my threat, but it worked. He opened the file drawer of his desk and brought out a handful of $100 bills. He paid the damage estimate in full. I signed a release and left.

The car was repaired by an excellent Kansas craftsman. I was pumped up with pride once more. A year later, when I left Fort Benning, I headed home on leave with orders to the Far East Command in Tokyo. It was early June 1950. On June 25 the Korean War broke out. I realized that a new infantry lieutenant was not about to sit around Japan while war raged in Korea. I sold my car with great reluctance, paid off all debts, and left for the Far East. True to the infantry, I was on foot once again.

The Pencil

Hill 300 overlooked the main supply route north out of the Pusan perimeter and ran through the village of Waegwan. Elements of the Eighth Army were waiting for 300 to be taken so they could move north to join MacArthur's forces landed at Inchon.

The hill was configured with a "gentle" slope from the west and a relatively sheer slope from the south. North Korean troops held off a number of companies of the 7th Cavalry Regiment for several days. They had been attacking from the west up the gentle slope. My Company C of the 5th Cavalry Regiment was assigned the mission late in the day on 18 September 1950.

We lacked one of our three rifle platoons and had to make do with the remaining two plus our weapons platoon. We elected the south slope as our route of attack. The crest was secured by 1800 hrs; about two hours after crossing the line of departure. The enemy continuously counterattacked us until dawn the next day. These were grenade-intensive attacks.

My platoon sergeant and I occupied a large foxhole dug by the North Koreans. During one attack that night, I saw a sparkling grenade on a trajectory toward us. My sergeant was behind me. I backed into him and spread my arms in a futile gesture of protection. The explosion hit me like a sledge hammer in my chest and knocked me into a state of semi-consciousness. When I regained my senses, I looked down and saw my left breast pocket torn up. My four-color Norma Steel pencil was bent double where a fragment had struck it. The pencil had kept the fragment from reaching my chest. However, another fragment had flown under my outstretched left arm and superficially sliced my sergeant's left side. He was treated and returned to duty. We were lucky that it was a concussion grenade, not a fragmentation grenade.

We held the hill, the enemy moved north, and we watched the Eighth Army break out of the perimeter. I partially straightened the bent pencil, used it in its immobile position through the remainder of my tour, and have kept it since as a memento of divine intervention.

Combat Chaplain

Our battalion chaplain was a bright-faced young captain who was married with children. One day an incoming mortar round turned him into a multiple amputee. He lost three of his four limbs. I wondered how God could have let this tragedy befall this man of goodness and his young family.

One cannot dwell on these sad events too long. The relentless inertia of combat simply does not allow it. His replacement arrived. He was older than all of us in the battalion. He had a bulbous "liquor nose" and had painted a white crucifix on his helmet at least two inches high. He virtually attached himself to my platoon, and we became close friends. He told me that he had been a railroad bum until he heard the word of God and turned to the ministry.

Our new chaplain would declare any quiet day of the week Sunday and always asked me to pump the portable organ. I never missed one of his services. He almost always was at my side during an attack. The "target" on his helmet worried my troops and me. They often yelled, "Padre, get your —— head down!" His response invariably was, "The Lord will protect me." However, when a round zinged by or glanced off his helmet, he launched into the most colorful, expressive expletives I ever heard. Bless him!

The Battle of Unsan

Pyongyang, capital of North Korea, fell to my division in mid-October 1950. The Eighth Army was soon ordered to continue northward to the Yalu River, the Manchurian border. The weather was beginning to turn cold. The North Korean Army was by then almost nonexistent except for a few units and remnants of others. We had to cross the Ch'ongch'on River at the so-called "narrow waist" of the Korean Peninsula. My company was ordered to take the high ground on the north side of the river. We crossed the river through water that was armpit-deep and brutally cold. We took the hill and received orders to stay there for the night—without blankets, sleeping bags, or the winter clothes that had not yet caught up with the Eighth Army. We were wearing cotton fatigues, field jackets, and had ponchos.

After spending an agonizing night in our wet summer uniforms in subfreezing cold, we continued north with the remainder of the Eighth. We received word to alter our route toward Unsan to help the Eighth out of a trap. Unsan was about forty miles south of the Yalu River. As it grew dark and we approached our destination, we heard the bugles of the CCF (Chinese Communist Forces). The Chinese Army had invaded Korea, much to everyone's surprise.

My unit, C Company, was ordered to hold the road open from Unsan for the 8th Cav's attempt to withdraw. I was acting company commander. My command post was at the front of the roadblock.

The 8th Cavalry Regiment had been attacked by three CCF armies consisting of three divisions each. My battalion unit, 1st of the 5th Cavalry, was attacked by one CCF army of three divisions. Their cavalry units were mounted on horses.

A small group of 8th Cavalry soldiers made it through our roadblock, with elements of the CCF a step behind them. My company was overrun by the CCF; I found myself, my radio operator, and a light machine gunner among a densely packed force of Chinese soldiers. Thanks to the confusion, darkness, and disorganization of the Chinese troops, we managed to escape (with the machine gun!). As we ran south on the road, the CCF opened fire in our direction with a large-caliber automatic weapon and two captured 81-mm mortars. As tracers bounced around our feet, we moved off the road, waded another frozen stream, and rejoined what was left of the company.

According to the official U.S. Army history of that battle, the 8th Cavalry lost close to 1,000 soldiers. My 5th Cavalry Regiment lost 350 men, of which 150 were from my battalion.

My personal survival, unscathed, had to be divine intervention.

My Seventy-ninth Mission

Three months before my rotation date, my regimental commander decided to temporarily detail me to division aviation as his personal air observer. He did this because I was one of the few lieutenants who had survived from the original group. I was also to adjust artillery fire, support armor, and assist the infantry forces. This was a welcome relief from ground combat. I found the work fascinating, yet I looked forward to rotation home.

I finally received my orders home and was to depart in two days. My flight log showed that I had flown on seventy-eight missions of two to three flight hours per mission. My seventy-ninth mission was scheduled for the day before my departure. Captain Herman Greer, my pilot, and I walked to the flight line. Our L-19 aircraft sat perched like a bird anxious to fly. We climbed in, buckled up, performed a radio and preflight check. Herman started the engine and we were cleared for take-off. As we cleared the end of the runway and reached about fifty feet above a rice paddy at the end of the runway, the engine quit.

Herman, a former crop-duster from Mississippi, deftly side-slipped the aircraft onto the road bordering the rice paddy. He made a perfect dead-stick landing. I stepped out of the cockpit and announced, "Herman, get yourself another boy. God is trying to tell me something!"

Several days later, I was standing on the fantail of the Japanese liner *Konga Maru* watching Pusan dissolve into the mist. I thought of the previous thirteen months of infantry and flight combat and realized that I was going home unscathed. I told myself, "Zickel, every day from here on out is a gift."

Bridging the Generations

On July 15, 1948, General of the Armies John J. Pershing, Class of 1886, died in Washington, D.C. I had just begun my First Class Year. The general was to lie in state in the rotunda of the United States Capitol and was to be buried in Arlington National Cemetery. The guard of honor consisted of a battalion of cadets and a battalion from the 101st Airborne Division. I was the sergeant major of the cadet battalion. We were in ranks from 9:00 a.m. until 6:00 p.m. It was a hot, muggy July day in Washington. Our uniform was dress whites (India Whites) under arms. Like all other dress uniforms in the cadet wardrobe, it included a choker collar. The cadet officers wore red sashes and carried sabers.

The funeral cortege finally moved forward at about noon at the traditional half-time pace to the slow beat of the drums. Shortly thereafter we were doused with a cloudburst. The red sashes ran onto the white cottons, and the wet cotton duck became almost transparent. As we started across Memorial Bridge, a broiling sun came out and baked steamlike water vapor out of the wet cottons. It enveloped our faces, making for a very uncomfortable day for all of us.

The worst was yet to come. At the grave site, the heat downed many of our cadets, and I had to escort them to an aid station tent nearby. The scene in the tent was reminiscent of the Civil War; pale men strewn about with white uniforms, white cross belts, and brass breast and waist plates. We were quite thankful when the general was laid to rest and taps sounded. It was 6:00 p.m.!

One year later I graduated and was commissioned a second lieutenant, infantry. After a short leave, I reported to my first duty station, the Ground General School at Fort Riley, Kansas. All bachelor officers were billeted in the old cavalry barracks. These were open squad rooms cleaned and maintained by retired cavalry sergeants who were quartered in small cottages on post. The master sergeant assigned to our area, whom I shall call John Brown here, and his co-worker, Master Sergeant Sam Smith, would banter and argue with each other until one became angry and demanded to know the other's date of rank. This question had an element of humor in it since both men had been promoted within days of each other in 1918.

John was seventy-eight years old and proudly informed me that when he joined the Army as a young stripling, he had been assigned to Second Lieutenant John J. Pershing as his orderly. When I told John that I had been in the guard of honor at General Pershing's funeral, he became emotional and literally adopted me. I never had to polish my leather or brass after that. Those were the days of the "old brown-shoe Army" and the uniforms of World War II. The current green and black uniforms with black shoes did not make their appearance until fifteen years later.

The following year, 1950, I was serving in Korea with the 5th Cavalry Regiment of the 1st Cavalry Division, actually fighting as an infantry division. During the winter of 1951 I became ill with infectious hepatitis. It erupted while I was en route to enjoy a one-week rest leave in Japan. Those of us on rest leave from Korea were flown to Japan in our combat gear and trucked to a processing center, where we showered and exchanged our field uniforms for dress uniforms, complete with decorations, badges, insignia, and shoulder patches. We were then transported to the locations designated for each of us. Instead, I was admitted to the 155th Station Hospital in Yokahama. There went the enjoyable part, and the one-week stay was to become two months.

Consequently, as the hospital orderly rolled me into the ward on a gurney, I was wearing my newly issued dress uniform. Suddenly I heard a strong, stentorian military voice from my left ask, "What outfit in the Cav, son?" I turned to seek the source of the voice and saw an elderly, distinguished patient in his bed. He seemed to me to be at least a full colonel and to have seen my shoulder patch. I respectfully replied, "Fifth Regiment, Sir!" He commanded, "Orderly, put him in the bed next to me!" I had little desire to be parked next to a high-ranking guy and was less than pleased with this location in the ward. My "senior officer" neighbor introduced himself as Pop Poneyman, sergeant major of the 5th Cavalry Regiment before it deployed to Korea. A severe cardiac problem had prevented him from going into combat with the regiment. I had never heard of him, because I had joined the regiment after it deployed to Korea and knew very little of its history in the Army of Occupation in Japan.

As we became acquainted with each other, Pop Poneyman told me that he had been with the 5th Cav. since 1916 and was with the regiment when General Pershing led the 1st Cavalry Division into Mexico to attempt to ferret out the bandit leader of the Mexican insurgents, Pancho Villa. Pop left the army briefly after World War I and became a police officer in the New York City Police Department. He rejoined the army a few years after, was assigned once more to the 5th Cav., and managed to stay in the regiment through its service with General Douglas MacArthur in the Pacific island-hopping operations of World War II. He remained a member of the regiment until his medical discharge shortly after I was returned to duty in Korea.

Pop was Jewish and was married to a Jewish woman from England. She was known as Mom Poneyman and was the total Jewish Mother. She fluttered around me as if I were her son and introduced me to the fair-sized military Jewish community in Tokyo and Yokahama. Knowing the Poneyman family and their friends was a wonderful adventure for me. Unfortunately, I never learned their first names, but I warmly remember this wonderful twosome as "Mom and Pop."

Several years after I returned from Korea, I was assigned to the First Army General Staff at Governor's Island in New York harbor. Mom found me and called my office asking for help. They were living in New Jersey. She was clearly upset. Pop was mentally deteriorating and posed a behavioral problem for her and their two daughters. She sought guidance for getting Pop admitted to a veterans' hospital. Fortunately, I had an uncle who was a physician in the VA hospital nearest to them. He provided guidance. I regret that I never kept in contact with them.

In 1995 and 1996 I managed the design and construction of the Rupert Johnson Memorial Stadium at Doubleday Field at West Point. The project was at the point where the contractor was building forms and placing reinforcing steel in preparation for pouring concrete. I received a telephone call from the head of the Department of Civil and Mechanical Engineering. He asked if he could bring his students to the site to witness the pour and examine the forms. I was delighted to have them.

The cadets arrived with their professor they were sharply turned out in their BDU's (battle dress uniforms, the old grads knew them as fatigues) and wore gray hard hats. Their professor introduced me as Colonel Zickel, Class of 1949. All eyes turned to scrutinize me and my physical condition. Their expressions seemed quizzical, as if to ask, "How come you're still alive?" I pondered their reaction later and realized that I probably would have reacted the same way if, while a cadet, I was introduced to an old grad from the class of 1902 who was still on his feet.

West Point, like Judaism, is steeped in tradition. Tradition provides continuity to an institution and enhances its longevity. New traditions are attempted in the hope that they survive. Few succeed, but those that do enrich the tenets of the institution and become part of the glue that holds it together as it strengthens its bonds. I shall describe three of recent vintage that have taken hold at West Point.

My class of 1949 celebrated its fiftieth reunion in 1999. We decided to expand and renovate the Class of 1949 Lodge. The original building was donated to West Point by my class in honor of our twenty-fifth reunion. The lodge, an Alpine-style structure, sits on a hill overlooking Delafield Pond. It has become the prime recreational facility on the post according to the West Point Club, which is responsible for booking parties there. Our class officers were seeking something more. Two ideas came out of that search and were implemented without delay. We designated the Class of 1999 as the group to which we would hand off the facility at a certain time. They readily accepted the offer. The second idea implemented was for our class to present gold second lieutenant bars to the members of the Class of 1999 engraved on the undersides: FROM 1949 TO 1999. These were handed out at the graduation ceremony as each cadet walked up to receive his or her diploma. Two of my classmates undertook the presentations. Every class since has adopted the same two activities. It appears that they are becoming traditions.

The section titled "The Alumni Gallery" in chapter 1 describes a new tradition at the Jewish Chapel, introduced for the bicentennial of West Point at the baccalaureate service in 2002. At each subsequent baccalaureate service we unveil the names of the graduating class, added to the names of all Jewish graduates from the first one in the class of 1802. This ceremony takes place with the graduates' families in attendance. It is an exciting ceremony for the cadets and all attending. It has also become a visible goal for the new plebes to strive to attain. The wall is drawn to their attention at the first Friday night service, and they are told that, when they are on the verge of graduation, their names will appear there for all time as they join the Long Gray Line. It has become an incentive for them to stay in the Corps. That wall bridges the generations; more than ten generations as I write this. Grip Hands! This is a mandate to bridge those generations.

Recently, the infantry detachment at West Point sent letters to all graduates in that branch asking them to send a pair of their old infantry branch insignia, crossed rifles, for distribution to those First Class Cadets assigned to the infantry. The response was overwhelming. I received a warm thank-you note from the cadet who received my rifles. It remains to be seen whether this will become a tradition.

The college class ring was an innovation of West Point and has become ubiquitous throughout the academic world at institutions of all kinds, including high schools. The Association of Graduates recently started a program of collecting the rings of deceased graduates and melting down the gold for use in the rings of the new graduating classes. This is another effort to reach across the generations, to tie the old to the new. The torch shall not burn out!

A Chance Meeting

It was shortly before the High Holy Days of 1965. I had just deplaned from a long flight at Atlanta's Hartsfield International Airport. It was somewhere close to midnight and the terminal was sparsely populated. As I rushed down the hall toward the baggage carousel, I noticed a trim young lieutenant colonel walking in front of me, apparently in the same direction. He was wearing the distinctive black-and-yellow patch of the 1st Cavalry Division on his right shoulder. A patch worn on the right shoulder indicates that it is the unit in which the wearer served in time of war. The "Cav" was my division during the Korean War. He was of the right rank, age, and from the right division to qualify as my contemporary and most likely someone I knew.

Without a second thought, I tapped him on the shoulder. He whirled around and loudly expressed his surprise at seeing me standing there, just as surprised and delighted as I was to see him. We were fellow alumni from West Point, comrades-in-arms, and friends. I had won the trifecta!

"Ed, Ed West, what are you doing in Atlanta?"

"I'm on my way to Fort Benning to spend the High Holy Days with my wife Marcie and the kids."

"On the way from where, and why isn't Marcie with you?

"I'm on a hardship tour in Korea. I command the 44th Combat Engineer Battalion. Remember the 44th? We supported your unit during the war. It's an eighteen-month tour without my family. I am located in Waegwan. Remember Waegwan? I am in the shadow of Hill 303. Remember 303?"

The combat history of the infantry soldier is punctuated with a legion of hills, all numbered and identified by their height in feet or meters above sea level. Hill 303 was infamous. It overlooked the village of Waegwan on the Naktong River. This hill was the site of one of the earlier atrocities committed against our troops by the Army of the PRK; People's Republic of Korea, short title, North Korea. They captured a number of soldiers from my regiment, the 5th Cavalry, tied their hands behind their backs, and executed all of them. The war started on June 25, 1950. This atrocity most likely occurred on August 16, 1950, and was recorded in the official history, *U.S. Army in the Korean War*, by Roy E. Appleman of the Office of the Chief of Military History, United States Army, as having been discovered on the following day, August 17,' by elements of the 5th Cavalry. They came upon the bodies of the twenty-six soldiers, mortarmen of H Company. The regiment was one of three; the 5th, 7th, and 8th of the 1st Cavalry Division. Hill 303 was located at the northern corner of the Pusan Perimeter, the southern limit of the advance of the PRK Army. We stopped their offensive along that perimeter. I was the leader of the second platoon of C Company of the 5th Cavalry. It was on this perimeter that I received my baptism of fire.

Between graduation from West Point in June 1949 and the first shot fired over my head, my ground arms classmates and I were fortunate to have had a year of branch and branch-immaterial training to prepare us for the unforeseen combat in our early future. All we lacked was troop-duty experience. Ed, on the other hand, graduated from West Point in June 1950, a few weeks before the war broke out. He and his classmates traded their cadet gray uniforms for combat fatigues. They were plunged right into combat. They paid a dear price in lives as a result of that personnel decision by the Department of the Army. Ed was commissioned a second lieutenant in the Corps of Engineers and was assigned to the 44th Combat Engineer Battalion. It supported a number of the combat operations of my regiment.

I remembered Ed as a cadet, particularly at Jewish services every Sunday morning. I remembered how young he always seemed to me, but was shocked to see how very young he appeared in the light of a flashlight as he peered at me out from under his steel helmet the night I saw him on the Naktong River in Korea in 1950, a few months after his graduation. His battalion supported us with assault boats for our river crossing that night. This was the only time I can recall meeting him during the war, though I know that his battalion continued to support us. Now, as a lieutenant colonel, Ed was back with the 44th, commanding the battalion he had served in as a new second lieutenant fifteen years earlier. What an exciting coincidence and experience, particularly with its proximity to Hill 303 and Waegwan!

Ed and I spent several hours in the Atlanta air terminal reminiscing and bringing each other up to date. I told Ed about my effort to sell my engineering services to the ROK government and that I expected to fly to Seoul in early 1966. I promised him, "Ed, when I get to Seoul and complete my business with the Koreans, I shall come to Waegwan to visit you."

"Sure you will. I'll believe that when I see it!"

We then went our separate ways. He had a flight to catch to Columbus, Georgia, and I needed to get some sleep.

In January 1966 I received a letter from the Department of State, Agency for International Development, advising that the ROK government wanted to negotiate a contract with me. After verifying this with the Korean ambassadors to the United States and to the United Nations, I planned my trip to Seoul.

After the close of business activities in Seoul, I managed to call Ed from Eighth Army Headquarters. The following dialogue took place:

"Forty-fourth Engineer Battalion, Sergeant Major ——— speaking, sir."

"This is Eighth Army calling Lieutenant Colonel Edwin West."

"Colonel West speaking, sir."

"Colonel, I don't know what you have planned for this weekend, but whatever it is, cancel it. I'm coming down there."

Silence. Then:

"Who is this, sir?"

"This is the SOB you didn't believe would keep his promise to visit you."

"Lew?"

"Who else?"

We made plans for me to fly to Taegu and take the train north to Waegwan. However, I ran into a snag. The ROK government had provided me with a bodyguard, Lim Duk Ok, a tall, impressive gentleman who was reluctant to let me out of his sight. His concern regarding the trip to Waegwan was that there had been a rash of airplane hijackings by the North Koreans. Lim worried about my safety and what would happen to him if harm befell me on that flight. I managed to placate him and promised to call him the minute I returned to Seoul.

The flight was exciting, over and above the fact that the Korea Air pilot flew our twin-turboprop, high-wing commuter monoplane as if it were a jet fighter. His low-level flying presented me with the rare opportunity to reacquaint myself with the peninsula while attempting to locate old battlefields. Upon deplaning at Taegu, I traveled by taxi to the local railroad station and boarded the train to Waegwan. The trip north up the valley afforded me with a panoramic view of the battlefields upon which we fought in that hot summer of 1950, the early days of the war.

Our weekend reunion was everything I expected; it was both exciting and enjoyable. We spent time seeking portions of the Naktong where river crossings were launched. We found other places of historical interest, attended a wedding of military personnel, and other social events. It was a memorable weekend, a perfect time for reminiscences.

Lim Duk Ok breathed a sigh of relief when I called him from my hotel upon my return to Seoul on Sunday night.

This business trip to Korea in February 1966 was made more interesting and pleasant by my traveling companion, John M. Murphy, Class of 1950. He was then a congressman representing Staten Island and Brooklyn, New York. Our friendship developed on the USAS *General Pope*, the Army troopship that transported us to San Francisco from Pusan, Korea, when our tours of duty there ended late in the summer of 1951. Our first stateside assignment was to the 9th Infantry Division, Fort Dix, New Jersey; Jack as the aide de camp to the division commander, Major General Homer Kieffer, and I as the commander of M Company of the 39th Infantry Regiment. Jack had congressional business to conduct in Korea and left for home about a week before I finished my business. As with Ed West, Jack and I spent enjoyable hours reminiscing.

When we arrived in Korea and were checking in to the Chosen Hotel in Seoul, a captain approached us. After we identified ourselves, he said that he was the helicopter pilot for the commanding general of the 7th Infantry Division. I asked for the general's name. He replied, Major General Johnson."

I asked, "Which Johnson?"

"Major General Chester L. Johnson," he replied.

"He was my economics professor when I was a cadet!"

He informed us that the general would like us to join him at breakfast the following morning at his command post. "Where is that?" I asked.

"Tongduchoni," he replied.

Another unusual coincidence. For the last three months of my duty in Korea, I was attached to the 1st Cavalry Division Aviation as the air observer for the 5th Cavalry Regiment. Most of my seventy-eight missions were flown out of an 800-foot dirt airstrip at Tongduchoni. It was a mere spot in the road about twenty miles north of Uijongbu, the location of the large MASH hospital portrayed in the movie and TV series of the same name, and approximately forty miles north and east of Seoul.

"How will we get there?" I asked.

"I will pick you up at the Eighth Army Headquarters helipad at 0600 tomorrow."

The next morning we flew up the Uijongbu corridor to Tongduchoni. When I had last seen this spot in September 1951 as I was leaving for home, the only structure standing was a large battered brick chimney with an enormous 1st Cav patch painted on the stack. I was dumbfounded to see the 1966 version of the village. In the ensuing fifteen years it had become a modern sprawling built-up community. Its population provided the civilian help needed in the 7th Division headquarters.

General Johnson met us at the helipad. We had a sumptuous breakfast followed by a detailed briefing on the DMZ (Demilitarized Zone) operations. This was an unexpected treat. General Johnson, Class of 1937, had been captured by the Japanese on Bataan in 1942, endured the Death March, was transported on three hell ships to Korea, and was held in a POW camp with two of the Jewish graduates from the Class of 1940, Melvin H. Rosen and Jules D. Yatrofsky (Yates). He enjoyed relating to his cadet students how they had devised a way of sabotaging the Japanese war effort. During the winter months, they manufactured uniforms for the Imperial Army. When they sewed buttons on the flies of trousers, they ran the needle through the cloth once and multiple times through the holes in the buttons. The knowledge that the Japanese soldiers donning the uniforms or answering the call of nature would suffer the disturbing event of losing the buttons on their trousers was a morale booster for these otherwise hapless prisoners of war. They did this for four years, but were never caught.

Major General Chester L. Johnson died on July 10, 1997, and is interred at the West Point Cemetery.

The Recruiter

It was the fall of 1972. I had been a bachelor living in New York City since late 1968 after fourteen years in Atlanta. One of my closest friends in Atlanta was Burton J. Epstein a staunch supporter of Jewish causes and of the State of Israel. One night he called and asked if I would provide lodging for an Israeli soldier for a few days. I agreed without hesitation and asked for his name. He replied, "Wellesley Aron." I asked, "What kind of an Israeli name is Wellesley?" Burt responded, "He was born and raised in England and immigrated to Palestine long before Israel became a state. He was quite important and instrumental in founding and fighting for the state." A few days later, an elegant, ramrod-straight, distinguished elderly man with a strong British accent appeared at my apartment. He resembled Abba Eban in many ways. Shortly after he had settled in and we were comfortable with each other, he told me his story.

Wellesley, while a student at Jesus College at Cambridge, had become disenchanted with the extremely assimilated social life of his parents. Though recognized as Jews, they attended Anglican Church services on Sundays for "social reasons." Other feelings of alienation, and a growing belief in Zionism prompted and eventually urged him to emigrate. He went to Palestine in 1926. His parents disowned him for this "un-British act." He became very active in preparing his adopted land for its eventual defense. He established a close personal relationship with Captain Orde Wingate of the British Army. Wingate was sympathetic with the Jewish desire for a homeland. At great risk to his career, he surreptitiously assisted in the military training of the future Jewish Army and helped equip the underground Haganah. Wingate eventually became a general in the British Army during World War II. He was killed in an airplane crash in the Burmese jungle on March 24, 1944. Israelis have never forgotten all that he did, at great personal risk, to arm and train them during the British Mandate. One can find many streets named after him in Israel in memory of his support.

When World War II broke out, Wellesley and other Palestinian Jews offered to organize a Jewish Brigade as part of the British Army. This was approved in time. Wellesley became a major and commanded the brigade's transportation battalion. The brigade fought against Rommel's Afrika Korps across North Africa and finally participated in the decisive Battle of El Alamein that denied Cairo to Rommel. After the battle, Wellesley heard that the then Colonel Wingate was a patient in the 15th Scottish Hospital in Cairo. This information came to him from Abraham Akavia, Wingate's personal assistant. Wingate had sent Akavia to find

Wellesley and bring him to the hospital. During Wellesley's visit, Wingate asked, "Wellesley, how did our boys do?" Wellesley gave a glowing accurate account of the fine performance of the brigade. He never saw Wingate again.

The Jewish Brigade was then moved to the Italian front and began fighting its way up the "boot" with other units, including General Mark Clark's Fifth Army. As it became apparent that Germany's military collapse was near, a final thrust was planned for the Italian front. Winston Churchill wanted the Jewish Brigade to spearhead the final attack against the Wehrmacht. Wellesley was flown to London to participate in planning at Whitehall, Britain's Department of Defense. It had been twenty years since he had last seen his mother. He made arrangements to meet her at a railroad station in London. Wellesley related the details to me of their meeting after twenty years of no communication. "A beautiful well-dressed dowager walked toward me on the station platform. It was my mother. I greeted her and she responded, 'Wellesley, must you wear your religion on your tunic? No other soldier does.' She was referring to the Shield of David shoulder patch on my uniform."

With a note of resignation he went on, "I knew then that the visit was a failure and that there was little chance, if any, of reconciliation. The next day she was killed in a V-2 missile attack on London."

In his book, *Wheels in the Storm*, Wellesley wrote about that last battle with the Wehrmacht:

> "D" day for the Brigade meant crossing the River Senio which was in no-man's land. Night patrols had probed the enemy's position on the far bank for several weeks locating mine-fields and endeavouring to fix the most favourable areas for the planned advance. When the battle began in earnest the troops moved forward behind the artillery barrage, the Sappers having cleared a passage through the mine-fields. The R.A.F. provided air support and fighter-bombers streaked over our heads on repeated missions. There was a story circulating that, prior to the first sortie, Air H.Q. had phoned Brigade H.Q. saying that the Squadron-Leader commanding the operation was an English Jew who had specifically

> requested the privilege of leading the air-strike and please would we note that the squadrons were flying in a special formation—that of a six-pointed star, the Shield of David. However, they were over and gone so fast in the welter of battle this courteous salute was never verified. Nevertheless it was an unusually friendly gesture.

In the years after World war II, as the likelihood of a Jewish State loomed on the horizon, David Ben-Gurion, the leader of Palestine's Jews and soon to be the first prime minister of Israel, was convinced that the Arabs would attack the new state without hesitation or delay. He decided that it was crucial for survival to begin amassing men and matériel immediately. He formed two groups that were to go to the United States for that purpose; one to recruit personnel, the other to obtain matériel. Wellesley was appointed chief of the personnel team. They eventually recruited Colonel Mickey Marcus, Class of 1924 (now resting in peace next to his wife in the cemetery at West Point) and a group of Jewish Americans they named the MACHAL (Oversees Volunteers for Israel). The surviving MACHAL members convene at the West Point Jewish Chapel every May to conduct a memorial service for Mickey Marcus, the first general of a Jewish Army in 2,000 years.

Wellesley's stories fascinated me. When he spoke of recruiting Americans, all of a sudden I recalled an event in my Second Class Year (1947–48). I told Wellesley that someone had approached me on the street at West Point and asked if I would be interested in joining the Haganah. I remembered turning down his offer and that he was eventually arrested by the military police and taken before Major General Maxwell D. Taylor, the superintendent. Wellesley laughed and admitted that he was the recruiter who had tried to enlist me. He went on to relate that General Taylor had told him that he was in sympathy with the Jewish cause, but could not tolerate Wellesley's recruiting his cadets. Wellesley concluded his story by saying that he and the general had become friends. I was dumbfounded by the coincidence of sitting in my kitchen sipping coffee with the man who, twenty-five years earlier, had tried to enlist me in the Haganah. We became fast friends until his death many years later.

In addition to *Wheels in the Storm*, the story of the Jewish Brigade, Wellesley appears in another book, *The Pledge*, by Leonard Slater, that describes his role as a recruiter for the Israeli War of Independence. I have also seen him in a documentary film about the founding of the State of Israel.

Wellesley Aron was like a phantom—appearing and then disappearing. In the summer of 1975 I was doing a tour of duty at Indiantown Gap, Pennsylvania. It was Saturday morning, my last day at the Gap. I was to leave for New York in the afternoon. I was called to the headquarters building to take a telephone call. It was Wellesley.

"How did you find me?"

"Your lovely wife told me where you are and that you are due home this afternoon."

"Where are you?"

"I'm at the home of Sam Pryor in Greenwich, Connecticut. He was the co-founder of Pan American Airways with Juan Trippe. You must pick up your wife and come here in uniform today. Sam never met a Jewish colonel."

"Wellesley, what the hell are you doing with Sam Pryor?"

"We've been friends for thirty-five years. Just come. Yael has the directions."

We made the trip. The Pryors were gracious hosts and most curious to meet this Jewish colonel and his Israeli wife. Sam Pryor, between entertaining us with a delicious lunch and stories about his tour with Interpol, was busy on the phone trying to find a suitable vice president for the new president, Gerald Ford, who had just occupied the White House. Simultaneously, he was trying to arrange a flight to Hawaii for his dying neighbor, Charles Lindbergh. Yael and I thoroughly enjoyed the afternoon and spending time with Wellesley again. As we were leaving, Mr. Pryor shook my hand and said, "Come back, son. You are my kind of man." I regret that I never returned. He has since passed away.

In his declining years Wellesley Aron founded Neve Shalom in Israel, a community for Palestinian and Israeli children to study together about ways to attain peace between their peoples. It operates to this day.

The New Orleans Belle

Harmon Charles Agnew, a true Southern gentleman from New Orleans, thoroughly enjoyed a good party in the tradition of his hometown. He gave the impression of being laid back with a happy-go-lucky outlook on life. Beneath that demeanor one could sense a hint of sadness and intensity. We were roommates Yearling Year, and despite our cultural differences, we got along famously and enjoyed each other's company.

Because of the great distance between New Orleans and West Point, most of Chuck's dating was with local women. He had a One and Only in New Orleans whose geographic separation from him was a cause for his concern. We all knew that many a young love relationship was sacrificed on the altar of such separation. "Dear John" letters came all too often to members of the Corps. Chuck, therefore, was delighted when he received a letter from his beloved that she was coming to West Point to visit him accompanied by her girlfriend, whom I shall name "Melanie" for this story. He asked if I would escort Melanie for this weekend "to end all weekends"! I, of course, agreed without hesitation. Chuck went on to explain that she was a local debutante from a famous family; famous both in New Orleans and nationally.

The big day finally arrived. The young ladies were all agog with the niceties of our military society set in the inspiring backdrop of monuments, cannons, forts, war trophies all shot into the steep hills of the Academy reservation overlooking the majestic Hudson River. Our impressive uniforms from the nineteenth century contributed in no small part to the overall romantic picture.

Melanie could have stepped out of the pages of *Gone with the Wind*. She was every inch the perfectly turned out Southern Belle. Though not a particularly pretty young lady, her demeanor, manner, and personality minimized any lack of physical attributes. She moved about with the effortless grace of a dancer and was engaging company. The day was pleasant and relaxed.

Chuck and I treated the two women to dinner at the Hotel Thayer followed by the usual Saturday night hop (dance). The pomp and circumstance of the receiving line was an exceptionally exciting experience for these young ladies; General Taylor resplendent in his highly decorated dress blues, Mrs. Taylor in a beautiful gown, the general's aide dripping in gold rope, and the cadets in full dress gray created an ambiance of elegance. It was the culmination of a perfect day.

We walked the ladies back to the hotel. Standing in front of the entrance, we planned for Sunday and bade them good night. Cadets were not permitted to enter the hotel at that hour, not even the lobby. Chuck suggested that both women meet him in the morning for chapel, after which we would all meet, walk around, go to lunch, and perhaps catch a movie. The mention of chapel brought up my non-participation in the morning's Catholic activities. I explained that I would be attending Jewish services.

Melanie's reaction was one of total horror. Her eyes opened wide and she clasped her hand over her mouth. She had discovered that she was dating a Jew!

Her extreme reaction caused Chuck and me to break up in laughter. I cannot recall the remainder of the weekend after that, though I expect that our laughter at her "predicament" did anything but assuage her reaction.

Chuck went on to become a pilot in the Air Force; and, yes, he eventually received the dreaded "Dear John" letter. He taught chemistry at the new Air Force Academy and left the service in 1958. Chuck died all too soon, on February 5, 1980. I regret that we never met after graduation, as was often the case between those of us who went Army and those who went Air Force. What meetings there were usually took place during class reunions, but I never saw him at one.

His laid-back casual demeanor often masked his deep feelings. My last recollection of Chuck was watching him at our Graduation Parade. He stood to my left front. Tears trickled down his cheek as the Corps passed in review. He was not alone.

The Marksman

For some reason that remains a mystery to me, I was less than a mediocre marksman during my four cadet years. Every trip to the rifle range ended in disappointment. Prior to becoming a cadet, I had little experience with firearms. Perhaps it was the condition of my M-1 rifle; but it is always easy to blame the weapon instead of the shooter. Whatever the reason, I barely qualified.

In June 1949 I graduated as a second lieutenant of infantry and spent the following year at the Ground General School at Fort Riley, Kansas, and the Infantry School at Fort Benning, Georgia. Both schools scheduled extensive marksmanship training and testing on every weapon in the infantry regiment from the .45-caliber pistol to the 90-millimeter tank gun and the 4.2-inch mortar.

As I began firing the first assigned weapon for the record, I realized that I was scoring quite high. Lo and behold, I qualified as an Expert Marksman! Weapon after weapon yielded the same results. I was dumbfounded but ecstatic to have broken the "curse." By the time I completed the year, I had fired upward of fifteen types of weapons for record and scored Expert on all but the 90-millimeter tank gun and the 4.2-inch mortar. My scores on these two weapons were just below Expert, falling into the First Class Gunner category. These successes were as much of a mystery to me as was my lack of capability to shoot a decent score as a cadet.

Toward the end of our six-month Infantry Basic Officers course at Fort Benning we were advised that the Army was planning to adopt a new marksmanship program for the M-1 rifle based on battlefield reality. The system in use was the traditional bull's-eye targets set at known distances from the firing line. The shooter always knew the range (distance) to his target. Firing was done from a relatively comfortable firing line in the standing, sitting, and prone positions. This course did not adequately prepare the soldier for the realities of combat.

The new system under consideration consisted of two parts called tables. Table I required the shooter to fire from a foxhole, the roof of a house, a tree, a pile of rubble, and other typical conditions that soldiers found themselves in during a firefight. The targets were man-sized silhouettes that popped up at unknown ranges from the firing line. Table II was marching fire. It consisted of man-sized silhouettes that popped up as the shooter walked forward from the starting line. They remained up for a second or two before they were dropped. The shooter had to fire at each target as it popped up briefly. This table required rapid response.

It was decided to delay our departure from Fort Benning by twenty-four hours to enable us to witness a demonstration of the new program. None of us was happy about this delay in starting our leave. We were itching to go. Somehow my classmates were led to believe that I had asked for this demonstration and therefore was responsible for the delay in our departure. This was untrue, but rumors are slow to die.

In a surly mood we were trucked to the rifle range to observe the demonstration and were seated in covered bleachers. The instructor explained the course and requested one of us to come forward to fire it. No one moved. He asked again, and someone in our group shouted my name. They all picked up on it. I found myself thrust into a most unwelcome limelight. As I stepped out of the bleachers, the instructor announced that to add interest to the event, I was to compete against Sergeant First Class Silverman, the rifle champion of the European Theater of Operations. My anxiety heightened. This generated catcalls and jeers from the stands. As I shook hands with the sergeant, we were soaked to the skin by a cloudburst. We took cover while my classmates laughed and hooted in the dry from under the roof over the bleachers.

The sun shone again and we moved toward the firing line of Table I. The Georgia red clay had become slick from the rain, and as I stepped forward, I slipped on the mud and fell forward, plunging the barrel of my rifle into the mud. A good infantry soldier never lets this happen. Its was sheer embarrassment. I learned later that the colonels who were also in the stands asked who that rookie was. My rifle was cleaned for me as I tried to regain my composure. We moved to the first position in the firing line.

Silverman fired first. The targets were raised at the near and then the far positions at unknown ranges. He hit both the near and far targets. I stepped up and also hit both targets. Silence from the stands, then cheers erupted. We went from position to position in Table I, each hitting both targets. The stands were cranking up with excitement as we both maxed the first table. We entered Table II, marching fire. Silverman went first.

I sensed that he had fired too fast. I followed with caution. He had missed two targets. I hit them all. I could not believe that I had beaten this champion. He was clearly dejected. I shook hands with him and said, "Sergeant, don't feel too bad, I am a landsman."

He lit up, "No kidding , lieutenant, you're Jewish?" We both smiled.

Meanwhile, the stands erupted into cheers. The two colonels walked up to me. I was covered with wet red clay and still wet from the rain. With some respect and sincerity in their voices, they asked, "Lieutenant, what is your opinion of this marksmanship course?"

Redemption! I have often asked myself if this really happened, or was it orchestrated to make me the winner. My only clues to the contrary were the dejected expression on the sergeant's face and the reaction of the two colonels.

PART 3
THEIR STORIES

The responses to my questionnaire produced an anthology of individual experiences of the cadet and army years of many of the alumni. These are stories that are separate from their comments on anti-Semitic experiences that appear elsewhere in this book (see chap. 1). I specifically requested "Experiences (positive or negative, humorous or otherwise) during your cadet years involving religious activities of interest, non-religious activities, 'beating the system', academic agonies; i.e., stories portraying the human aspect of your life as a cadet."

Most of the more than 200 questionnaires returned to me included one or more such stories. A number of responders included stories of experiences relevant to their Judaism while on active duty. Chapel-related activities, particularly those of the Jewish Cadet Choir, dominated the responses. For those from the classes of 1985 and forward who were cadets after the Jewish Chapel opened, there were special comments that highlighted the importance of the Chapel to their spiritual well-being and often to their decision not to resign. One recent graduate expressed his feelings to me about the chapel after his bar-pinning ceremony in 2003. He said, "Sir, there are two things I recall from Beast Barracks; one was a bottle of brass polish that opened in my pack soaking everything, and the other was your speech at the first Shabbat service when you said, 'Consider this chapel your home away from home. We built it for you.' I never forgot that."

All of the stories in this anthology appear with the permission of their authors. In some instances the names of the authors are omitted at their own request. The stories are reproduced here word for word, as written and submitted. Each questionnaire, when received, was provided with a sequence number that also became the file number of the responder.

Tales of the *Shinyo Maru*

The Japanese attack on the United States on December 7, 1941 at Pearl Harbor was meant to cripple the U.S. fleet to render Southeast Asia more vulnerable. The Philippine Islands were a major point of the Japanese effort. Of key importance in the archipelago were the Bataan Peninsula and the island of Corregidor. Both had been heavily fortified by the U.S. Army years before the war began.

Among the Jewish graduates from the USMA class of 1940, four were assigned to the Philippines prior to the outbreak of hostilities: Morris L. Shoss, Jules David Yates (name changed from Jules Yatrofsky), Walter Wald (name changed from Israel Wald), and Melvin H. Rosen. All four became prisoners of the Japanese and worked as slave laborers until 1944. They survived the brutal death march and were shipped out to Japan in prison ships called "hell ships."

Eleven "hell ships" sailed from the Philippines, none of them bearing the prisoner-of-war markings commonly used in that era. Four of these ships were sunk by U.S. subs and aircraft whose crews were unaware that they had American prisoners aboard. All told, 5,271 U.S. soldiers died during these sinkings and in the surviving ships.

The survivors from the years of Japanese captivity convene periodically to support one other and to swap stories about their experiences. In September 1998, at their convention in San Antonio, they assembled all sort of documents relating to their capture and events leading up to, during, and subsequent to their captivity. Morris L. Shoss and others wrote detailed accounts of their experience that were published under the title *The Shinyo Maru Survivors Reunion*.

I sent Colonel Shoss a copy of my questionnaire and did not learn of his death until I was contacted by his daughter, Marie Haas, who found it in his mail. She recognized the historical importance of her father's story to this book and to American military history, and took it upon herself to authorize me to see his story. I felt that it deserved to be reproduced in its entirety. Colonel Shoss's story follows.

Morris L. Shoss, Class of 1940

I was the Executive Officer of Battery C, 91st Coast Artillery, Philippine Scouts, which was commanded by Capt. John Gulick (deceased). Our organization, at the time of interest, had an air defense artillery mission on Bataan until it fell on April 9, 1942. Then we acquired a gun artillery counter battery mission on Corregidor until we had to surrender on May 6, 1942.

On Bataan, we actually operated as a provisional two (2) battery battalion with a battery of four 3-inch anti-aircraft guns, a T8E3 electro-mechanical director and a stereoscopic rangefinder, plus a battery of two 50-caliber air cooled machine guns, equipped with speed ring sights. Our strength had been increased to about 200 men due to an augmentation of Filipino Army troops. We were assigned to the 200th Coast Artillery, AAA (New Mexico National Guard) for tactical employment on Bataan, since our parent 91st Coast Artillery Regiment was stationed on Corregidor.

Around February/March 1942, we received four aviators from the 17th Pursuit Squadron—Lt. Majors, Page, Lt. Krantz, and Lt. Bolfanz. At that time, we were occupying a position adjacent to a tactical landing strip at Cabcaban on Bataan. Our permanently assigned officers were Capt. Gulick, Lt. Shoss as Executive Officer, and Lt. Howard Irish as Fire Direction Officer. Since we operated on a round-the-clock schedule, Capt. Gulick assigned Majors and Page as Assistant Fire Direction Officers, and Bolfanz and Krantz as Assistant Executive Officers.

During the first week of their detail with our unit, both Majors and Page were killed. The Cabcaban airstrip came under an enemy attack and we countered with our 3-inch guns. A faulty fuse (WWI vintage—powder train type) caused one round to detonate over our position (muzzle burst). Several Filipino scouts as well as Majors and Page were killed instantly by shell fragments. Both Capt. Gulick and I received wounds. Our rangefinder was demolished and our unit was out of action for several days.

It was a terrible and sad blow to lose Majors and Page so early in their new roles as artillerymen. Both were eager to continue their duel with enemy aircraft, albeit from the ground. We never got to know them well. Both Bolfanz and Krantz remained with us and became proficient artillerymen. Bolfanz never fully recovered from the shock of losing Majors and Page and underwent a gradual change of personality and behavior. During the fall of Bataan, April 7–9, 1942, we activated our plan to escape to Corregidor, following the demolition of our air defense weapons and ammunition, which we could not take with us. Bolfanz was sent ahead to Corregidor to arrange accommodations for our men, should we succeed in getting there. We never saw or heard from him again.

Krantz was a superb combat officer. He gained the respect and admiration of the men and officers by his coolness under stress and remarkable skill in developing field expedients to handle problems. He was a natural leader who would have enjoyed an illustrious career had he survived. Following our miraculous escape to Corregidor, our unit was assigned two fixed seacoast artillery batteries facing Bataan, Battery Grubbs, two 10-inch seacoast artillery guns on disappearing mounts and Battery Morrison, two 6-inch guns also on disappearing mounts. I was placed in command of Battery Morrison, which was located on a promontory and nearest in distance to Bataan. Capt. Gulick divided the men into two equal complements, and took Lt. Irish with him to Battery Grubbs and assigned Lt. Krantz to me as my Executive Officer. We underwent intensive training and preparation for the artillery counter battery duel we knew was coming. Following the fall of Bataan, the Japanese lined up all the Americans and Filipino captives along major roads which they used to bring up battalion after battalion of artillery, primarily their deadly accurate 240-mm Howitzers. We were under restrictions not to fire on them for fear of exacting a heavy toll on our unfortunate comrades who were being used as human shields.

My station during action was a pillbox observation post located immediately above our fire control plotting room and connected to it by a vertical shaft. Lt. Krantz's station was in the gun pits located on each side of a reinforced concrete ammunition bunker.

By coincidence, my close friend and West Point classmate (1940) Lt. Herbert Pace, occupied a fire direction post for the 60th Coast Artillery, AAA, on high ground behind us. He was in excellent position to locate targets for us and to help in adjusting our fire. We ran communication lines to his position and with his help had developed firing data on many lucrative artillery targets.

On the fateful day around the middle of April, 1942, when we received a command to initiate our program of destruction fire against enemy artillery, we managed to neutralize two targets before Japanese counter battery responded. For several hours, which seemed like an eternity, we were subjected to accurate direct hits by all caliber of Japanese artillery. My observation pillbox received a direct hit and collapsed. I was saved by my helmet from serious injury and it took several men to extricate me from the rubble and pull me down the shaft to the plotting room. When the Japanese finally ceased fire, both our guns were destroyed. We were all shell-shocked and sorely grieved to find Lt. Krantz dying from a small shell fragment that penetrated his stomach. The recovery party sent by Capt. Gulick notified us that Lt. Pace's observation post took a direct hit that obliterated him. Pace Hall at Fort Bliss, Texas is dedicated to his honor. I regret no comparable honor was ever given Lt. Krantz who succumbed shortly after our first and only counter battery duel.

Battery C, 91st CA (PS) continued the battle following the loss of Lt. Krantz. The survivors of Battery Morrison joined Battery Grubbs, which suffered the same fate as Battery Morrison a few days later. We were then assigned two mobile 155-mm guns that were maneuvered over Corregidor, sniping at the enemy of Bataan. One piece was the last weapon to fire before the surrender of Corregidor. Our officer staff had been reduced to the initial three: Capt. Gulick and Lts. Shoss and Irish.

Shortly after the middle of 1944 when American aircraft were able to reach targets in Mindanao, Japanese authorities began to move American prisoners to Luzon. However, 750 of the youngest and healthiest were sent first to Lasang, near the southeast coastline of Mindanao to serve as coolie laborers alongside hundreds of natives, whose members included women and children, to build airstrips. Our American compound was located on the extension of the airstrip and lighted at night as an intentional invitation to Allied bomber aircraft to attack us. That they did. Irish and I were on this detail. Fortunately, the night raiders missed our compound but put enough craters in the landing strip to discourage its continued use. The decision was made to evacuate the 750 prisoners by ship to Luzon. We were marched to a nearby dock and placed in the hold of a decrepit cargo ship. We were crowded in a small hold with barely enough room to lie side by side on the floor. The temperature was high and we sweltered in our perspiration. Latrines were buckets, which were pulled up by ropes twice daily for emptying. Food, consisting of steamed rice, as well as drinking water, was lowered in buckets. We were so cramped for space that equitable distribution of food and water was impossible. Many prisoners became dehydrated and lapsed into unconsciousness. We were tortured for lack of oxygen, water, and food. We soon lost interest in food and beseeched the enemy to allow us to rotate people on deck to breathe fresh air. This was done once, on which occasion prisoners were hosed down with salt water pumped from the sea.

After several days without incidents or attacks by Allied planes or submarines, we arrived at Zamboanga. There, a convoy of several ships was being formed to make a run up the Sula Sea to the San Bernadino Straits. We were to be escorted by gunboats and seaplanes. Our freighter was moved alongside another with holds in the bow and stern to accommodate prisoners and we were transferred to the larger ship. Once in the holds, the long ladders were pulled up and the hold covers were pulled shut. We were in darkness, in horrible, suffocating heat and stung by the warning shouted down by the interpreter. He told us that in the event the ship was hit by Allied aircraft or submarines, the guards were to annihilate us by throwing hand grenades into the hold. Our convoy underwent sporadic bomber attacks but no bombs fell on our ship.

On the seventeenth day of our voyage, about late afternoon on September 7, 1942, the convoy was astride the wide mouth of the Sindangan River, which fed into the Sulu Sea. This was a stretch of deeper water which our American submarine packs used as an ambush spot. Our ship was one of the first hit. Following noisy commotion on topside, accompanied by loud clatter of machine gun fire, the first of two torpedoes tore into the side of the freighter. I was knocked unconscious by the first explosion. I had a vision of diving off a high diving board into a front flip. As I began my recovery from the front flip, I was propelled into a back flip. This must have been when the second torpedo hit.

On regaining consciousness, I was impressed by the stillness. The explosions made me partially deaf. The section of the ship I was in was listing. Dead bodies were strewn all over the hold. I was the only person stirring among all the dead or unconscious. I could not get my bearings or locate my close friend in whose group I had been sitting. Obviously, the explosion had flung me away from them. Steel beams and decking had collapsed into the hold. I realized I had best get topside before the compartment capsized and sank. A line dangled down from a gaping rent in the deck and I stumbled over bodies to grab it and pull myself up to the deck.

In desperation, I found enough strength to slide my body onto the sloping deck. As I turned over to survey what remained of the ship, I was surprised to find most of the superstructure gone. Dead Japanese guards were sprawled haphazardly on the deck. One dazed Japanese guard stood over me and monopolized my full attention. He had his weapon pointed at my chest and followed me as I raised myself and backed to the high side of the listing ship. When I reached the edge, I threw myself overboard to escape this wild-eyed demon, only to find, on looking down, that I was headed almost on top of a wood raft, crowded with Japanese guards.

Their impulse to protect themselves kept them from firing at me. I splashed clear of the raft and sank as deep as my momentum would take me before swimming underwater as far as I could away from the raft. On surfacing, I discovered that there were many prisoners in the water, some in obvious distress for lack of swimming ability. I started pushing flotsam toward those in difficulty and helping others swim toward this flotsam. I hastily took a panoramic view of the sea around us and noted several ships in various stages of sinking.

Two more ships were already beached. Gunboats maneuvered in the area, picking up Japanese survivors. To my horror, I identified machine gun tracers emanating from gunboats aimed at us on the flotsam and occasionally, at prisoners swimming toward the distant shoreline. Everything was like a scene in a silent movie. In fact, it was like a dream. I experienced exhilarating euphoria, my body bathed in refreshing cool water and my nostrils sucking in delicious fresh air.

It was apparent to me that the Japanese were bent on killing all American survivors as they had threatened. Shore was not too inviting in daylight with tracers ricocheting off the surf. The gunboats would eventually circle the flotsam and kill any Americans on it. I decided to follow the tide out to sea and after sundown, face the problem of making shore. As I moved away from the scene of action using a lazy sidestroke, I was fascinated watching the torpedoed ships go down. Of the ship I was on, the *Shinyo Maru*, only one section remained, possibly the stern. It was now covered with people who, like ants, crowded the diminishing portion still above water. Finally, it slipped completely under, ending the scene. I was awakened abruptly from this reverie by sharp stinging sensations along my right chest that moved upward. A gunboat or beached ship, one or the other, had found my range while sweeping the water with machine gun fire and I had received superficial wounds. I submerged immediately, bobbing to the surface only for a bit of air. Once I got the impression that a gunboat was bearing down on me and swam frantically as fast and as far as I could underwater. Much later, I was relieved to note that the gunboats were concentrating their fire toward shore to cut off those trying to escape the cordon they formed between open sea and shore.

Night came quickly. The tracers continued intermittently and pointed the way toward shore. I soon could make out the surf along the coastline from the phosphorescence created by wave action. As darkness deepened, I found to my dismay that I created phosphorescent illumination when using vigorous swimming strokes. Occasionally, a tracer was directed toward me from one of the beached ships, indicating sharpshooters were still at their cowardly task. After years of being cramped like a sardine in close quarters with hundreds of fellow Americans, here I was, all alone, possibly the only American survivor. I felt that I had to live to bring back word of the fate of those who lost their lives that day. I also recognized that my chances were getting slim because the pain in my chest was getting more severe, breathing was becoming painful and difficult, and I was tiring.

It must have taken most of the night to reach the surf close to one of the beached ships. Cruel fate had another ordeal to try me. The surf pounded on jagged coral reefs. First, my palms were sliced in my effort to prevent my body from contacting the coral. I was completely naked and had no protection against the razor sharp coral. I tried to float on my stomach until I reached the shallow water. Soon my feet, my chin, stomach and knees were sliced and each cut burned like bee stings. At last I was over the coral on a narrow strip of sand but too weak to stand. My mind kept repeating the warning that the Japanese from the beached ship were here, too. I barely could raise my head to look around in the dark. However, my hearing had improved a little.

Then the odds changed in my favor. A heavy, refreshing rain squall commenced. I started crawling away from the beach toward the tree line. I was so weak that I would have been content to find a comfortable hide-a-way and go to sleep forever. As I entered the jungle, I crawled over a fallen tree trunk that had a hollowed-out section filled with rainwater. I drank almost all the water in that reservoir. A sturdy branch I found nearby served as a cane but I struggled for almost an hour to get on my feet. Then, slowly bobbing in painful steps, I penetrated the jungle. As twilight came and the rains stopped, I started looking for my hide-a-way. I was enveloped in a cloud of mosquitoes. The stinging bites sent me reeling through the jungle until the cloud left me. I now knew there would be no resting until the following heat of day. Somehow, I came upon a trail, which I followed through several deserted native villages.

I must have lapsed into delirium. I am vague on how many days I hobbled around before a friendly tribe of Cebuanos aborigines found me and administered to my basic needs. After several days of treatment, I was carried on a bamboo stretcher to the nearest Filipino guerilla organization. Being incapacitated, I was placed with a family of Filipinos. While I convalesced, several other American survivors were with me, and I learned from them that of the original 750, only 82 were accounted for. Several of these survivors died or were dying from wounds. Howard Irish was not among the survivors. Eventually, we were integrated into the guerilla organization and resumed active combat against the enemy. When our supply submarine, the USS *Narwhal*, made a rendezvous in our area, it had instructions to evacuate all survivors of the *Shinyo Maru*. Most of us who were in the vicinity boarded the vessel and were evacuated to New Guinea. From there, we were transferred to the 42nd General

Hospital in Brisbane, Australia. By November 1944, we were returned to the United States by ship. Capt. Gulick survived prison camp and the sinking of a Japanese POW transport by US aircraft to return to the states in 1945. He died March 6, 1967 of cancer.

Here is Morris L. Shoss's response to the Reunion Inquiry (where he presumably described his life). He is a retired colonel and a retired tenured associate professor of technical mathematics at San Antonio College.

I was born in Houston, Texas, April 10, 1915, the third of five siblings. I graduated in June 1933 from Jefferson Davis High School, Houston, as the top male student and applied through my congressman for an appointment to the US Military Academy at West Point. I also applied to Rice Institute (now Rice University) for a full scholarship which was approved. In 1936 after completing three of a four-year course in chemical engineering, I transferred to West Point. I graduated in June, 1940 and received a regular Army commission as a second lieutenant in the Coast Artillery Corps.

I married Flora Gordon Shoss of Wharton, Texas on September 22nd, 1940. Flora had finished three years toward a bachelor of journalism at the University of Texas, Austin. We spent our honeymoon almost a month, first by car from Wharton to San Francisco where our car was placed aboard an ancient Army transport ship, the *USS A.T. Grant*. We sailed to Manila, Philippine Islands by way of Hawaii and Guam.

I was assigned as Executive Officer of Battery C, 91st Coast Artillery (Philippine Scouts) of the Harbor Defense of Manila and Subic Bays, located on Corregidor Island. Flora and I had been married only seven months when she was evacuated with all the other military dependents back to the U.S., during May and June, 1941. We would not see each other again until November 1944.

My unit's first contact with the enemy was shortly after the attack on Pearl Harbor, Hawaii. We were on Fort Wint Island in Subic Bay manning anti-aircraft guns when enemy aircraft attacked the U.S. Naval Base Olongapo in Subic Bay. We got credit for two kills. Two weeks later we had to evacuate Fort Wint and withdraw into the Bataan Peninsula where we shot down 13 more enemy aircraft before Bataan fell. My unit was the last one that managed to escape to Corregidor after the fall of Bataan. While on Bataan, I was awarded a Bronze Star for Valor and a Purple Heart for wounds. On Corregidor, my unit in a Field Artillery counter battery role, manned a series of fixed large caliber cannons which were destroyed by overwhelming enemy superiority. On the fall of Corregidor and our military forces in the Philippines on May 6, 1942, we had little left to fight with. We were exhausted and short on food, water, and clothing. I was awarded the Silver Star for heroism and another Bronze Star for valor. As a POW, I spent six months at Bilibid and Cabanatuan prison camps and two years at the Davao Penal Colony on Mindanao Island.

In August 1944, the enemy started moving from the southern islands northward ahead of advancing Allied forces. I was on the Japanese prison ship, *Shinyo Maru,* which was carrying 750 allied POW's and was sunk September 7, 1944, in the Sulu Sea, off Sindangan by the U.S. submarine, *Paddle.* I was one of the 82 survivors who escaped and joined the Filipino guerillas. I was awarded my second Purple Heart for wounds received during my swim to shore. The enemy had told us that in the event the ship was sunk, all prisoners were to be killed. We survivors were collected and given aid by friendly natives and guerillas in the area. A few weeks later, we were evacuated from the Philippines by the U.S. submarine *Narwhal* and ended up at the 42nd Army General Hospital in Brisbane, Australia. After extensive medical treatment, we were processed for return to the U.S arriving about Thanksgiving Day, 1944.

Early 1945, I returned to active duty by attending the Army Command and General Staff College to catch up on military developments. This was followed by a short stint at the Army Anti-Aircraft Artillery School at Fort Bliss, Texas to prepare for an assignment to Brazil as an advisor to the Brazilian Army Schools and Commands on Seacoast and AA. We lived in Rio de Janeiro from 1945 to 1948.

I received several decorations and awards from the Brazilian government. I was selected for graduate school in nuclear physics. This involved a year at the Naval Academy Post Graduate School, followed by two years at the University of California, Berkeley. Upon graduation in 1951, I was detailed in the Army Chemical Corps and participated in nuclear weapon atmospheric and underground testing at Nevada test site. This was followed by three years on the staff of the Military Liaison Committee to the Atomic Energy Commission in Washington, DC. Returning to the Artillery Branch with an assignment in Germany as Commander of the 25th Field Artillery Battalion of the 10th Infantry Division, I was moved up to headquarters, U.S Army Europe, as nuclear operations officer. From 1958 to 1962, I was assigned at the Artillery and Missile School, Fort Sill, Oklahoma in weapons research and development, then back to U.S. Army Europe Headquarters in Heidelberg, Germany, as Deputy Inspector General of Nuclear Warfare Organizations. In 1965 I returned to Washington, DC, for an assignment with Defense Intelligence Agency. My last assignment brought me back to Texas to Headquarters, Fourth U.S. Army, Fort Sam Houston as Deputy Assistant Chief of Staff for Operations and Training. I retired June 30, 1970 at Fort Sam Houston with a chest full of medals and decorations.

By September 1970, I was employed at San Antonio College to set up a technical mathematics program that I headed for 11 years before retiring as a tenured associate professor in December, 1981.

We have two children, Dr. Robert Shoss, MD, and Maurie Lynn Haas. Robert was born December 11, 1945 while we were stationed in Brazil. He is a dermatologist and has a practice in Albany, NY, where he took his residency following his graduation from the second graduating class at the University of Texas Medical School in San Antonio, Texas. He has three children. His oldest daughter is in the psychology graduate program at Penn State. His youngest daughter is in high school and his son is studying architecture at Syracuse University.

Maurie Lynn has two sons. The oldest is in the furniture business with them in McAllen, Texas. The youngest graduated, Phi Beta Kappa, from Rice University in May 1998, and is staying at Rice to work toward a Ph.D. in history.

My wife, Flora, did finish her BA in journalism in 1942 at UT. She was inducted into WICI and during WWII worked on the Houston Post as a reporter and feature writer. Her last assignment was to cover my return from the Philippines after which she resigned to be with me for the rest of our lives.

My hobbies after returning to San Antonio in 1968 include volunteer work with the American Red Cross in water safety programs, teaching swimming and life guarding until 1981. Since then, I have volunteered for senior citizens in giving classes of yoga on mats and in water. I compete in Senior Olympic Swimming events and have garnered over 50 medals.

A Sample Questionnaire

Before proceeding with the stories extracted from the questionnaires, as explained at the beginning of this chapter, I am here including one questionnaire in full, both because of its general interest and also so that the reader will have a sense of the questions to which the graduates in the final section were responding.

Roll Call Questionnaire

Name: Elad Yoran **Class:** 1991 **Cullum No.** 48808

Admitted to West Point (City or Town) Pound Ridge **State** New York

At what age did you aspire to attend West Point? I started to think about it at 15.

What generated or who influenced your aspiration?

Four specific people influenced my aspiration to attend West Point: my self-appointed 'godfather', Pete Pietrobono, my step-father Leonard Schonberger, my father, Chaim Yoran, and my high-school friend, Stephen Cook, each of whom played a different role. Once the idea of attending West Point started to germinate and grow within me, a series of experiences that directly exposed me to West Point accelerated its development.

I am the first son born to immigrant parents and the first American in my family. My parents came to America in 1968 for my father's residency following medical school and for my mother's graduate schooling. They came here from Israel, at that time a 20-year old country born out of the ashes of the Holocaust with a soul that cried, 'Never Again' and a creed that Jews should know how to defend themselves, because no one else would protect them. I was born a year later, on Memorial Day of 1969. My mother often told me that she could see American flags waving outside the hospital room window that day, so she knew that I would be different. For a long time, 'different' to me meant having an unusual name. I was named Naftali Elad Yoran; my first name after my maternal great-grandfather and middle name, Elad, a modern Israeli name, meaning God for eternity. My parents believed at that time that eventually they would return to Israel and that I had to have an Israeli name. (When my brothers Amit (USMA 1993) and Dov were born, they had the similar naming experiences. By the time my two youngest brothers were born, both my parents were naturalized American citizens, and they were named Ron and Adam respectively!)

Our family chased the American dream, struggled and ultimately suffered through a divorce. Nonetheless, both my parents worked hard, accomplished a lot professionally and established themselves. We bought a house, made close friends and became active in the community. This was most evident at our Passover Seder meals which have always had Jews, Christians, and even Moslems at the table. Though there were many difficulties, we were living the American dream that has inspired generations of immigrants like ourselves.

As I progressed through high-school, the decision that lurked ahead was not whether I would attend college, but rather which. I had always excelled academically. In addition, I had always been engaged in athletics and other extracurricular activities, so that by my senior year in high school, I was in the fortunate position of being able to decide to attend either West Point or one of several Ivy League colleges that had offered admission to me. As I approached high school graduation and contemplated college, the idea of serving this country grew from a passing thought to something that took on a life of its own. To me, the decision was obvious; clearly, my path led through the gray granite gates of West Point.

This decision was influenced by my own experiences and by several role models in my early years of development. My role models included a second-generation Italian-American named Pete Pietrobono who, at the entry of America into World War Two, volunteered to join the Navy at 17 and served aboard the aircraft carrier USS Yorktown at the Battle of Midway. When the Yorktown was destroyed by the Japanese, he floated in the Pacific for hours until pulled aboard a rescue boat. Later he served in both Korea, where he earned a battlefield commission, and Vietnam. Pete called himself the "Iron Major of the Pacific" and it was he who first brought me to West Point where I was awed not by its solemnity, but by the statue of General Patton in front of the library and that of MacArthur and Eisenhower on the Plain. That visit struck a chord in me. A dear friend of the family, Pete and his stories were a constant presence at our house. He was perhaps the most enthusiastic and open about the idea of me attending the Academy. On one of the proudest days of my life, Pete and my stepfather pinned my lieutenant's bars on my shoulders. Pete died in 1997 and I miss him terribly to this day.

My second role model was my stepfather, Leonard Schonberger, Len to us, himself a son of Czech immigrants a generation earlier. He had served as an US Navy officer and a high-altitude researcher in the 1950s when jets began to replace propeller driven planes and higher-altitude flying became a possibility. During his research, he developed a mask valve that enabled pilots to fly higher than they previously could. Today that mask is still displayed in the Smithsonian Air and Space Museum in Washington, DC. Len was a patriot and proud to have served as an officer in the United States Navy. As children, he would march us around conducting a mock "OCS" program (as he had once attended in the Navy) for my brothers and me in which tests such as keeping the fire burning all night in the wood-burning stove in our kitchen became a test of manhood rather than a chore. Len was a value-driven person who loved his country and community where he was a long-serving family doctor, and the people in the community loved him for it. Long before West Point, Len taught us to live according to simple values, integrity, humility and loyalty. He also taught us not to smoke. He died of emphysema in 1998. When I wonder how to resolve a difficult situation I turn to the lessons he taught me. He raised me as his own son and I will always love him for it. He is in my heart daily.

My third role model was my father who had served as an armor officer in the Israeli army in the 1956 Sinai Campaign and 1967 Six-Day War. In 1973, during the Yom Kippur War, while we were living in Israel (We were living in Be'er Sheva in the Negev Desert at the time), he again served in war, this time as a doctor. Born in Israel, 10 years before the creation of the state to early Jewish pioneers, my father is the epitome of the modern, secular, Israeli Jew who is not only hard-working and accomplished, but also strong and capable of defending his homeland and family. My father became a naturalized citizen of the United States when I was just 10 years old and I can remember both his preparation for the exam as well as the pride he felt on the day in 1980 when he voted in his first US election and pulled the lever for Ronald Reagan. During our annual summer childhood trips to Israel, my father led us on tours of the country. Over the years, it seems we covered every square inch of Israel together. On his tours, we did not visit many museums or too many beaches. Rather, we visited places of Jewish history, both biblical and of modern Israel. From Jerusalem to Jericho to Masada by the Dead Sea, to Gamla in the Golan Heights, to Mt Tabor in the Galilee where Deborah led the Jewish Army in victory over the Canaanites, to the caves of the Maccabees, from where the Jews defeated the Greeks, ancient Jewish history was filled with great military struggle and victory. But these places were only part of the story. My father showed us other places that meant much more to him, and by consequence to me. He took us to see the burnt vehicles along the windy mountainside road where modern Israelis, led by a West Point graduate, COL Mickey Marcus, were killed as they struggled to break the siege to Jerusalem in 1948. We visited the Latrun memorial at the base of the foothills and walked the DMZ that separated East from West Jerusalem between 1948 and 1967. He took us to see the trenches on the Golan Heights where so many died, and the border fence with Lebanon. We stopped at Army bases along the way and watched Israeli soldiers shooting target practice in modern Merkava tanks. My father beamed with pride, as he had been an Armor officer; by then I already knew from his oft repeated stories, that in those days, they fought in World War Two era Sherman, and then later Patton model tanks. It did not occur to me at the time that these tanks were both named after West Point graduates. As we crossed Israel from the Golan to the Negev, we picked up soldiers hitchhiking home or to their base; experiences in which the soldiers would inspire me with their strength and determination. Whereas Pete and Len taught me to love America and the idea of serving as a way of expressing gratitude and giving back to my country, my father added the dimension that Jews had an obligation to know how to fight and protect themselves.

Ultimately, it took my close friend Stephen Cook, who was three years older than me who attended Annapolis to demonstrate that serving in the military was something that members of my generation could do as well. When Steve enrolled at Annapolis, I saw a friend and a peer volunteering to serve, and I understood that I could not only be accepted at West Point, but also be successful there.

Growing up, I had visited West Point twice, once with Pete and once with Len, but knew of it mostly through Pete's stories. Then, at 17, I attended the Invitational Academic Workshop, a weeklong academic introduction to West Point. We lived in the barracks, ate in the mess hall and attended class lectures. In addition, we experienced a bit of the other aspects of cadet life by having PT in the morning and marching to events. Later, I attended Boys State where I met other high school students also thinking about West Point. This direct and indirect exposure to the Academy and others my age that were thinking about West Point solidified something in me that, heretofore, was a dream.

That dream took one step closer to reality when in the autumn of my senior year in high school I entered a large room with six strangers seated across a large conference table and sat in the single chair facing them. My interview lasted an hour or so; I do not recall it all. Two weeks later, I had the opportunity to meet Senator Daniel Patrick Moynihan of New York State as he nominated me to West Point.

Looking back at it now, I realize that I attended West Point not despite my Jewish identity, but because of it.

Did you expect to find other Jews at the Academy? I believe that the answer was yes, but I do not remember thinking about it very much. I guess that I always felt that there would be.

Were you aware that Jews had been attending West Point throughout its history? No.

Did you encounter or experience anti-Semitism during your cadet years? If so, please explain. Perhaps I was naïve and anti-Semitism did exist at West Point, but I never experienced it. Certainly, I did not ever experience institutional anti-Semitism. To the contrary, I found West Point to be the place that helped develop my sense of Jewish (religious) identity.

That said, I do think it would be difficult, if not outright impossible, for someone who is much more observant than me, to be Jewish at West Point. For example, I believe, that it is not possible for someone to keep the Sabbath at West Point. During my cadet years, we still had academic classes on Saturdays, as well as inspections, parades, football games and many other activities. Much of that is still the same today. Is this anti-Semitism? I do not think so.

The only anti-Semitism I did experience at West Point came at the hands of my fellow cadets. Many cadets came to the Academy from places where there are not many, if any, Jews. Some of these cadets, when they learned I was Jewish would express either interest in learning more about me and what being Jewish meant or, on much rarer occasions, others would tell stereotypical Jewish jokes or make anti-Semitic remarks. I did not take the latter group seriously.

I was raised in the modern 'Israeli' sense of being Jewish, i.e. speaking Hebrew and keeping traditions such as a Passover Seder and fasting on Yom Kippur, but being secular. We did not belong or attend a synagogue and, for the most part, had no association with any organized or structured Jewish organization or entity. For me, all that changed at West Point. During Beast Barracks, I identified myself as Jewish and, at our first introduction to the chaplains and religious services at West Point, I met the few other Jewish cadets. We were marched to the Jewish Chapel where we met the Rabbi (then Rabbi Leinwand), members of the Jewish community both at West Point and in the surrounding area, and most important of all, Jewish Firsties, who, the second we stepped into the Jewish Chapel, stopped hazing us and treated us as equals. Being someone who was unaccustomed to going to a synagogue, at first the Jewish Chapel was simply a sanctuary from the stress of daily life at West Point. Eventually, I developed a desire to learn more about Judaism and learn the traditions and prayers. I looked forward to Friday evening services and to Rabbi Leinwand's guitar playing and sing alongs.

I found the Jewish community to be warm and supportive. Perhaps because we were such a distinct minority, we paid more attention to it. Among other things, we had special tables for Passover and a small but close knit cadet Jewish Chapel Choir, of which I served as CIC during my cow year. Rabbi Leinwand taught Hebrew classes through the Department of Foreign Languages, which certainly helped my GPA that semester. My family also became active members of the greater West Point Jewish community. My stepfather Leonard got a job at Keller Army Hospital. My family attended services and holidays at the Jewish Chapel. We became close to members of the community, especially the Rabbi and his family and Col Sydney Lawrence's family. Col Lawrence was a doctor at Keller and he had three daughters with whom I became good friends, which of course added to my popularity amongst my fellow cadets. Rabbi Leinwand officiated at my brother Dov's Bar Mitzvah which was held at West Point.

Did you earn academic awards such as stars? I achieved Dean's List all eight semesters and I earned the Commandant's Award (the wreath) for excelling academically, in military leadership and physical fitness.

Were you awarded a Rhodes Scholarship or other post-graduation scholarships, appointments, fellowships, honors, etc? Please explain. No.

Advanced Academic Degrees: Masters in Business Administration (MBA) from the Wharton School of the University of Pennsylvania.

Were you a Corps Squad athlete? No **What sport(s)?** N/A

I skied on the competitive ski club team which competed against other colleges.

In addition, in my intramural athletic career, we won the Brigade Championship in swimming, and were once runners up in wrestling. Also, out of many dozens of teams, including those from other academies and other countries, we won the tough Sandhurst military skills competition.

Did you break any athletic records? No **Please explain.** N/A

Did you enter the Army, Air Force or other service upon graduation? Army

If Army, what branch? Engineers **If Air Force, flying or non-flying?** N/A

How long did you serve in the regular service? I served just less than three years. I was medically retired after I re-injured my knee during a parachute jump at Ft. Bragg, NC. I tore the Anterior Cruciate Ligament (ACL) in my left knee during intramural wrestling firstie year (we were practicing for the Brigade Championship!) and had it reconstructed at Keller Army Hospital at West Point. After intense rehabilitation the rest of the year, despite my better judgment, I wanted to be Airborne and serve as a paratrooper. So, on branch and post selection, I was lucky to be high enough in my class to pick Ft. Bragg. My knee wasn't so lucky. Less than three years later, I tore the ACL again in the same leg in a parachuting accident . . . and that was the end of my military career.

Did you serve in combat? Yes **What war(s) or action(s)?** Operation Restore Hope in Somalia, Africa 1992–1993

Earned awards and decorations.
Army Commendation Medal; Armed Forces Expeditionary Medal; Humanitarian Service Medal; National Defense Service Medal; Army Achievement Medal (2x); Army Service Ribbon; Air Assault Badge; Airborne Parachutist Badge

Highest grade in Regular Service? First Lieutenant (1LT) **In reserve service?** Same

Civilian Occupation or profession.
I was an investment banker for three years and then made the plunge into entrepreneurship and started a computer security company called Riptech, Inc. Today, I am on my third start-up. I am building and running an early-stage private equity fund called Security Growth Partners LLC to invest in and develop emerging security technologies.

Please relate an experience or experiences (positive or negative, humorous or otherwise) during your cadet years involving religious activities of interest, non-religious activities, "beating the system", academic agonies, i.e., stories portraying the human aspect of your life as a cadet. (Use an extra sheet or the reverse side of the questionnaire)

The highlight of my and all cadet experiences are the friends we made that were forged by many hours of tough experiences together, youth, and mutual respect.

As far as Jewish activities, my memories of Choir Trips are vivid. To us on the choir, the trip or two that we took every semester was something to look forward to. Generally, we would visit a congregation where we would perform once or twice over the weekend. We would be hosted by members of the congregation and stay in their homes. The performances consisted of, more or less, the same set of songs that the Jewish Chapel Choir had been singing for generations—military songs, West

Point songs, and Jewish songs, including favorite show tunes from Fiddler on the Roof. The performances always started with the singing of the Star Spangled Banner and Hatikva. We would answer questions about West Point and about being Jewish at West Point, including the ubiquitous, "What is a nice Jewish boy like you doing at West Point?" The audiences loved our performances, even though I cannot say much about the quality of our singing. We were, after all a group of young, fit, Jewish (for the most part!) cadets in uniform. What was not to love? However, to us, these trips had almost nothing to do with the performances. The performances were largely a means to an end. To us, these trips were about food, alcohol and girls, and not necessarily in that order. As we would sing, every cadet's eyes would scan the audience for the first pretty girl that he could find. After the performance, during the oneg, each cadet would make a beeline for that special girl, stopping only to grab a bagel on the way. It was the lucky cadet who had the good fortune to have as his host a family with a pretty daughter. The unlucky ones would have to make due with raiding their hosts' refrigerators and with trying to meet a girl at a local bar. Needless to say, when I became CIC of the choir during my cow year, we had some of the best trips, this time not only to visit local synagogues, but also to nearby colleges, where the selection was much better, and even a trip to Miami.

One day during my plebe year, I was ordered to report to my company commander's room. Unknowing what I had done to cause this stress-filling event, I was nervous. Nevertheless, I had to do it. My roommate checked my uniform to ensure I would not get in any more trouble than I already was in, and then I left to face the consequences of my actions. When I reported, my company commander let me know that former Israeli Prime Minister and at that time serving Minister of Defense, Yitzhak Rabin, and several Israeli generals were coming to West Point and that I was invited to eat on the poop deck with them, the Superintendent and other dignitaries. Following lunch, I would help escort them around the post. "Who do you know, Yoran?" my company commander asked me. "Sir, no one," was my reply. "Well, enjoy. Now, get out of here." I saluted and left as quickly as possible, not wanting to linger in this dangerous environment a moment longer than was absolutely necessary. When I returned safely to my room, I could not believe what had just happened. That night, I braved the barracks hallways once again to wait in line to use the payphone to call my parents and tell them the good news.

On the day of Rabin's visit, I brought a copy of his autobiography, "The Rabin Memoirs" with me to lunch. The view from the poop deck was awe inspiring. Below, I could see the entire Corps of Cadets eating as one in a huge star-shaped room with stained glass windows, chandeliers and, on one wall, an enormous mural depicting historical battles and military leaders. The room echoed with upperclassmen talking and the sound of plebes being hazed until the room was called to attention; and then, silence. The announcement was made that Rabin was present as a guest of honor and immediately the Corps started cheering for him and waiving their napkins in a sea of white commotion.

Over the course of the meal and then subsequently as I led him on a tour of West Point, I had the chance to speak with him openly, and at times, in Hebrew. We walked around the Academy grounds and I explained the history of some of the memorable sites (lucky I had remembered all my plebe knowledge!). We visited the Jewish Chapel and Rabin was impressed that we had a synagogue at West Point. As we walked, Rabin asked questions about me and my family. He asked how I was managing. I told him that I was doing well and about my family in Israel and my grandmother in Rishon Le'Zion. He told me that he was proud of me. I asked him to sign his book and whether he would let me have my picture taken with him. He willingly did both. In all, our time together lasted almost three hours. Even then, I did not want it to end.

One day, about a week later when I called home, my mother told me that she had just spoken with my grandmother. Apparently, upon Rabin's return to Israel, he telephoned my grandmother to tell her that he had met me, that I was well and not to worry. She was in shock, but overjoyed, that this man, a national hero in Israel, personally telephoned her to tell her about her grandson. For a little while afterwards, she became a celebrity in her circle of other grandmothers! In addition to being a hero, Rabin was quite a mensch.

Football games were always memorable at West Point, especially Army/Navy games. During my cadet years, we beat Navy three out of four years. During my cow year, we were particularly good and went to a bowl game for the first time in many years. The West Point football experience included 'spirit missions' in the middle of the night. As a plebe, it was terrifying and exhilarating at the same time to be woken up by upperclassmen dressed like ninjas, from head to toe in black, and be told to get dressed and be ready in two minutes. Sometimes the spirit missions were to hang up a banner on an off-limits building or statue. Sometimes, they were just to explore the network of steam tunnels that ran under the Academy grounds, and sometimes they were a bit more mischievous than that. As they were always at night and after Taps and lights out, the trick was not to get caught by the MPs and others that patrolled the Academy. On one particular mission, the MPs were out in force, and I came within inches of being caught. We were just getting started and were sneaking behind MacArthur Barracks when a group of MPs spotted us and gave chase. Our group split, but two of the MPs followed me. I had nowhere to go, but up. So, I started to sprint up the steep hill and stairs toward the cadet chapel. Lucky for me, I was in better shape, and soon I had left them panting on the side of the hill. But, I was too scared to stop running or turn around until I had gone at least a quarter of a mile up hill and then found a place to hide so I could catch my breath. I made my way back to the barracks and safely into my room. What a night! Of course, that night's spirit mission was postponed until the following week and the next football game.

The world was changing rapidly during my cadet years. It was a powerful but strange experience to be in the protected environs of the Academy while the world went on around us. On the one hand, we felt isolated. But, on the other, we felt as if we were a part of it all and we tried to stay informed and aware. Certainly having to memorize the front page of the NY Times every day before the 6:18 AM breakfast formation helped ensure that we would.

Ronald Reagan was president for the first half of my cadet years. He was a hero of mine even before I attended the Academy. But, at West Point, I could experience firsthand the changes in the Army that were the direct result of his leadership. The Army I knew was a far cry from the demoralized and ill-equipped Army of the post-Vietnam era. By 1987, the year I entered West Point, the Army had entered a renaissance and was in the midst of a profound change that continues to this day. But, the leadership, including the NCO corps, had experienced the harder times, and they worked hard to instill in us pride in the transformation that was taking place and the notion that the future of the Army, and much more, depended on us. It sounded good to me, in theory. Not surprisingly, somehow these lessons did not really sink in when I had a "Juice" WPR to study for or a constitutional law paper to write. I knew that I was training to be an officer to lead soldiers in combat, but the idea of actually going to war seemed remote and not a concern of mine. After all, the only military activity in recent memory was the invasion of the island of Grenada and the disastrous peacekeeping mission in Beirut, neither of which seemed too important to me. Besides, both took place in 1983, during my freshman year of high school, surely too long ago to matter. In the mid-1980s we were still preparing to fight the Soviet Union, and we all knew that was not going to happen.

But, the world kept changing. In 1989, during the first semester of my cow year, two things happened that transformed my thinking. In November, the Berlin Wall came down, effectively ending the Cold War and in December, the 82nd Airborne Division parachuted into Panama to oust the dictator General Noriega. I could feel the world changing around me and the thought of leading a platoon began to take on a sense of reality.

In August 1990, I was attending Air Assault School at Ft. Campbell, KY. It was the summer before my firstie year when we heard that Saddam Hussein had invaded Kuwait and that President Bush was sending in the 82nd Airborne Division to Saudi Arabia. As the situation with Iraq intensified, the Army's buildup in Saudi Arabia continued. Soon, the Army had several hundred thousand soldiers, including many recent West Point graduates and friends of mine, waiting in the desert.

Life at West Point changed for us all, including the staff and faculty. Our class lectures adjusted to discuss what was going on in the desert. Professors and other Academy staff were now deployed. We were particularly aware of the threat of chemical weapons and the size and quality of Saddam's elite units, the Republican Guards. As Cadets, we were living, breathing, and sleeping the news from Iraq. War seemed real and the sense that I needed to be ready to lead a platoon in combat that had begun to develop in me during the invasion of Panama less than a year earlier was growing quickly.

Saddam's Army was very large and well equipped. He had chemical weapons. The entire world was legitimately concerned that a war with Iraq could take a long time. When the air campaign began, I was less than a semester away from graduation. My entire firstie class was getting emotionally, intellectually and physically ready to go to Iraq. While life at West Point kept going, WPRs and papers, for the first time in my cadet experience, did not matter as much to me anymore.

This war was personal, in many ways. I knew and cared for people that were deployed. I knew their families and loved ones. My sponsor with whom I was very close, LTC Lawrence, a doctor at Keller, was deployed. His daughter Naomi's boyfriend, Robert (USMA 1989) was also deployed. She and I were good friends, and sometimes Naomi would call me to talk since she would get in fights with her mother because her mother did not understand how she could be as worried about her boyfriend as her father. (Naomi and Robert have been married now for 14 years and have two beautiful children of their own, Benjamin and Rebekah).

This war was also personal because it involved Israel. Saddam was threatening Israel with SCUD missiles armed with chemical warheads. The threat was real and the Israeli government issued gas masks to all five-plus million people in the country. Everyone in Israel, including my grandmother and cousins with little children, had to convert a room in their home to a chemical attack shelter by covering windows with plastic, stocking up on supplies, and by using filtration systems where possible. President Bush sent several air defense batteries, including Patriot anti-missile batteries, to protect Israel. US Army soldiers were deployed to protect Israel.

Until the Gulf War, some in my family in Israel did not understand why I decided to attend the Academy and volunteer to go to the US Army. They argued that if I really wanted to serve, I should do so in Israel. They, after all, were doing it because, unlike me, they had to. In the years prior to the Gulf War, I had tried to explain my reasons and American patriot-

Tablets outside of the Jewish Chapel.

Ark on the Bimah.

Ark (Parochet) covering.

Alumni Gallery.

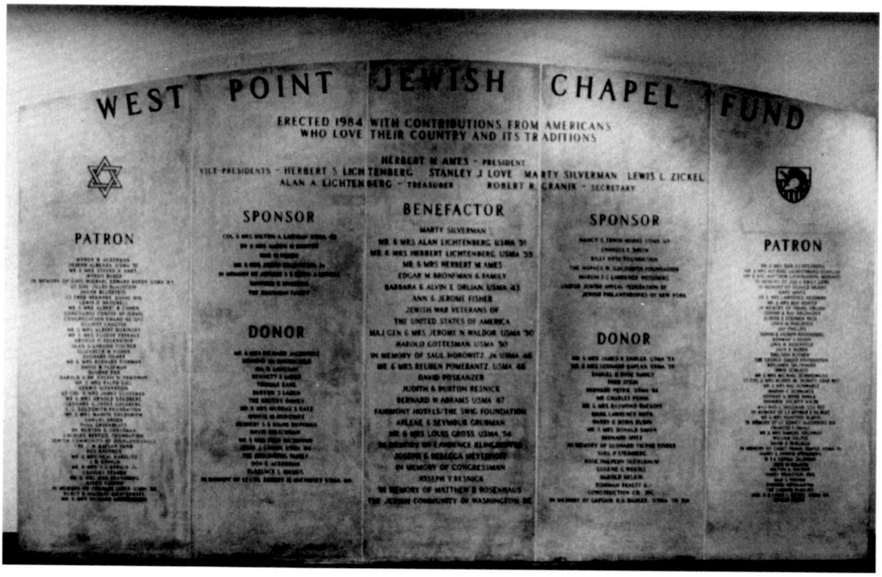

Founders and Contributors.

Recipients of Aaron and Hur Award. Lou Gross (right), Herb Lichtenberg (left), Lewis Zickel (center).

Jewish Chapel Choir then and now.

Deputy Secretary of Defense, Paul Wolfowitz, with cadets on the Day of Atonement (Yom Kippur).

Jewish Chapel Choir with President and Mrs. George W. Bush, at the White House, celebrating the lighting of a Menorah during Chanukah.

Cadets reading the Passover Haggadah at a Seder.

Lewis Zickel walking down the center aisle of the West Point Jewish Chapel.

Cadet Lewis Zickel, 1949.

ism to them many times, apparently sometimes unconvincingly. The Gulf War changed that immediately. My aunt Leah, a well-known journalist in Israel, wrote a moving piece that appeared in the leading newspaper in Israel that she finally understood why her nephew had volunteered to serve in the US Army and that she was grateful and thankful for it.

The Gulf War ended as quickly as it had started. Saddam's Army was defeated convincingly and Kuwait was liberated. While we openly discussed the wisdom of stopping the war so quickly, we were caught up in the euphoria that swept the nation. The Army had performed magnificently. My friends serving in Iraq had performed magnificently. The country loved us and we felt as if we were on top of the world. The media again treated West Point as the bastion of leadership and all that is good in America, and a West Point graduate, General Norman Schwarzkopf, was the leader that had made it all possible.

In May of 1991, New York City held a tickertape parade for the returning troops. Later that same month, the Corps of Cadets gave General Schwarzkopf a full brigade review in his honor. That evening, Schwarzkopf addressed the Corps at Eisenhower Hall. It was a memorable address, but the highlight was when a classmate of mine, asked not whether Schwarzkopf would run for office or anything about the war, but rather whether the General would let him buy him a beer! To our surprise General Schwarzkopf replied that he would be honored to have a beer with him, and that he was inviting the entire graduating class to the firstie club for a beer. One of my favorite photographs to this day is a picture of General Schwarzkopf and me toasting a beer together! That night, after Taps, all the plebes came running out of their rooms, and despite the MPs and breaking the rules, they headed straight for the Supe's house, where Schwarzkopf was staying as a guest of the Superintendent. Soon, the entire Corps was rallying in front of the Supe's house. The Supe came out and urged us all to go back to our rooms, but we were having none of it. We wanted to see him again. Then, a few minutes later General Schwarzkopf came outside and stood on top of an MP vehicle in his pajamas and led the Corps in a Rocket. It was an incredible day.

I graduated from West Point a few days later. President Bush was the commencement speaker. It was a hot June morning and we were wearing our India Whites because our Full Dress uniforms had been soaked during a rainy parade the day before. The President delivered his remarks and then handed out diplomas to the distinguished graduates. The agenda then called for the Superintendent and Commandant to hand out the diplomas to the remaining ninety-five percent of the graduating class. Those of us in the audience that had not yet received our diplomas wanted to get them from the President. We started cheering and rooting for him. President Bush seemed invincible then; he had just maneuvered the United States through a brilliant and painless victory over Saddam. His popularity was sky high and he fed off our enthusiasm. The President paused for a few minutes and asked for a glass of water because it was over ninety degrees. Then, he turned to the Corps and said, "Let's do it." When my name was called, I walked across the stage and saluted the President. He saluted me, handed my diploma to me and shook my hand. He repeated that experience more than 900 times that hot June day. It was a remarkable performance which I will never forget. As I passed on stage, for some reason, the President smacked me on the rear and said, "Congratulations Lieutenant." When I would next see President Bush almost a year and half later, he would look like a different person, worn, tired and defeated. That afternoon, we had a celebration at home. Len and Pete pinned my lieutenant's bars on my shoulders. I had made it. Shortly I would be off to EOBC and then to Ft. Bragg where I would be a platoon leader.

Perhaps the two most significant experiences of my short military career were my deployment to Homestead, FL following Hurricane Andrew and my service in Mogadishu, Somalia during Operation Restore Hope. Ironically, both experiences contained a strong Jewish element.

In August 1992, the most powerful Hurricane in recent memory devastated the Southern end of Florida, just below Miami. A relatively poor area of Dade County was the hardest hit. I really did not know anything about it until that night. I had arrived at Ft. Bragg less than six months before and was a new platoon leader in the 20th Engineer Brigade, a separate Airborne Engineer Brigade that had a long and illustrious history from the Civil War through Desert Storm. I was living in an apartment about eight miles outside the gates of the fort and, even though I had been there six months, I had not yet had a chance (or the money) to furnish my apartment. The next night, I was sleeping on a mattress on the floor when I received a phone call in the middle of the night. We were having an alert. Immediately, I called my platoon sergeant, SFC Carroll, and activated the recall process. I dressed quickly and drove to our battalion headquarters all the way thinking two things, one that I would soon be deploying to Bosnia because of the civil war taking place there, and two, that my mother would kill me if she knew that I was going.

When I arrived at the battalion HQ, my commander, LTC Slusar, called me into his office and told me and the others that a large Hurricane had hit Southern Florida and that we believed that the president was going to order the Army to deploy to conduct humanitarian relief, disaster recovery, rescue and emergency rebuilding operations. This was going to be an engineer mission, and a small contingent party was being sent immediately to conduct reconnaissance and damage assessment for the larger force that would follow. I was to be part of that lead element. Other than the thrill of being deployed on such an important mission, my second reaction was a sense of relief that I would not have to tell my mother that I was deploying to combat in Bosnia.

I flew several hours later to a part of the country that looked like it had been through a war. Two days later, the Army deployed in large scale numbers to help the Hurricane victims. Soon, about 25,000 soldiers and marines were working around the clock in the sticky Florida summer heat. One of my unit's first jobs was to clear the roadways of huge quantities of debris so that other vehicles could pass and clear the canals so the next rainstorm would not flood the region. Once these were accomplished, another of our missions was to repair the schools so that they could be ready for the thousands of children waiting to attend school on opening day, only a few weeks away. The work was difficult, but we were sustained by the significance of the mission and the support of the local community that was grateful for our presence. Within days of the large-scale deployment, we received communication from above that religious services would be available for the servicemen at such and such location. Of course, religious services meant Christian services.

Even though I did not attend religious services other than at West Point, I felt it was important for Jewish services to be available for those that wanted to attend, and it was my responsibility as an officer to make sure they could. So, I decided to volunteer to lead Shabbat services on Friday evenings and wrote a memo to the commanding general informing him of such. The next Friday evening, about a dozen Jewish soldiers and marines arrived at my battalion TOC looking for me. I assembled everyone together and asked whether anyone knew how to lead services. No one volunteered. So, it fell upon me to get things started. My principal experience with prayer had been at the Jewish Chapel at West Point, at which I was a regular attendant. So, I had some idea what to do. But, the truth of the matter is that soon I discovered how little I really knew, and before too long, was making things up. That Shabbat evening was a lot of fun. The following day, I resolved to come up with a better alternative going forward, especially as the high holidays of Rosh Hashanah and Yom Kippur were approaching.

So, what should a veteran CIC of the Jewish Chapel Choir do in such a predicament? I knew that the answer lay in my cadet experience. One afternoon I commandeered a humvee, a local yellow pages telephone book and drove north toward Miami. It stood to reason that the sizable Jewish community of the Miami area should be willing to host Jewish soldiers and marines as other congregations had hosted the Jewish Chapel Choir during my cadet days. Randomly, I called a rabbi I found in the telephone book, explained who I was and asked to visit him. Rabbi Goodman of the Alper Jewish Community Center in Kendall happily received my visit and was gracious to welcome all Jewish soldiers and marines deployed to Southern Florida to their congregation for as long as needed. We arranged for members of the community to host the soldiers and marines in their homes during Rosh Hashanah and Yom Kippur.

Later, on one of my visits to the Rabbi's house, he pulled two small prayer books off the shelf in his study and handed them to me. They were "Prayer Book for Jews in the Armed Forced of the United States" and "Jewish Holy Scriptures" prepared for Jewish Personnel of the Army of the United States. The books were printed during World War Two and were signed and dated by the officer to whom they belonged, CPT Robert Lycams in 1943. Rabbi Goodman told me that he wanted me to have them as a token of appreciation for what I had done for the Jews that were deployed. To this day, these prayer books sit on the shelf in my living room along the prayer books that I received at West Point at my baccalaureate service.

In early December of 1992 families all over Ft. Bragg prepared for the upcoming holidays that bring them together, if only for a few days at the end of each year. 1992 had been relatively quiet, and a good year for most, without the tension and stress of family separation that accompanies deployments to hostile environments. Ft. Bragg soldiers spent two of the previous three holiday seasons far from their families and homes. This year, they eagerly looked forward to their time to relax. For some, this would not be the case.

Graphic images of emaciated Somali children living and dying in dusty, fly-infested refugee camps and news of armed gunmen that terrorized the countryside and stole food from United Nations relief workers filled our televisions and radios. Somalia was in the midst of two simultaneous tragedies, a famine in which hundreds of thousands of people were starving to death and a civil war in which armed militias terrorized civilian populations. We could not permit such horror to continue, and on December 9th, 1992, in the glare of the media spotlights, the first wave of United States Marines landed on the beaches of Somalia's capital city, Mogadishu. Two days later, I received word that my platoon would be deployed to Somalia as part of a humanitarian relief effort that became known as Operation Restore Hope.

My company was part of the 30th Engineer Battalion, a unit that contained an assorted collection of engineering assets, including a bridging company, a heavy construction company, a survey detachment, two topographic companies, and more. The 30th was part of the 20th Engineer Brigade, which had two other combat engineering battalions, and together we numbered over 1,500 airborne engineers. Out of this large unit, my platoon was the only unit that was being sent to Africa. As a second lieutenant, I would be the only officer and the senior most person deployed from the brigade. Life at Ft Bragg was certainly not boring. Our primary mission was to ensure the safe distribution of food and medical supplies to the famine victims. But, we understood that we were being deployed into a hot area of operations. I knew that this deployment would be different than the one from which I had just returned following Hurricane Andrew.

The urgent mission left us little time to prepare. Soldiers picked up desert camouflage uniforms, flak jackets and desert boots from the Central Issue Facility (CIF). We made final checks on vehicles in preparation for air movement and inventoried and secured our personal gear that would remain behind. Everyone in the platoon went through Personnel Overseas Review (POR) where we prepared our wills. Some received as many as seven vaccinations. All started taking anti-malaria pills. Under the strict supervision of the non-commissioned officers, we prepared for a six month deployment. Soon, all was ready. A day before we were to depart, I received word not to bring any equipment other than our personal gear. We would be assigned to the Joint Task Force (JTF) headquarters, specifically the J-2, and the J-2 would provide us with all required material.

The first leg of our trip was to McGuire Air Force Base in New Jersey where we were to link up a squad of marines from the Defense Mapping Agency (DMA) that were being attached to my platoon. We waited at McGuire AFB for two days for their arrival and the arrival of more than 40 tons of maps, imagery and other important intelligence and topographic material that we would bring with us into Somalia. Our initial role would be to provide these products to the US and various other United Nations forces that were being deployed. These maps were vital so that critical things as convoy routes could be planned and truck drivers could navigate to the refugee camps. They would also be used for planning military operations against the various militias. Operation Restore Hope had been conceived so quickly that the units arriving in country would do so without maps in hand. Instead, they would acquire them upon arrival.

Our C-5B flight was relatively uneventful, the most interesting events being the two times we refueled in-air and the five hour layover in Jiddah, Saudi Arabia. It was a mild shock to our Desert Storm veterans to visit Saudi Arabia, a place some hoped not to see again. We arrived in

Mogadishu early in the morning; the heat and humidity were not yet oppressive. The earth was sparsely vegetated with scrub trees and low lying bushes. The dirty brown soil, littered with debris and refuse, blew in the wind and covered every exposed object with a fine layer of dust. As we stepped down from the C-5B we gazed at the deep blue water of the Indian Ocean to our right and the remnants of what must have once been a beautiful city, now in ruins, to our left. The early morning sunrise covered everything with a warm glow. It seemed at odds with the hectic movement of men and equipment on the tarmac. The smell of JP-4 jet fuel filled my nostrils and the deafening roar of the jet engines rang in my ears. These noises and odors would be our incessant partners during our deployment.

Once we had established this 'map depot' our task would be to consolidate new information about the situation on the ground about the various routes, including changes in terrain, condition of bridges, obstacles (natural and manmade), hostile action and much more, and then disseminate updates to the different units. Where possible I would go along the convoy routes to inspect bridges or other structures, verify that routes were passable and gather additional information. As things changed we would help maintain the flow of information from the field to various units and the command structure.

I made daily trips to the site of the US embassy in Mogadishu, where the task force was headquartered, to find out about upcoming requirements and to pick up our ration of supplies, including water and MREs, and of course, mail from home. We never received any equipment from the J-2 and supplies were in short order. I perfected the science of scrounging and improvising. It did not take me long to learn that the best friends to have in a place like Somalia, where even drinking water was scarce, were people in the Air Force. After all, an Air Force person could ask his pilot friend to bring some of the conveniences from home on his next flight to Mogadishu. So, while we in the Army struggled to find basic supplies, Air Force people were well stocked and slept in air-conditioned tents with televisions and VCRs. I would barter with my friends in the Air Force to get supplies from them. As I had nothing to trade, I bartered with information. Most of the Air Force personnel were confined to the airport compound. For them, Somalia, although past just a few strands of concertina wire, was a distant land. They yearned for stories from the field and wanted to feel part of the mission outside the gates of the airport. And, I was happy to trade what I had, information, for supplies. This way I was able to acquire a generator, wire and even light bulbs from my friends in the Air Force. We built a makeshift shower, and I negotiated with the Air Force fire department to fill it with water.

Units from the Pakistani Army had been serving in Mogadishu before the arrival of the first US forces, and they had the responsibility of providing security at the airport. However, security remained a constant concern. Somalis loitered around the airport perimeter and stared at the ongoing operations. Children often climbed through the concertina wire barriers and played on top of abandoned rusting vehicles and Russian MIG fighter jets. They begged for food and anything else that we could provide; and if they were not satisfied, as was usually the case, they resorted to stealing. Within a day of our arrival, I realized that the Pakistani-provided security was not adequate and I felt that it was better to be safe than sorry. I implemented a 24*7 security watch at my platoon level, and despite the difficulty of maintaining a round-the-clock watch with so few people, we kept it up the entire time we were in country.

While the drives along the convoy routes were, for the most part, long and dusty, the drive to the embassy snaked through some of the busiest and most dangerous sections of Mogadishu. Every time one left the perimeter of the compound, one wore all protective gear and chambered a round in their M-16. The rules of engagement were simple; we were authorized to use force if felt threatened or at risk. The environment in Mogadishu was tense. Crowds filled the streets and one could never know from which direction the next sniper would emerge. Sniping was a fact of life. The sound of gunfire did not surprise us. From time to time, Somali "Technicals", as the bandits were called, opened fire at us with AK-47s. Usually in small groups and poorly organized, the Technicals shot at us from concealed positions behind walls, from distant windows or from the midst of bustling crowds of civilians as we drove through the narrow city streets. We were lucky, most of the time they were bad shots.

Throughout the day, many Somali men chewed a leafy plant called Kat, a mild narcotic. By evening they would be not only well armed, but also high and emboldened. Nights were, as a result, far more dangerous than days. On three separate evenings in a one week span, groups of Technicals in the open shot at us. In all three situations we took cover and returned fire. Twice we recovered the bodies of dead Technicals; the third time, they got away. We were becoming quite good at reacting to these ambushes.

Several memorable moments marked our stay in Somalia. The holidays, as always, were a time for celebration, even in the midst of such a hostile environment. While we were unable to spend the holidays with our families, we were enlivened by a Navy Santa Claus from one of the ships off-shore, in full costume carrying his goody bag full of cigarettes, candy and other treats.

US military personnel were prohibited from drinking alcohol in Somalia. As it was an Islamic country, alcohol was not readily available and it was not a problem. But, it seemed reasonable to me that we should be able to toast New Years Eve. I turned to some of my friends from the Air Force and managed to get my hands on three bottles of champagne. I hid the three bottles near our platoon area. That evening, I led my platoon sergeant, SFC Carroll, near to where I had hidden the bottles and told him I had a present for him for New Year's Eve. I pointed to where the bottles were hidden. Then, I reminded him that drinking alcohol was prohibited in Somalia, and I told him that that rule was going to be strictly enforced for the soldiers on guard duty that night. Other than that, on that single night, what I did not know would not come back to hurt him. I winked and told him that I would make myself scarce that night. SFC Carroll was a veteran soldier. He had served in Vietnam in 1973, in Panama in 1989 and in Saudi Arabia and Iraq in 1990–91. He and I had served together in Florida after Hurricane Andrew. I knew that I could rely on his judgment and felt confident in his ability to manage without me for an evening. One would think that bending the rules as I did would have led to disciplinary problems in the platoon. My experience was the exact opposite. Through my actions, I demonstrated a human side to my soldiers that brought us closer together. They understood that I cared for them deeply and would not put them in harm's way callously, and as a result, platoon cohesion and discipline increased.

President Bush visited Somalia in December to spend the holidays with the troops. He had just lost the election the previous month to Bill Clinton, in an election that a year earlier no one would have predicted he would lose. Despite the loss, President Bush was still immensely popular with the soldiers. They loved him, and it was clear that he loved them. On the day of the President's visit, we gathered at the airport. Upon his arrival, we all cheered loudly. He spoke briefly and thanked us for our service. Then, in an unscripted move, the President left the podium and walked into the crowd of soldiers. He ambled and chatted freely with the soldiers and it seemed that he was truly enjoying himself. It was eighteen months since I had met President Bush at my graduation from West Point. A lot had occurred during that time, but it was still remarkable how much he had changed in such a short time span. President Bush had visibly aged. He looked tired and worn, a different person than the confident man he was at graduation. But, when he was among the troops he had the same sparkle in his eye. I took a photograph with the President and told him that I had met him once before at my graduation at West Point. We chatted for a few minutes and then he moved on and continued mingling.

I celebrated Chanukah in Somalia that year. The Jewish Chaplain for the task force led services at the JTF headquarters by the embassy. We stacked our M-16s outside the designated chapel area. I put on my camouflage yarmulke, said the prayers and lit the Chanukiah. Chanukah is the celebration of the Maccabees victory over the Greek Empire and the Seleucid King Antiochus around 200 BCE. The Greek rulers imposed great hardship and cruelty on the conquered Jews and desecrated the Temple in Jerusalem. The Maccabees were a family that rallied the Jewish people, trained an army and eventually led the Jews to victory over the much larger and stronger Greek Army. After their victory, the Maccabees visited the desecrated Temple and discovered that the Lamp had only enough oil in it to last one night. However, in a miracle, the oil lasted for eight nights. It is from this experience that Jews have the tradition of lighting candles during the eight nights of Chanukah in commemoration of the Maccabees victory and the miracle of the oil lamp. A common Hebrew blessing, the Shechianu, is recited during Chanukah. The Shechianu celebrates and expresses gratitude for enabling us to reach this day and this milestone. It is a celebration of life and contentment. That evening as we recited the blessings, I felt that it was wonderful irony, and entirely appropriate, that we were reciting the Shechianu in Mogadishu; despite the continuous violence, we were there as peacekeepers and humanitarians distributing needed food and supplies to a starving population.

In addition to the few soldiers and marines, the services were attended by a squad of reporters who covered the event. Covering the troops as they celebrated religious holidays away from home was a favorite human interest story of theirs. Nevertheless, I was glad that they were there. Even though I knew it would not happen, I hoped idealistically that the site of Jewish and Christian soldiers conducting such magnanimous humanitarian work to help Moslems in need would cause some good for our relations with the local population, and the West's relations with the Islamic world broadly speaking. Perhaps the opposite occurred as the sight of Christians celebrating Christmas and Jews celebrating Chanukah in an overwhelmingly Islamic country enabled religious demagogues and intolerant leaders to spew further hatred and violence. To these cruel and inhumane people, our mission in Somalia was irrelevant; they would rather let hundreds of thousands of their own people starve to death than accept support from Western infidels. I do not know whether the press coverage affected anyone's political views. I do know that everyday the situation on the ground deteriorated.

My platoon rotated home several weeks later as our mission was transitioned to a Canadian unit. It was a joyous day for me when we departed from Somalia and all the members of my platoon returned safe and sound.

Shortly after returning, I was promoted to First Lieutenant and assigned to the 362nd Engineering Company, a heavy construction and combat engineering unit in the same battalion, where I would lead a platoon of more than 40 soldiers. Several months later, we received word that the 362nd would rotate to Mogadishu for a six-month deployment.

While disappointed on the inside to be going back to Somalia, I immediately began to prepare for the upcoming rotation. This time, I would know exactly what to expect, and because we had ample advance notice, I could prepare not only my platoon, but the whole company. I conducted training classes based on my experience and assigned homework to the soldiers for them to research Somali culture, terrain, weather, medical conditions, history, politics and more. I would review their research and facilitate where possible. Then, they would present their findings to the platoon in a classroom setting. The 362nd would deploy to Somalia better informed and prepared as a result.

About a month before we were to deploy, we had a parachute jump. Being an airborne unit, training jumps were a regular part of our routine. I had always wanted to be a paratrooper and very much looked forward to the jumps, even though they always made me nervous. The training jumps were tense events. Military parachuting is different from civilian sky diving. The jumps were usually at night and we carried heavy loads. We jumped from low altitudes, fell fast and hit the ground hard. Often, we carried out additional missions out after the jump as part of the exercise. Sometimes, the jump was only the first part of an extended field training exercise. But, on this particular night, we jumped for proficiency purposes; during our several-month-tour in Mogadishu we would not be able to jump. That night, in a freak accident on a bad landing, I blew out the ACL and tore other ligaments and cartilage in my left knee.

Instantly, I knew something bad had happened. Nevertheless, I gathered my gear and walked off the drop zone.

The next day, I went to the hospital to confirm what I already knew, that the same knee I had injured during my cadet years, was severely injured again. A few days later I had the second operation on it. Everything from that moment forward happened fast. I could not go with my platoon to Somalia. I was disappointed, because despite not wanting to go there again, I desperately wanted to be with my men. Now, another lieutenant was leading my platoon. On the day they left from Pope Air Force Base, adjacent to Ft. Bragg, I stood on the tarmac holding my crutches and waved good-bye.

The situation in Mogadishu continued to deteriorate. A few weeks later, one of the squads in my platoon was ambushed while clearing an obstacle. Two of the NCOs, SGT Malasig and SGT Gilbert, were wounded by shrapnel from an RPG round. They were medically evacuated out of Somalia back to Ft. Bragg where I visited them in the hospital. One day soon after they left the hospital, I chatted with them. That day, they turned to me and said, "LT, you should have been there with us. If you were there, all of this (meaning their injuries) would not have happened. We needed you there with us." I turned and walked away as tears welled in my eyes. It was then, and is to this day, the greatest compliment anyone has ever given me.

In October of that year, 18 US servicemen were killed in Mogadishu in a fierce battle commemorated in the book and subsequent film, "Black Hawk Down."

A few months later my paperwork was complete and I was medically processed out of the Army.

May I include your personalized story or stories in this book? Yes

May I mention your name in conjunction with the information you provided? Yes

Signature **Date**

The personal information and stories that you provided in the above questionnaire will be used *solely used for writing of this book* and will be used without identifying you unless you specifically authorized otherwise hereon. Your wishes will be honored. None of this information will be released to any other entity, group or organization.

Thank you for your help!

Selections from the Questionnaires

And here, at last, are some of the stories and experiences related by those who responded to my questionnaires, in their own words, with nothing changed.

Kristen Beyer, Class of 2005

I was not raised in a Jewish family; however, my best friend at home is Jewish and their family always included me in all of their activities, religious-based or not. Upon arrival at West Point, It seemed only natural to me that I turn to the Jewish Community here as a place to fit in because of the close-knitted group there, as well as one that is very accepting and friendly. I have made numerous good friends and have always enjoyed being a part of that community.

Larry Waters, Class of 1962

I entered West Point the same year as General John K. Waters' (Patton's son-in-law) son entered. He was Catholic. At the end of the first semester he flunked out. No one thought that they would kick Waters' son out so they thought it was me. Every Sunday A.M. they called my name at Catholic Chapel formation. My roomie, a Catholic, would always say for several years, "He's not coming." At the start of senior year an official order was issued transferring me to the Jewish Chapel (Squad). I was also in the choir. We all were!

Throughout my short career, senior officers thought I was the General's son and showed partiality toward me until I told them otherwise. When I was at the 82nd Airborne, the General was USAPAC (U.S. Army Pacific Commander) when (I was) in Okinawa. Sometimes it was too funny for words.

Anonymous, Class of 2008

My time at West Point so far has been short but perhaps the best example of the human aspect of my life as a cadet has been from religious activities. They were the outlet for socializing during beast barracks and meeting people after services or during Chaplain's Time. Later during Plebe year some of my best friends and times have been experienced in the Jewish Chapel Choir. Religious life provides humanity here, even during the worst of it.

Dr. Paul J. Kantrowich, Class of 1965

I have written 340 pages for a book about my Plebe Year, "Jew at West Point" that has gone untouched for 6 years because I'm a terrible writer! I have so many stories to tell about my career at West Point that I have become a legend in my own mind . . . and that's not only dangerous . . . it's also boring!

P.S. I applaud your effort and would be happy to release my experiences to you with an understanding that this was a satirical view by an immature young man who developed into an immature older man. I would even release my title of "Jew at West Point" for a good salami sandwich from Mendy's Delicatessen plus a Dr. Brown's cream soda.

Terry A. Bresnick, Class of 1969

I kept kosher before coming to West Point; while there, I didn't eat shellfish or pork products. Beast Barracks table commandant wanted me to eat crab cakes, and wouldn't let me respond as to why I couldn't. ("Sir, may I make a statement?", "No, Smackhead!") I refused to eat them; problem was resolved, but only after "driving around to his room".

I used to bring kosher salami back from weekend leaves and, during the winter, I'd preserve them by hanging them out my window in a metal tin. This worked well since I had a room in the "lost fifties" that faced the mountain. Nonetheless, my TAC spotted it and I was written up for "unauthorized salami hanging from window."

Plebe year, I took Jewish choir trip on Supe's plane to West Palm Beach. It was in February and Florida was having a cold spell, so weather was in the 40's. But I'd be damned if I was going to go back to USMA and not be able to tell my roommate that we went swimming in the Atlantic. Despite the cold weather, we made sure we took a 'polar bear" dip (at least in Florida terms.)

[In explanation of the cadet slang used here by Terry, "Smackhead" was one of a number of belittling appellations upperclassmen used to address plebes in lieu of their names. It was part of the plebe system that emerged from the earlier years; a plebe was considered a social nonentity. One of the punishments an upperclassman could inflict on a wayward plebe was to require him to come to the upperclassman's room to receive a variety of uncomfortable punishments. The TAC was (and still is) the company tactical officer (a commissioned officer) in charge of good order and discipline in the cadet company assigned to him. Being "written up" was to receive a citation for a violation of regulations. Terry currently is an active member of the West Point Jewish Chapel Fund.]

Richard E. Entlich, Class of 1963

During the first night of Beast Barracks, I roomed with two individuals—a USMA prep school individual and an individual who had just graduated from high school in Florida (He was Jewish!!—2 Jewish cadets in the same room—the Class of 1963 had a total of 12 Jewish cadets out of approximately 760). That night the Jewish cadet reached under his bed and pulled out his suitcase and started packing. I asked him where he was going and he said— "Home!" My roommate and I finally talked him out of going AWOL on the first night. He actually made it through 4 years and was one of 5 Jewish cadets to graduate in 1963 out of a class of 504.

Mark A. Sweberg, Class of 1975

Every Jewish cadet was in the Chapel Glee Club (choir), whether or not he could sing a note. When we went on Glee Club (choir) trips those who could not sing stood in the back and mouthed the words. No one ever knew—or let on anyway.

I made Academy history when I was commissioned. My father was a CWO-4. He arranged, with the help of the Superintendent, for Army orders promoting him temporarily to the rank of Colonel for the purpose of commissioning me. Upon completion of the ceremony, he reverted to CWO-4. I am the first, and only, cadet legally commissioned by a noncommissioned officer.

[A CWO-4 is a chief warrant officer, grade 4. Mark's brother Victor graduated in 1979. Their mother, Eva Sweberg, was a tireless volunteer at the chapel until her retirement a few years ago. Mark is currently with the Department of State as a senior planner for peacekeeping operations, complex contingency planning. He holds the civil service rank of GS-14.]

Gerald D. Goldberg, Class of 1956

Jewish Choir—best deal on campus.

Robert Goodman, Class of 1985

The event I remember was a West Point Jewish Choir trip to NY City. First of all, I could not sing to save my life. But as a Plebe, the choir was a great way to escape from West Point on great trips. This particular trip was to a famous N.Y. nightclub. We actually got on TV. I think that maybe 3 people could actually carry a tune. The other great trip I remember was a Jewish Chapel retreat to Grossinger's resort. What I remember about this trip was that first of all we were probably 30–40 years younger than anyone else at the place. Secondly, we were hit by a big snowstorm and had to stay an additional day.

[Robert was a plebe in 1981–82. The nightclub was the "Red Parrot," and the event was a major fund-raiser for the construction of the Jewish Chapel. The superintendent authorized the Cadet Glee Club and Cadet Chapel Choir to augment our less than professional Jewish Choir. He also sent the Hellcats, the Academy's rousing fife, bugle, and drum corps. It was a gala event carried on the news of all major television networks. Construction of the chapel commenced in January 1982.]

Amy (Dickinson) Stredler, Class of 1988

I experienced much more angry sentiment from others about my being a *woman.* [This response was entered under the question about anti-Semitism in the questionnaire.].

My experience was unique because I entered the Academy as a non-practicing Christian, and I was converted by Rabbi Leinwand. I was also married at the Jewish Chapel. My husband is Dan Stredler, Class of 1986.

We were featured in the magazine "Reform Judaism" as only the 2nd cadet/cadet couple to be married at the Jewish Chapel. My biological mother died when I was 4 years old. My father remarried to a Jewish woman. My "mother" had the most influence on me, so I was very familiar with a lot of the Jewish customs. My favorite Aunt & Uncle (Jewish) lived 20 miles from West Point (in Spring Valley, NY). They both absorbed the brunt of my anxiety of cadet life.

The way I met my future husband was from a newspaper article published in the Spring Valley paper. The article featured a Jewish cadet attending a Passover Seder. My Aunt gave me the article. The cadet was an upperclassman in my company! We were married 2 days after my graduation on 27 May 1988. Seventeen years later, we are happily married with 2 great children. Lauren Rose just had her Bat Mitzvah, and Grant is working toward his Bar Mitzvah. Rabbi Leinwand relaxed some of the conversion rules, as long as I promised to have Jewish children! I was in the Jewish Choir, of course, knew *none* of the songs. They let me travel on the trips, regardless and I had a great time. Good luck with your book.

Norman M. Smith, Class of 1955

Out of sheer desperation, and armed only with inspiration & no training, I led the Jewish Chapel Choir for over two years, on many trips. One of my stalwarts was a Mormon who joined up because he liked early Sunday breakfasts.

Norman Levy, Class of 1956

In Plebe year I joined the Jewish Choir since this was the only way for me to get trips away from the Academy. I was the best monotone singer in the choir.

Gideon Sinasohn, Class of 1982

Friday nights sponsored by the JFW [*sic*] probably got me through Beast Barracks, Plebe Year, and was a nice homey experience, even after that. The locals from nearby, including Highland Falls and Monsey made it feel like home. Jewish Chapel Choir got us off post, a chance to meet "some nice Jewish girls." We often had Catholic/non-Jewish cadets in the

Choir, who could actually "sing." (Sometimes we would only "mouth" the lyrics.)

Matthew D. Lampell, Class of 1949

[The stated objective of the writer of this story was to support with personal examples his statement "To point out my feeling of never having had anti-Semitism affect me." His response to the questionnaire on anti-Semitism was "No—none quite the reverse—I always felt there was total acceptance of all cadets by all cadets." I have abbreviated his story in the interest of clarity.]

When I was in Hyde Park High School in Chicago I was a member of the ROTC. In Sept of '42 I entered the University of Wisconsin to study electrical engineering/communications. I joined Signal ROTC. An announcement was made about joining the enlisted reserve. I went to the Signal Captain to inquire. He revealed a list of serial numbers, knew when they would be called to active duty, but without names to go with the numbers. He suggested that I notify him when I got drafted. At the end of the academic year I got drafted and contacted him.

When I arrived at my induction post, a WAAC filling out my info said, "I don't know who you know, but you have a direct assignment from the pentagon to the Signal Corps." I was sent to Camp Crowder for basic training and specialist training as a radio operator, low speed. From there I was sent to Fort Monmouth for advanced specialist training as a radio operator, high speed. In late 1943 I was shipped to Puerto Rico to the 596th Signal Company.

In the spring of 1944 there was an announcement about selection of army candidates for 60 appointments to West Point. There were 180 candidates for the 60 appointments. The Caribbean Command would have one candidate. Five of us in the entire command were eligible. First they gave us the entrance physical . . . now there were only two of us, both of equal rank. My commander promoted me immediately. We were interviewed by a team of officers. I was first. The last question asked was, "Which two teams are leading their respective leagues?" I answered that I didn't have the foggiest idea. After interviewing the second man, the Captain who asked me the last question came out smiling and pointed to me . . . "You're our boy—the last question made the difference—he guessed and was wrong!"

I was awaiting the date to be in the US to attend an assigned college to prepare for entrance exams to West Point. I was to go by ship, but the Captain from the interview (also Aide to the Commanding General) arranged for me to fly to the mainland on the General's plane.

I prepared for the entrance exam, passed it, entered West Point and finished the four years well.

While at West Point was a member of the Jewish Chapel Squad Choir. Our Chaplain was the Rabbi from Vassar Temple (Congregation Brethren of Israel) in Poughkeepsie. He wanted his congregation to know what he was doing on Sunday mornings so he had the choir come to Poughkeepsie to participate in a Friday night service. Bernie Sabel (a classmate) and I were being housed together in a member's home. We were there with two young ladies. Bernie and I went upstairs and flipped a coin to see who would get which girl. I won and chose Muriel—who is now my wife of 55 years.

Two weeks prior to the start of the Korean War, the Chief Signal Officer at Fort Monmouth gave us the option of being assigned to Germany or the Far East on a 50/50 split. Seven of us chose Germany. We thought that the war would cancel all deals for overseas assignment. The assignments were honored for members of the classes of 1949 and 1950.

I served in the Constabulary which was absorbed by the 7th Army. In all of the assignments in Europe I found myself placed in positions calling for two or more grades above me. As a 1st Lt., I was appointed Battalion Adjutant despite the fact that the company commanders were all Captains.

While I was Adjutant, we were going to be in the field over Easter Sunday. We had a chaplain assigned to the battalion and I told him that I expected him to conduct Easter Sunday services where we had men. He told me to go to hell. When his service was over at the post chapel and he walked out, he was flanked by 2 armed guards who put him in a jeep, drove him to an air strip and we flew him wherever we had men. A few days after we got back I got a call from the Chief Chaplain of 7th Army (a Lt Col, Catholic and he knew me and knew I was Jewish). He told me he had just heard about our battalion chaplain and Easter Sunday. I started to apologize and he told me not to. He said he had called to thank me for teaching one of his chaplains his duty.

I was assigned as Company Commander of a special mission signal company. I was a 1st Lt with the highest MOS in the Signal Corps, a career assignment (almost never seen below Lt Col), on the 5 % list for promotion to Captain.

As we were returning to the States, I realized that I was in a lot of trouble . . . others, particularly those in command of me, would wonder who the hell I knew, who was looking out for me, etc. So I decided to get out and left active duty in Nov or Dec of 1953 accepting a commission in the Reserve. In 1960 there was a provision that if you were in the reserve, had 10 years active duty (including time at USMA) and service in both WWII and Korea, you could ask to be retired. I did.

In many cases (not all) I think anti-Semitism is felt or suspected rather than actual. In some cases I think it is because non-Jews don't know what will/will not bother Jews.

Stephen L. Weisel, Class of 1964

My attendance at West Point was, in some respects, a fluke. I had received a work scholarship (waiter/bus boy) that enabled me to spend my four years of high school at the NY Military Academy (NYMA) about ten miles away from West Point. I did not go there with thoughts of joining the military. NYMA was one of 40+ Honor Military High Schools that could nominate candidates to compete for "honor Academy appointments." Since I stood at the top of my class I could have received the nod to compete for any of the Service Academies. I was leaning toward Annapolis, but read one of their brochures that indicated you incurred a four-year service obligation when you graduated. The West Point brochure said three years. My motivation was not to become career military. Rather I was impressed by my high school instructors and coaches who were USMA graduates and I reasoned, "If the Academies have men like them, that was what I wanted to be part of." Of course the obligation for attending both West Point and Annapolis was the same. It just so happened I read a West Point brochure that was out of date.

As a side bar to all of this was that I came from a relatively affluent community that sent dozens of kids to Ivy League schools every year, but no one I could find knew anyone who went to any of the Service Academies. Also, my grandmother who was born in Eastern Europe, was quite upset when she learned that I was going to join the military.

When the class of 1964 entered USMA in 1960 we had 13 Jewish plebes out of about 830 in the class. By graduation the Jewish contingent had dropped to 5 out of 565. I was somewhat disappointed by the high dropout rate and the meager 1% representation of our classes total graduates. On the other hand, although I never have spoken of it, I was pleased that four of our group of five Jewish cadets were in the top one third of our class.

As cadets we assembled with all other cadets on Sunday (yes Sunday) morning for Chapel services and then marched for our service to the Old Cadet Chapel at the Academy cemetery. I found the chapel and the setting to be pretty inspiring.

The total number of Jewish cadets at any one time during my tenure at the Academy ranged from very low 30's to the very low 40's. We were referred to as the Jewish Chapel Squad. All of the members of the Jewish Chapel Squad were members of the Jewish Chapel Choir. I guess we could have opted out, but nobody did. It was a proverbial "good deal." In those days, opportunities to get off post were few and far between. But the Jewish Chapel Choir made several trips every year to Jewish communities in the NY/NJ area to perform. What we did was harmonize at Friday night services. Then there was always some sort of Oneg Shabbat or party where we were fed, introduced to girls, and usually put up for the night with families from the community. I recall that on one occasion while in Scarsdale during my "cow year" I met a girl who was the most serious friend of my time at the Academy.

During my plebe year the choir was pretty disorganized. The next year, the firsties decided we needed to improve our act by having us stand grouped by the kind of voices we had. To place us they had each one of us sing individually. The net result was that myself and Dan Schwartz—classmate and one of my best friends, were told to stand in the back and mouth the words. Sometimes I tell people I was in a choir. If they ask what part I sang, I respond, "Pantomime." Sadly, I never got close to the other three classmates who were Jewish. In some respects that reflects the positive aspect that I didn't feel any special need for such clustering together. During my four years as a cadet I can't recall ever experiencing any sort of bias or even being made to feel uncomfortable as a Jew.

Don Schwartz and I were also both Corps Squad wrestlers. He was about ten pounds heavier so we didn't work out against each other, but just recently, 40 years later reminisced about the sport. This was the first time we had seen each other since graduation. My luck as a wrestler was both good and bad. I did not have the sort of background most of the other Corps Squad wrestlers had. I had just a few years experience in a fairly uncompetitive small school environment. Most of the others had intimidating credentials—Iowa State Champion, Pennsylvania regional champion, etc. However, I came on strong. I wrestled in the vast majority of Plebe matches and as a yearling and cow, most of the B-Team matches and a couple of varsity matches. The bad luck (for me) was that in both my yearling and cow years West Point had a fellow a year ahead of me (Mike Natvig) who was a two-time national champion. Then, as a senior, I broke my hand just as the season was beginning, so I became the cadet coach of the plebe team. I always regretted not seeing what I could do on the mat that last year.

I also played lacrosse in high school and played Corps Squad lacrosse as a plebe—anything to get on athletic tables. After plebe year I played intramural lacrosse and became a "big man" on those playing fields. It was real fun.

Overall my cadet experience was a very positive one. I treasure being an Academy graduate and particularly feel that my class was full of men I admired then and continue to admire. Being in the Washington, DC area, usually my class has get-togethers several times a year, and I am an enthusiastic and regular participant. I also have participated (albeit sporadically in recent years) as a member of the Ft Belvoir Jewish Community where my son was bar Mitzvah since 1981.

As time has passed I have come to treasure my good fortune at having attended West Point. I have found that over the years it has been a source of pride, with minor exception, positive regard both in the Jewish community as well as in all my other life experiences.

[Colonel (Retired) Stephen L. Weisel served on active duty in the infantry for twenty-eight years. He served in Vietnam, where he was awarded the Silver Star, Legion of Merit with Oak Leaf Cluster, the Bronze Star for Valor with three Oak Leaf Clusters, the Purple Heart, the Air Medal, the Meritorious Service Medal with two Oak Leaf Clusters, the Army Commendation Medal with two Oak Leaf Clusters, the Vietnamese Gallantry Cross with Gold and Silver Stars, the Combat Infantryman Badge, Ranger Tab, and Parachutist Badge. This is the man who entered West Point with the initial intention of leaving after his service obligation expired!]

Alan H. Gould, Class of 1947

My first look at the faces of my classmates as we made the long walk up the hill to old Central Barracks on that momentous day of June 3, 1944; the excitement and feeling of elation when walking through the Sallyport of Old Central and the utter shock of my first exposure to an upperclassman which marked the beginning of one of the longest years of my life—Plebe Year, the memory of which gets totally blurred. Great memories of my classmates and roommates and company C-2. The Plebe year hunger which drove me to try out for "B" Squad football to get on a training table which after a few scrimmages I quickly realized that I was going to be broken into small pieces by Poole Blanchard, et al; so I decided that I wouldn't chicken out on my classmates and would make the best of it by assuming my regular seat at the plebe end of the table.

I helped organize the Cadet Glee Club by auditioning the greater part of the entire Corps and becoming the director and also participating in all three 100th Night Shows.

Fortunately, as I look back I can now appreciate the humor which at the time didn't appear funny at all. During my Yearling Year I had four VIP generals mistakenly enter my room thinking they were going to visit one of their sons, a plebe whose room was directly opposite mine. The visit occurred after a Saturday Parade and I was in my skivvies, relaxing, when the door burst open and I popped to attention to stare at four star General Hap Arnold, Major General Sinclair Street and two other General Officers whose name I can't recall—all the while standing at attention in my underwear, believing that my military career was coming to an end, since I had caused one of their sons to be slugged for conduct unbecoming a plebe, i.e.; urinating in the sink outside my door on the fourth floor of old North Barracks.

During my plebe year after "beast barracks" I was invited to dinner at the quarters of Col. and Mrs. "Biff" Jones, director of athletics, along with Tucker, Davis, Blanchard, Poole, Fuson and all the other super football stars of our class. I assumed, since I was a second string quarterback for the University of Rochester, that I belonged in this illustrious group but as we sat down to the wonderful dinner we were individually introduced by Mrs. Jones, after which she realized she made a major blunder since she introduced me as being the son of Alan H. Gould, Sports Editor of the Associated Press. I politely explained that my father's name was Peter C. Gould and she graciously allowed me to stay and partake of the finest food I had during my entire plebe year.

My most difficult cadet experience was getting slugged during the last three months of First Class Year and walking the Area for those three months—all for missing a lecture, the only one I ever missed, and unintentionally so, since I had fallen asleep after evening chow and was rudely awakened by the Cadet Officer of the Day, too late to attend. Since I should have known better the standard reply of "no excuse sir" applied and I attended graduation ceremonies sans stripes, saber and velvet sash—a buck cadet private—little embarrassing particularly when the Mayor of your hometown, relatives and dear friends were in attendance. Since then I'm never without an operating alarm clock.

Traumas in life impact us all. On March 30, 1986 we lost our second son, Howard, in an airplane crash. He was 33 years old at the time and well on his way to a successful career as a pilot for UPS. Those of us that had the misfortune of losing a son or daughter never fully recover but we continue to thank God for time we had and all the other blessings such as our grandchild, Mimi's recovery from major cancer surgery, and being part of one of the greatest classes our Alma Mater ever produced.

[Alan spent eight years in the Air Force, part of which was as a B-29 pilot. More of Alan's story is told in *A Tale of Three Cadets* by his fellow alumnus Irving Schoenberg, and included in this book. Alan was blessed with an almost operatic baritone. He sang in the Jewish Chapel Choir along with my classmate Chet Trubin, also blessed with an outstanding voice. I sang with both of these gentlemen in the choir, but "by a singer I was not a singer!" His story about sleeping and missing a lecture mirrors one of my experiences, but without the punishment. As a result I, too, always keep a working alarm clock. Sixty-one years later I still avoid being late to a degree that annoys my wife! The word "slugged" warrants explanation. It is the extreme form of official punishment to which the command can sentence a cadet. It includes reduction in rank to cadet private, confinement to quarters except for classes and official duties, loss of all leave privileges and a mind-numbing number of punishment tours; walking to and fro on the Area of Barracks for hours at a time. The football players Alan listed at the Jones dinner were the stars of the famous Davis-Blanchard team of the 1940s.]

Lorintz Gleich, Cass of 2006

The Jewish Chapel Choir allows me to live a different cadet experience than others in my company. Ever since Plebe year I have been traveling on the monthly choir trips all over the east coast. Even though I am now a cow, I still enjoy "beating the system" and missing Saturday Comm's training and SAMI's. Meanwhile, I am at some college in civvies having a great time. Thank you Jewish Chapel!

[Lorintz is an outstanding young man. I worked with him in his role as cadet in charge (CIC) of the Jewish Chapel Squad and Choir during his first class year; academic year 2005–2006. He has demonstrated excellent administrative and leadership skills.]

Alan M.R. Dean, Class of 1951

I did not know the Army football team was from West Point. Someone asked me on or about 4 June '47 if I would like to go to USMA . . . I said "sure" . . . 27 days later I was a cadet!"

[Lieutenant Colonel (Retired) Dean served on active duty in the Army as a field artilleryman for twenty years and two months. He served in Vietnam for two years, where he was awarded the Silver Star, the Legion of Merit twice, the Distinguished Flying Cross, the Bronze Star Medal for Valor, fourteen Air Medals, the Army Commendation Medal for Valor, the Purple Heart and "some foreign stuff."]

George M. Dell, Class of 1947

Had no aspirations to attend West Point until offered a principal appointment by Congressman Chet Holifield at age 17 while first year student at University of Southern California. Declined because I had failed eye exam for Naval ROTC and felt I could not pass USMA eye exam. A few months after reaching age 18, after I joined the Army and attaining the high rank of PFC, my commanding officer recommended me for the USMAP program and I signed the necessary papers. Completely forgot about it, was assigned to ASTP program ay Indiana University and was there only a week, at which time I was told get on a train to Amherst College for the USMAP program and nine months later was one of 10 Army enlisted men appointed to West Point.

My major extracurricular activity in high school and college before West Point was debating, and that interest remained when I was a cadet. I was involved in debate for my entire cadet career and participated with some success in numerous debates and tournaments. My debate partner and I were the recipients of an Omega watch presented to the outstanding members of the debate team. I wore it proudly until I lost it on the golf course a few years ago.

The other side of the coin is a bittersweet memory. One of our debate team members was LeRoy Majeske, a thoroughly enjoyable friend who never lost his sense of humor. Math was never my strong suit and when calculus came, I found myself eventually in the seventh section, in which LeRoy was the section leader. He had been turned back from the class of 1946 and so as he drove the section to class did not need to do so at attention; in fact he "fell out" and hummed the tune of "The Gallant Seventh" to our delight. LeRoy was killed in Korea on September 1, 1950.

On graduation I entered the Air Force. I had hoped to go into flying training, but it was not to be, perhaps for the best. I passed up the opportunity to be sent to law school by the Air Force, a decision I realized was a mistake. When the four years of obligated service was reduced to three (for those of us in the class of 1947), I decided to return to civilian life and go to law school, courtesy of the GI Bill.

After eight years in private practice I was appointed a court commissioner and later served two years as a municipal judge and three years as a superior court judge, in which capacity I served over 18 years. I retired at age 60 and commenced hearing cases—which I am still doing—as an arbitrator, mediator, referee and temporary judge.

[Some explanation is needed to clarify the Majeske story. In the 1940s classes in each academic department were divided into small sections of twelve to fifteen cadets. They were assigned according to class standing in each subject and were "ranked" within each section. The cadet with the highest grade in a subject was the leader of the First Section; the cadet with the lowest grade in the entire class was assigned as last man of the Last Section. As the sections marched out of the Area of Barracks, the section leader reported any missing cadets to the cadet guard. Plebes marched at attention. Majeski was a "turnback" from the previous class. This means that he had failed only one subject and was allowed to repeat the year. A turnback was relieved of repeating the restrictions imposed on plebes, hence he was allowed to "fall out" as he marched the lowly Seventh Section to class. The singing was illegal! Cadets no longer march to class.]

Anonymous, Class of 1954

As a Firsty, I had the brilliant idea to find out if the toilets at OSMA were the strongest in the world. On a Saturday Morning I had the Plebes put a roll of TP in the toilet in the basement of Old North Area, then string the paper up the stairs to the 3rd floor. On my command, the toilet was flushed and the paper, traveling at warp speed, proceeded to travel the four flights and was socked into the toilet. Unfortunately, the TAC entered the barracks in the middle of the episode and you know he didn't have a sense of humor. I was in confinement for two months.

[This man served twenty-nine years in the Army in the armor branch. He fought in Vietnam and Beirut. He was awarded the Legion of Merit three times, the Meritorious Service Medal, Joint Service Medal, and "some campaign stuff."]

Michael J. Ungor, Class of 1980

I was lucky to have a Jewish roommate—Jacob Kovel. I was an exchange cadet at the Air Force Academy cow year. We were the first class with women. If you can imagine arriving at Academy wondering about what it would be like to have women living next door, and landing in a Beast squad with not only women, but also a Jewish new cadet, Dana Maller. I remember the second day of Beast. Our squad leader was teaching us how to square away our rooms. Dana asked our squad leader, "How do I fold this?" and handed him her bra. He did not know how to answer her, handed her the bra back, and left the room. My Jewish experiences were very special. Rabbi Soltes was great. I grew up reform and am now Conservative Jew as a result of the Academy. I really enjoyed singing in the chorus. From time to time, I recall being told, "Mr. Ungor, you need to mouth the words for this song." I recall singing the songs I learned in Chorus to my kids when they were infants, to help them get to sleep. I am fortunate today to be able to host the choir in South Carolina for a trip section to our Synagogue this April.

Marvin S. Weinstein, Class of 1946

When going through Plebe indoctrination, I sang for Mr. Meyer, director of Chapel Choir, who asked me to join Choir. Instead, I sang with Glee Club and referred to myself as an "Honorary Protestant."

Stephen M. Herman, Class of 1968

One afternoon, walking across the Plain in a blinding snowstorm during my first year, a staff car pulled up beside me and BG Bernard Rogers, the Commandant of Cadets, opened the car door and invited me in for a drive to Central Area. I was CIC of the Jewish Chapel Organization at the time, which was a fact apparently known by the general. The general inquired about current activities of Jewish Cadets at the time which inevitably led to an observation of mine. "You know, sir," I said, "A couple of us hold pretty high rank in the chain of command this year. Mr. Ederman commands the second Regiment, and I command a battalion, nevertheless, we are not as prominent today as Jews were in the class of 1802 when fifty percent of the grads were Jewish." The general was a brilliant and kind-hearted man who looked at me with amusement and disbelief, obviously certain that I was putting him on. Some moments later, I had the privilege of dining in the general's home. He pulled me aside, over a drink, and said, "You know, Herman, you were right. One of the two graduates in the class of 1802 was Simon Levy, a Jew. Fifty percent of the class was Jewish!" He sure was a great general, that general Rogers.

[Lieutenant Colonel Herman served in the Army's armor force for twenty years. He fought in Vietnam and was awarded the Bronze Star Medal, Purple Heart, Army Commendation Medal twice, Meritorious Service Medal, Air Medal, and Ranger Tab. He was airborne and an aircraft crewman.]

Mark. M. Weimon, Class of 1971

Memorable moments: 1. Service at Mickey Marcus' gravesite . . . Plebe year. 2. Amnesty granted by Anastasia Somoza from a severe punishment . . . Junior year. 3. Presented SABRE to Rabbi while CIC . . . senior year. 4. Sitting in my grandmother's pew at Chapel while the commander of NATO gave the address.

[His grandmother's pew had her name plate on it in recognition of her donations to the Jewish Chapel.]

Michael K. Stein, Class of 1957

During yearling summer at camp Buckner, I wanted to check out a canoe to paddle around the lake. When I got down to the boat house there was a long line of cadets. I got in line and waited and waited. The line was moving very slowly and finally I asked the cadet in front of me if this was the line to check out boats. Without a snicker he said, "No. This is the line for Catholic confessions."

Charles S. Adler, Class of 1945

Corps squad summoning interfered with riding instruction, but in first class I was dropped from the team and had to attend horseback riding, a disaster—had never been on horse! Medics learned my schedule and hence were always close by to polish up my bruised body when thrown. Hospital ER got tired seeing me—excused from further riding. Became swimming instructor for cadets deficient in this skill.

Robert M. Haas, Class of 1947

My attendance at weekly Jewish religious services, first as a Plebe with the opportunity to "fall out" with the upper classmen in the squad, and finally as the squad leader as the ranking Jewish Cadet (captain), provided me with a welcome respite from the daily routine.

As for the various comedic situations, there were many, including during plebe year, a fellow classmate's reaction of rubbing noses with an upper classman while undergoing a face-to-face shouting reprimand; and during yearling year, the pre-flight training exercises at Stewart Field wherein the instructors were gambling with their note boards, writing instruments, helmets, etc. (if not their lives) every time they instructed their cadet front-seaters to stall the aircraft and then pull out of same by pushing the throttle ahead, with the possibility that the cadets would over-correct and put the aircraft into a 180 degree maneuver flying upside down in the opposite direction (I later learned from a former Japanese naval pilot that their instructors sat behind them with baseball bats at the ready, which they readily used, in those instances where their students fouled up, thereby forcing the instructors to take control) and during summer ground maneuvers, wherein as a tank commander I was following the point man, who happened to be one of my roommates, affectionately referred to as "Knucklehead," up to an impassable stone wall and whose response to my "What do we do now?" was a sheepish grin and, "Beats me," as we, therefore, concluded our participation in the exercise. From a personal standpoint, the Academy, in addition to instilling the credo of "Duty, Honor, and Country," gave me the confidence to believe that obstacles experienced during cadet training, subsequent military service, in the business world, as well as in personal life situations, could all be handled effectively assuming they were approached with a positive attitude. Finally, in addition to its influence on an individual's moral fiber, the relationships developed and the camaraderie experienced at the Academy, fortunately continue to this day.

Michael Sirkis, Class of 1956

Member of "Century Club"—walked well over 100 hours on the area.

[Colonel Sirkus served twenty-nine and a half years in the army as an air defense artillery officer. He served in Vietnam and was awarded the Defense Superior Service Medal, Legion of Merit twice, Bronze Star Medal twice, Meritorious Service Medal twice, Air Medal twice, Joint Chief's Service Medal, Army Commendation Medal four times, and miscellaneous service medals.]

Igor D. Gerhart, Class of 1959

I went to the Citadel before West Point and therefore had two plebe years back-to-back. I won best new cadet at the Academy two weeks in a row. I was forced to take Russian because I had one year of German at the Citadel. A classmate of mine of Russian descent, was also forced to take a class in a language (Russian) he already spoke fluently. He wanted to take Spanish in college before going to West Point. The reasons given for forcing us into Russian was to avoid giving us an unfair advantage over our classmates. Guess who was the number one student in Russian and who had to work his fanny off just to get by. Be careful when people want to be "fair."

[Lieutenant Colonel Gerhardt served twenty-three years in the Army infantry airborne. He was a Ranger, Pathfinder, and a Special Forces Officer. He fought in Vietnam for two years where he was awarded the Silver Star, three Bronze Stars for Valor, the Air Medal for valor, two Army Commendation Medals for valor, and the Purple Heart. As a cadet he was a superb diver on the swimming team.]

Norman H. Rosner, Class of 1959

During my cadet years, 1955–1959, it was common knowledge that the Jewish Chapel Choir was perennially short of tenors. Invariably a non-Jewish tenor would join the Jewish Chapel, more inspired perhaps by the prospect of three-day choir trips than by a religious transformation. On one such trip to a Manhattan synagogue, choir members were called, in pairs, for Torah "aliyahs." One of our "new" tenors sat next to me. He asked, "What do I do when I get up there?" I said, just stand next to me, and when I recite the blessing, in Hebrew, just "mouth" the words. This seemed like a good idea at the time.

When our turn came we dutifully walked up to the Torah reading table. The "shamus," looking at my friend, recited the Hebrew introduction for a person to receive an honor . . . and which requested my friend's Hebrew name. I leaned over and whispered to the Shamus, "He's not Jewish!" The Shamus, immediately repeated his introduction and again looked to my friend to recite his Hebrew name. Again I whispered, "He's not Jewish!" The Shamus looked at us with a blank expression. Suddenly I realized the problem. Like many other Shamuses' of that era, he was a Holocaust survivor, new to this country, and who spoke Yiddish . . . not English. Mustering up my best Yiddish I whispered, "Er is nicht Yuddish" (He is not Jewish). The Shamus' face lit, half in shock that a non-Jew was on the BEMA (alter) and half in enlightenment. Without hesitation, he again launched into the introduction, this time supplying a Hebrew name for our tenor. The name he used was, JESUS BEN JOSEPH (Jesus son of Joseph). The rabbi's eyes rolled . . . and those of us in the choir who understood what had transpired, had all we could do to stifle our laughter!

In the late spring of 1959, graduation year, classmate, and fellow Jewish Chapel Member, Paul Sper, and took off in Paul's Sabre, an Israeli-manufactured car he bought from my brother-in-law on a weekend pass. We headed North to New Paltz, where I knew a girl attending the State Teacher's College. After an evening of "partying," which consisted of going to a local bar with some of the students, Paul and I decided to make use of the most attractive feature of the Sabre. The seat-backs rolled down creating a double bed. We found a very dark grassy knoll, parked the car, put our clothes in the trunk, pulled out our respective "Brown Boys" and then "official" Cadet-issue comforters, rolled the seat-backs down, and went to sleep in our Cadet-issue underwear. Dawn broke to the sound of church bells. I'd slept through the blast of the reveille cannon, so I ignored the bells and kept snoozing. Paul nudged me and said "I think we are being watched." And we were! Curious churchgoers peering in the window surrounded the car. The grassy knoll was the front lawn of a church. In case anyone spotted two cadets, racing out of New Paltz, New York that Sunday morning, it was us.

By August 1962 I had spent 2-1/2 years in Schweinfurt Germany with the third Infantry Division. From the time I arrived in December 1959 until that August, I never dated an American woman, in part because there were so few of them, and in part to avoid the temptation of marrying out of the Jewish faith. Late August was when the new American schoolteachers arrived for the September opening of the dependant's school year. As a senior First Lieutenant, I pranced over to welcome (check-out) the new arrivals. I knew that the next spring I would return to the States and I figured I might date one of the new arrivals to re-acquaint myself with American dating habits. I focused on the best looker of the new arrivals, a gal named Elva. I "cut her out" from the herd and asked for a date. She agreed. That evening I went to pick her up at the Bachelor Women's Quarters ("BWQ"). I knocked on her door. She answered and let me in. She had just arrived that day so her trunk was in the middle of the room.

On the trunk was printed her name and address. I saw, "Elva," "Rosenburg," "Gonzales," and "Texas." I knew a cadet from Gonzales, Texas, so my mind went into overdrive. This was the first Jewish woman I had met in almost three years! WOW. We had a wonderful first date. I was smitten . . . and so was she! I was ready to call my mother with the good news. Then when I took her back to her room I took a second look at the trunk. Now, I read, "Elva Gonzales, Rosenberg, Texas." She was Mexican-American, from a small town 20 miles southwest of Houston. Rosenberg had been named for a pre–Civil War Jewish dry-goods merchant, who's "RB Department Store," was still operative. How did I know it was still operative? Because I saw it the next year on my first visit to meet my in-laws.

Elva and I have been married since 1963. We have two children and two grandchildren. Elva was responsible for creating the kosher kitchen at our new synagogue building, and is President-elect of our local chapter of Hadassah. Our parents are gone now, but we visit Rosenberg at least twice a year. While the RB Department Store has long-since been closed, the site still remains as when I first saw it . . . a wonderful reminder of how I once transposed Rosenberg with Gonzales.

Peter Stark, Class of 1989

During Beast Barracks, I remember being in the regimental formation on the apron every Sunday morning before religious services. The Adjutant would call off each religion one by one to form up in a separate formation per the location for their respective religion. Once all service groups were called out, the main formation went from 1000 cadets to about 12 Jewish beanheads scattered throughout the length of the apron. The adjutant then told us to fall out and spectators would see the 12 Jews in the class pinging back to their barracks.

The local Jewish War Veterans Posts were extremely kind every week when they sponsored the Oneg. Once it was over, there were always leftovers. I used to bring back a dozen bagels, knishes, pastries, and herring to my classmates in the barracks. This was heaven during Plebe year when meals were never relaxing and food wasn't exactly plentiful during mealtimes. People often asked me if I experienced anti-Semitism at West Point. My experience involved classmates and friends asking me how they could sign up to be Jewish so they could get that kind of food every Friday night. I spent four years in the Jewish Chapel Choir and can't sing a note. We had approximately 30 Jewish cadets in the corps and all 30 were members of the choir. I always believed that we sang for the Jewish retirement homes because they were too old or too deaf to hear us. Both my parents who still believe that I can do little to no wrong spent many hours laughing at how bad we all were. There were truly many memorable moments on those choir trips.

Anonymous, Class of 1951

As a member of the Jewish Chapel and Jewish Choir, one of my goals was to have frequent trips away from the Academy. On one such trip to Poughkeepsie where we sang at a Temple, I was billeted at the home of a prominent family, with two unmarried daughters. The parents evidently liked me and encouraged the older daughter (who I think also liked me) to pursue a relationship. I had an OAO back home and found myself in constant retreat from the daughter!!

Abraham M. Glass, Class of 1944

I am the last person that you should ask about Anti-Semitism. I was raised in a community of 4,000 families. The village contained two Jewish families. I enjoyed the friendship of six boys and their parents. Anti-Semitism never arose. During my service, I was a Company Commander in Camp Fanning, Texas. I received a phone call from the Jewish Chaplain asking if I was an anti-Semite. I had placed charges against a boy who had stole $18.00 from a camp-mate. The mother of the theft contacted the Chaplain claiming that I was an Anti-Semite. I didn't remember seeing the boy at the Chapel. At West Point I lived in barracks with two other cadets. Neither were Jewish. They would ask me about the Jewish religion. Anti-Semitism was not a topic. In 1941, each cadet had to have a religious faith. There was 12 Jewish Cadets in the Academy. We met each Sunday in a field-house room. I don't think the smallness of the room was assigned with bias.

Robert L. Kaplan, Class of 1953

Although involved in private flying since 1945, and having extensive R & D experience in Army Aviation, Army would not send me to flight school in view of vision problem—gave up after five applications in 10 years and reverted to USAR—completed another 23 years as a mob designee at HQDA.

Herbert I. Stern, Class of 1941

Jewish Services on Sundays initiated in 1939. NY Jewish Welfare provided Rabbi—Lt. Col Tintner. Tintner knew everyone and received much to ensure continuation of Jewish services. My class had seven Jews, one of whom later converted. Cadets referred to us as the "Ham eaters." I have original order establishing Jewish services—sent to Chapel.

[Colonel Stern served in the Army field artillery for twenty-seven years. He fought in World War II in the European theater where he was awarded the Silver Star, Bronze Star twice, Legion of Merit, and the Army Commendation Ribbon.]

Ben Diamond, Class of 2007

I think Shabbat services and the promise of bagels and lox kept me in my first summer. The Jewish Choir and Hillel are what every club wishes they could be. A very relaxed and social club that conducts official enough business that the BTO rarely disapproves our trip section requests so we "get out" often.

Eric M. Lowy, Class of 1985

I grew up in a non-religious house (I didn't get Bar Mitzvah's, etc.) so on the 2nd or 3rd day of Beast Barrack, when my squad leader asked me to indicate which religion I was (for what services I would be attending), I said that I was Jewish, but that I was not religious and therefore did not desire to attend services at W.P. Well, he took me aside and said, "Lowy, let me explain something to you: you're going to have me and the other upperclassmen making your life miserable here every day. So if you can escape us for a few hours every Friday night to relax and be yourself, I strongly suggest you do so!" Well, that sounded like some pretty damn good advice to me, so I said, "yes, sir." That I would go. So that Friday night, after taking a good few days of abuse, I showed up at Jewish services in Bartlett Hall just to escape as he had suggested. And after meeting all of the quality, caring people there that night (civilians, fellow cadets, etc.) from that first Friday night on, I rarely missed a service for the rest of my four years. The support I received from the W.P Jewish community was absolutely essential in helping me through the hard times at W.P (because of this, I am a consistent donor to the W.P Jewish Chapel Fund every year.)

Daniel Stredler, Class of 1986

I played football from 1982–1985 and was a three year letterman as the long snapper for the team during the Cherry Bowl in 84' and the Peach Bowl in 85'! I was the only Jewish cadet on the team in those years.

Bill Schwartz, Class of 1959

Every Sunday morning we, like our Christian classmates, marched off to Chapel. It was mandatory. When we entered the Academy we had to declare our religious preference and we had only three choices: Protestant, Catholic or Jewish. In my case, being forced to march off to the Old Cadet Chapel in the West Point Cemetery on Sunday had its elements of both humor and irony.

First, we were being marched off to Jewish services that were not even being held on the Jewish Sabbath. But if the Protestants and Catholics had to march off to Chapel for their Sabbath services on a Sunday, then by golly, the Jews should join them on this singular day of religious devotion. Second, I wasn't exactly religious—a gross understatement. I would have much preferred sleeping in. Finally, some of the cadets marching off to the Old Cadet Chapel for Jewish Services, weren't even Jewish. They'd elected to become Jews, for purposes of chapel attendance, because Jewish Chapel was held early on Sunday morning, which meant "Jews" had most of Sunday to spend with their dates or to hustle one up "Trolling the plain."

In fact, the cadet in charge of the Jewish Chapel Squad my Yearling year was Wally Summer, a Chinese-American with a Jewish father, who was known as "Genghis Goldberg." Wally definitely did not "look Jewish." He was also a strict disciplinarian and a tough cadet company commander. In fact when the class of 1957 broke ranks at graduation parade, and ran across the Plain, only Wally's company classmates continued to march. Why? Because Wally drew his sword and threatened to run anyone through who broke ranks. His classmates knew that that was no idle threat. But that's another story. When we went on a Chapel Choir trip and Wally stepped out front to introduce us, you could see the civilian congregants turning to each other with a 50's equivalent of a "say what?" look.

Which brings up the other, most important, reason why Christians became Jews while at West Point. This temporary "conversion" enabled them to participate in the Jewish Choir—the ultimate good deal for a Plebe. Why was this a good deal? Because those were the days when Plebes were not permitted to go off post for the entire year, except for attendance at the Army-Navy game. The only other way to get through those gates to freedom, as a plebe, was to join the Jewish Choir which frequently sang at Temples and Synagogues in the New York area and

Northeast. Since the percentage of Jews at West Point pretty much mirrored that of the population as a whole (2% or so), and we only had 2000 cadets in the Corps, the Jewish Choir needed all the help it could get to fill its ranks.

As I recall, some of the guys couldn't even carry a tune. They lip synched the words. And those were Hebrew words in many cases. Picture the scene at Choir rehearsal. Here is the enlisted Choir Director (Protestant bandsman) teaching Hebrew liturgical songs to Jewish cadets, many of whom never sang them before, and WASP's who didn't know shalom from adios. So for the sake of good PR, the authorities permitted any cadet who was selected for the Jewish Choir, to include Plebes, to take these weekend trips. To make it an even better deal, and add some more irony, we were billeted at the homes of the congregants, many of whom had daughters whom they would like to fix up with gentlemanly, Jewish cadets. Can you imagine, these parents actually trusted our intentions with their daughters? Amazing the effect of good PR and a gray uniform.

I used to chuckle at the thought of some of these parents introducing their little princess to some WASP from Cowflop, Texas, thinking they had the possibility of acquiring a good Jewish cadet as a son-in-law. By the way, I have nothing against Cowflop, Texas, or its citizens. Just a metaphor.

From my standpoint, and Jewish classmates with whom I've reminisced about Chapel, there were some very tangible non-religious benefits to attending those Sunday services. It mostly related to the effect on us of the plaques on the walls of the Old Cadet Chapel. As you face the alter, in the left rear of the Chapel, was a plaque placed by the Jewish War Veterans which honored the first two graduates of USMA, one of whom was the Jewish American Simon Levy. On the other wall space were plaques commemorating the battle deaths of grads of the early 1800's, in combat actions that were almost footnotes to history. There were other plaques honoring graduate participation in America's wars. The plaques served to remind us that we were at West Point to become soldiers and that we were part of a glorious and heroic military tradition. Seeing those plaques every Sunday made us aware that it was now incumbent upon us to continue the tradition and the values of the long gray line. Just as it is for the Jewish American cadets who attend West Point today and who will in the future. Grip hands.

[Lieutenant Colonel Schwartz served twenty-one years in the infantry branch of the Army. He fought in Vietnam and was awarded the Legion of Merit, four Bronze Star Medals, the Air Medal, the Defense Meritorious Service Medal, four Meritorious Service Medals, Commendation Medal, Ranger tab, Senior Parachute Wings, and Vietnamese Ranger Badge.]

Joseph Katz, Class of 1958

As you know, at the tables in the Mess Hall, a Plebe can "fall-out" if his team won a big game, told a good joke etc. At one meal, I told the table Com "Katz is the oldest surname in the Bible related to Aaron, the brother of Moses, page 495, believe it or not! The table Com wasn't impressed and said Katz continue to eat a square meal.

Billy Jo Cory, Class of 1954

Never did anything noteworthy. However, the instructor always kept the class overtime on Saturday mornings and we all received two demerits for being late to the next class. I placed an alarm clock inside the top drawer of his desk, and it went off on time. The class froze. I don't remember if I ever got my roommates alarm clock back or not.

N. D. Greenberg, Class of 1943

Your research will probably confirm or reject my recollections concerning the Jewish Chapel activities. Since I am a turn-back from the class of 1942, I recall that at that time there was no Jewish Chapel. In fact, I attended the Protestant services and for a brief period was a member of the USMA choir, based on my ability to sing "Glory Of God." I was soon released from the choir when the leader (and WP organist) learned that I really had no musical talent. In 1930 I recall that the Jewish Chapel Squad was very informal. We usually met in the gymnasium or theater and came to the group individually. Later (perhaps 1940), the Jewish Chapel Squad was formalized by a special order from HQ USMA. After that the group assembled and marched to services. My recollection is that the group numbered about 19 and that the leader was a 1st class cadet, named Leonard Kaplan. During my cadet days, I recall two chaplains—one from the Jewish community of New Rochelle. He was orthodox and very dull. Later on we had a much more charismatic rabbi, by the name of Tintner. He was a good speaker.

[Colonel Greenberg served thirty years as an Army field artillery officer. He fought in France in World War II. He was awarded the Legion of Merit, Meritorious Service Medal, and the Army Commendation Ribbon.]

Alan D. Sapowith, Class of 1947

During Bayonet practice as a Plebe, Mr. Sharkorff, 2nd class, who was coaching/criticizing, said "get some hate in there!" I replied, "Get in front of me, sir!" Sharkorff stayed away.

Donald Benjamin, Class of 2008

I was in such a state of shock during my first week of Beast that I was sure I had made the worst decision of my life in attending West Point. On the first Thursday night of cadet Basic Training all of the new cadets assembled in Robinson Auditorium to fill out cards and receive information about the religious opportunities afforded us during our tenure at the Academy. At the end someone asked all of the Jews to meet in the lobby with the Rabbi. It seemed like I was the only person who stood up although about ten of us met up in the lobby. The rabbi told us to come to services the next night. I waited impatiently all day for the evening to roll around. Walking up to the Chapel relieved me a little from my oppressed state, although I still had numerous doubts about my future. Major Huerta led us through the service and began his usual weekly sermon. The rabbi, however, didn't just deliver a sermon; he gave the most motivating speech I will probably hear in my entire life. I felt like Major Huerta knew exactly how I was feeling. He reminded me why I wanted to come to West Point in the first place. I was convinced that Beast was a small price to pay for the opportunity to be an officer and alumnus. When I returned to the Barracks my roommate saw me smile for the first time. "You look reJEWvenated," they said. They were right, my depression had disappeared and I made it through Beast in one piece.

Martin B. Zimmerman, Class of 1956

In 1954, the Jewish community in NY decided to commemorate the 300th anniversary of the initial entry of Jews to the "New World." They invited the then President, Dwight D. Eisenhower, to attend and he accepted the invitation to be a speaker at the Waldorf Astoria. The planners of the event heard that there was a West Point Jewish Choir and decided to invite the choir to tie in the President to the Jewish community. There were two problems inherent in the invitation: although we had 48 (or so) members of the choir, we were not very good. Most joined as a means of getting away from the Academy for a limited number of weekend visits to Synagogues in the NY, Conn, PA area, and the invitation went directly to the head of the choir—avoiding the chain of command. Approximately a month before the event, the NY Times printed an articled describing the celebration, including the choir in the article.

As I understood it, the "Supe" read the article and called the "Com" to see what he knew of the event. When the answer came back, that he knew nothing of it, they decided to call Capt. Barry Drew, who was the head of the Academy's Glee Club (the real pros). They asked him to check out the Jewish Choir to assure that the Academy and the President wouldn't be embarrassed. We were lined up, as a result, and asked individually to sing, "Glory to God." When we all sang—as well as we could—only one of us passed muster. He was a member of the Glee Club (Irwin Mayer—a friend—who subsequently died in an air accident in the China Sea).

The commandant, when told the result of the audit, decided to take members of the Glee Club and teach them the Hebrew songs (transliterated) and send them to the Waldorf titled as the West Point Jewish Choir. I guess that having a single Jewish cadet in the group assuaged their conscious. The stories I heard after the fact from classmates who participated were really funny.

Alvin J. Marrow, Class of 1963

The one event that I can still remember was my first experience going to Jewish Chapel services. It was a Sunday morning, about 0730 hours, and 10–12 of us Jewish Plebes lined up in the South Barracks area to march to the Old Cadet Chapel. Not knowing what to expect, we entered the Chapel and took seats in truly historic surroundings. The cadet in-charge went to the front of the Chapel where a large "Cross" was sitting on a rotating pedestal. He turned the pedestal 180 degrees and suddenly a "Star of David" appeared. What a site to behold! For the first time in nearly a week of Plebe Barracks I felt a sense of belonging. The experience—the rotating pedestal—was the beginning of my four wonderful years as a Jewish cadet at West Point.

Alvin E. Orlian, Class of 1945

My father organized the first Seder at the Thayer—Gen Wilby the Supe, and Col. Gallagher the Commandant attended—this was in 1941 (12 cadets). My father was Israel Orlian. My Appointment was from Andrew Sommers through Congressman Emanuel Celler.

[Al Orlian saw combat as an infantry officer in Europe during World War II. He landed in Normandy on Omaha Beach, where he joined the 29th Infantry Division. He was wounded at St. Lo. He was awarded the Bronze Star Medal, two Purple Hearts, Combat Infantry Badge, "and the others in the ETO."

Al is a dear friend of mine and a colleague on the West Point Jewish Chapel Fund. He contributed a considerable sum of money to the fund and continues to serve on the fund. His father started a tradition of Passover Seders at West Point that now are limited to cadets and families, but occasionally the cadets bring roommates or friends.]

Harold H. Lusky, Class of 1960

The only way I "beat the system" was to be a member of the Jewish Chapel Choir (all four years)—many trips to New York and other adjacent cities. I was taken in by a family from Patterson, New Jersey my Yearling year and they allowed me to stay at their house when I was away from the

Academy—I needed their friendship and acceptance to make the years away from California and family not feel so lonely.

Elliot "Stud" Heit, Class of 1950

I suppose the truly outstanding memory of my cadet years was the deep and enduring friendship with fellow classmate Joseph McCrane (Joe passed away last September and I was invited by his family to address the crowded Catholic Cadet Chapel). During our cadet years we were inseparable, even though I was 2nd regiment and he was in 1st regiment. We had some common threads that served us together and I know most of class were well aware of our presence (we were, for the first time ever, selected as Co-directors to produce the traditional 100th night show). Part of the common thread, we were part of the 38% of '50 that served in WWII. Joe did his time in the Marines, including a stint in Guadalcanal, and I was a sky-jock, who got his wings on or about the time I just turned 19. But one of the many, many funny incidents came about by our mutual love of football. Joe was an outstanding player and was assisted by backfield coach Andy Gustafson (he coached Blanchard and Davis). I was also a pretty good lineman at Erasmus Hall H.S. in Brooklyn, and coincidentally, it was Andy Gustafson who got "the ball rolling" with my congressional appointment from Brooklyn. My line coach at USMA was famous Herman Hickman; it took him about ten minutes to figure out I was a no-go. The same thing happened to Joe. We were both relegated to B-squad and this is where we met while scrimmaging with A-squad. Joe was Quarterback and I was Right Guard. The ball is snapped and my position was flooded and overrun with the big "A" boys. There we both were—never met before and under 1000 pounds of A-squad. Meat! Neither of us can move; Joe manages to yell out to my crushed body close to his, "Are you the guy who opened the door and let all these guys come in?" I laughed and said, "yeah, that's me; my name is Stud Heit." He says, "Okay, my name is Joe, but see if you can keep the door closed a little bit better." That was the way our friendship started and it never stopped until Sept, 2004.

Harold L. Blank, Class of 1950

Approximately 60% of my class, 1949, fought in WWII or served in some capacity. They varied in rank from Private to Major. There were many Lieutenants in the group. The officers were willing to relinquish their rank for an appointment to West Point. The Jewish veterans in the group included.

During 2nd class summer training at Ft. Bragg, OIC of our glider orientation ride was a crew member of "my brother's" B-17 in WWII. While performing Non standard maneuvers, our _____ tow rope snapped. The rope took out the wind shield and a hidden stump in a farmer's field took out the fabric under side of our craft, filling the interior with plowed earth. There were no injuries to the pilot or the cadets. It was the height of our trip.

[Colonel Blank served in the Army Corps of Engineers for twenty-eight years. He served in Vietnam and was awarded the Army Commendation Medal four times, the Meritorious Service Medal, Legion of Merit twice, and the Bronze Star Medal.]

Robert B. Peltz, Class of 1950

While returning from track practice as an upper classman, my work-out uniform was quite disheveled. I was stopped by Col. A.S Collins, a tough Irishman. He said, "Mr. Peltz, you're a mess! Straighten out your shirt, pants, and everything else!" I complied, after which he said, "I'm going to make a Christian out of you yet." I replied, "I don't think so, sir." "Why not?" he asked. "Because I'm a Jew." We both laughed and I went on my merry way.

Wilbur Kahn, Class of 1944

I never rode a horse until I was a cadet at USMA. I was the only cadet to request extra instruction in Equitation because it was an authorized absence from my room when I was in confinement. I could check out a horse from the stables and ride all the many trails. I attended the Advanced Equitation course and Ft. Sill after graduation and joined an all horse and mule pack artillery battery in the 10th Mountain Division. I taught riding classes at Cornell University when I was an ROTC instructor there.

[Major General William Cohen, class of 1959, did not provide information outside of what is listed here, yet because of his outstanding achievements in combat I felt it only right that he should be mentioned. Major above it is Major General Cohen reported that he flew combat missions in Vietnam and in the Israeli Air Force during the Yom Kippur War. In Vietnam he was awarded the Distinguished Flying Cross four times, and the Air Medal twelve times, plus a variety of other decorations.]

Herbert Y. Schandler, Class of 1952

I graduated 80th in my class (of over 500 graduates), which happened to place me as the 25,000th graduate from West Point. One of the NY papers did a feature on graduation and the milestone in the Academy's history (I believe the paper was the NY Daily News—but I am not sure). My picture apparently appeared in newspapers around the country, because my parents received many nice notes from friends who had seen it. To this day, at reunions and class functions, I am remembered by classmates for this occurrence—which seems to be my major "claim to fame." Interestingly, it took the Academy 162 years to produce 25,000 grads!

[Dr. Herbert Yale Schandler was born on January 2, 1928 in Asheville, North Carolina. In 1952, he graduated from the U.S Military Academy at West Point, and was commissioned in the infantry. In 1953, he served in Korea as a platoon leader and company commander in the 2nd Infantry Division. He later served in Germany with the 10th Special Forces Group and as Special Warfare Plans Officer at Headquarters, U.S. Army, Europe. He served two combat tours in Vietnam with the 1st Infantry Division in 1965 and as a battalion commander with the 101st Airborne Division in 1969-1970. He also served in the Revolutionary Development Division, Military Assistance Command Vietnam (MACV). He served as an assistant professor in the Department of Social Sciences at the U.S. Military Academy from 1957 to 1960. Other assignments included service in the Strategic Plans and Policy Directorate of the Army Staff, as Assistant for Southeast Asian Affairs in the Office of the Chief of Staff of the Army, as a member of the faculty at the National War College, and in the Plans and Policy Directorate, Joint Chiefs of Staff. He also served as a military social aide at the White House from 1967 through 1969 during the Johnson and Nixon administrations. He graduated from the Army's Infantry School, Special Warfare School, the Command and General Staff College, and from the Air War College. Colonel Schanler's personal military decorations include two awards of the Combat Infantryman's Badge, four awards of the Legion of Merit, three awards of the Bronze Star Medal with V, fourteen awards of the Air Medal (two with V), two awards of the valorous Unit Award, the Meritorious Service Medal, and the Army Commendation Medal, as well as awards from Vietnam, Korea, and the Netherlands. He received a master's degree and a doctorate from Harvard University. His Ph.D. dissertation was published by the Princeton University Press in 1977 under the title *The Unmaking of a President: Lyndon Johnson and Vietnam*. He lectured and wrote on the Vietnam War; and was a contributing author to the books *Foreign Policy and U.S. National Security* (1976), *Vietnam as History: Ten Years After the Vietnam War* (1985), and *Regular Armies and Insurgency* (1979). In 1998, he traveled to Hanoi to interview Vietnam's wartime leaders. Based on these interviews, he contributed to the book *Argument Without End: In Search of Answers to the Vietnam Tragedy,* by former Secretary of Defense Robert S. McNamara, published in 1999. Upon his retirement from the Army in 1975, Dr. Schandler joined the Congressional Research Service as a specialist in national defense. In 1983, he became professor of political science at the Industrial College of the Armed Forces, National Defense University, in Washington, D.C.; and from 1990 to 1996, served as chairman of its Department of Strategy. During the Persian Gulf War, he served as a commentator for the NBC *Today* show. In 1999, he was appointed George C. Marshall Professor of Grand Strategy. He served on the board of directors of the McLean Citizens Association and as a member of the Human Relations Advisory Committee of the Fairfax County School Board. He has also served on the Social Studies Curriculum Advisory Committee and the High School Curriculum Advisory Committee of the Fairfax County Public Schools. He is a member of the West Point Society of D.C., the Special Forces Association, the Asia Society, the Society of the 1st Division, and the Disabled American Veterans.]

Sigmund T. Weiner, Class of 1964

Late one November night during Plebe year, just before the Army-Navy football game, I was pressed into service to accompany a prank detail to swipe a cannon from Trophy Point and deposit it in the Mess Hall. Since pushing was easier than pulling, plebes appeared to be at the front as we worked up a head of steam on the gravel road by the practice football field in order to hop the curb and proceed across the plain.

My last thought before the steel wheel of the cannon crushed my foot was that when I stopped hearing the crunch of the gravel I'd better look for that curb. I hopped on one foot back to barracks where the ambulance picked me up. Unfortunately, the duty Sergeant didn't consider the injury serious enough and so by the time that Colonel Parvin saw me on his morning ward rounds, gangrene had already set in.

It took three operations and nearly six months for that superb surgeon to save enough of my foot (all but the last digit of my big toe) to keep me in the Corps. During that entire time I was told to keep my foot elevated above my heart and I did thanks to an old, specially rigged wheelchair. Since a cast wouldn't work, the bones were wired and corks popped onto the ends extending out of my foot to protect the innocent and my bed sheets. I seem to recall that they were eventually removed with a power drill in reverse. During my lengthy wheelchair tenure, that model became obsolete and I recall having to continually cajole the staff to let me keep mine beyond its expiration date. In time my seniority in the orthopedics ward earned me bed one.

I don't recall ever getting gigged for my myriad infractions. I had no trouble with academics but staying awake for the first class after lunch wasn't easy when it was a large group in one of the lecture halls. Usually the P's were able to awaken the drowsy by casually telling the class to ignore the next command and then belting out a "Group Atten-HUT" which got the sleepers precipitously and alone to their feet. Apparently at one such class, I was the only sleeper so the P took a different approach, bouncing a thrown eraser off of me. The instructor was Frank Borman.

Joel Bernstein, Class of 1964

On a Jewish note, I recall the delight in qualifying for the Jewish Chapel Choir (which fortunately didn't involve much musical ability) and getting some rare trips away from the Academy during those years. Our hosts, invariably parents or eligible daughters, over-indulged us (probably still do), but those were wonderful times. The one trip I made from the Academy plebe year, before my injury, was to New York, my hometown, for the Army–Notre Dame football game. I brought my roommate back for a home cooked meal after the game and I recall that my working mom, who had a limited cooking repertoire (basically things she likes: Swiss steak, fried chicken, breaded veal cutlets, cheesecake. Period.) couldn't figure out which I'd prefer, so she made them all. Quite a doggy bag we took back.

Joel Gartenberg, Class of 1966

During Beast Barracks I often got in trouble for not being serious enough and was placed in a "laughing bag," a laundry bag placed over one's head. The Upperclassmen also sometimes put me in their closet with the laughing bag over my head and had me double time in place, but I continued to laugh, having retained my sense of humor despite their attempts to get me to stop. On another occasion during Beast, I was in an Upper Classman's room bracing against the wall next to the door while another classmate knocked on the door to request entrance. After a couple of knocks I noticed that he banged even louder and that paint chips were flying off inside of the door. I learned later from a classmate who also was waiting outside to enter that the one who caused the paint to chip had banged the door with the butt plate of his M-1 rifle.

[Lieutenant Colonel Gartenberg served in the Army for twenty-four years in the infantry. He fought in Vietnam, where he was awarded the Legion of Merit, the Meritorious Service Medal five times, the Army Commendation Medal for Valor twice, the Good Conduct Medal, and a variety of service medals.]

Alan Scheinwald, Class of 1987

My greatest honor as a Jewish cadet was that during my senior year, my mother was allowed to get married in the new Jewish Chapel. This occurred in March 1987 and was the first civilian wedding in the new chapel. Mr. and Mrs. William Schmier were married with the blessings of LTC (Rabbi) Abramowitz, and sanctioned by the Academy.

Michael D. Mahler, Class of 1958

My father was a New Yorker who grew up in an Irish-Catholic Parish in Tremont in the Bronx. One of his high school classmates went to USNA and one to USMA, and he turned down an appointment to USNA because of conditions at home and the need to contribute to the support of his family. He kept up with both, and was a corporal in the artillery during WWI, though he never left the United States. He was a newspaperman for all his life, working for the *Brooklyn Eagle*, various Hearst papers, and finally the *New York Daily News*. In fact, he started the Westchester supplement to the *News* in the early '50's. I grew up, therefore, hearing stories about Mickey Marcus and the military.

We lived initially in Peekskill, and then moved down to White Plains in 1947. Both were close enough to visit USMA, and I can remember going down to old Camp Smith, at the entry to the Bear Mountain Highway to watch the troop trains leave during WWII. The witnesses at my parents' marriage were a Sandy and Florence Weisberg from New Rochelle. Their daughter, Natalie, married Jules Yates, known as David, Class of 1940. I was at that wedding as a youngster of four. David Yates was captured at Corregidor and spent the war in a Japanese prison camp. In fact, there was a recent *Assembly* ring story about a nurse who married a guy from the class of '40 against policy. The husband died during his captivity and David took the surviving nurse to Tiffanies to buy her the miniature she had never had. There is, by the way, a *Life* magazine from 1942 that shows Natalie in a WAC uniform. She joined up after Jules was captured, and was one of the first into the WAC. David survived by not being on one of the prison ships that were sunk because a doctor lied and said he had berri berri, which terrified the Japanese. He actually had typhus, I believe. He returned after the war and took up his career again. He was stationed at USMA as a Russian Instructor, maybe during your time as a cadet.

The mother-in-law, Florence Weisberg, lived with them at that point, and my family visited frequently during their tour. They lived in those old quarters overlooking Thayer Road just past the road that used to go to the Hospital side entrance. Neighbors were David Eisenhower, whoever was married to a Wainwright daughter, and some other famous Army names. All of that solidified my interest in things military that my father had encouraged. I initially went to the Citadel in Charleston, SC, while my dad tried to get me an appointment. After about six months, he managed to get Representative Arthur G. Klein, later NY Supreme Court Justice Klein, to appoint me. Klein's last appointment prior to mine had been Paul Lansky ('54) the son of the mob accountant, Myer Lansky. Klein had taken some flak over that.

So much for how I got to USMA. With regard to stories, I would offer two: Your classmate, John Hodes, accused me of being anti-Semitic when I was on the Beast Detail. He was the New Cadet Company Tac and I was on the cadre. We had an absolute disaster of a new cadet named Ginsberg from Brooklyn—he left shortly after Beast—and I was accused of being too hard on him at one point. During that conversation, Hodes suggested that I might be anti-Semitic. I never said a word, and I never knew if he had a clue that I was Jewish.

The Tercentenary of Judaism in America took place while I was a cadet. The Jewish Chapel Choir, such as it was, was invited to sing at the official celebration at the Hotel Astor in New York. The Academy didn't quite trust us to perform in a way that would do credit, so they assigned a number of Glee Club members to augment our small group. Nobody noticed or remarked on the number of fairly obvious WASP cadets in the group, but there was considerable comment about why there was an oriental cadet in the group. That cadet was Wally Summers ('57), who was an official member of the Jewish Chapel Squad, though I don't really know to this day whether he was a Jew by birth or by choice. Wally came from a missionary background and was also my cadet company commander.

[Colonel Mahler served in the Army for twenty-four years as an armor officer. He fought in Vietnam from 1967–68. He was awarded the Legion of Merit twice, the Bronze Star Medal twice, the Meritorious Service Medal twice, the Air Medal three times, the Army Commendation Medal twice, the Vietnamese Civil Action Honor Medal, the Vietnamese Cross of Gallantry with Valor, Parachutist Badge. and the Army General Staff Identification Badge.]

Robert D. Wolff, Class of 1965

Max Thurman was my tactical officer. One night I was caught by Max calling my girlfriend (now my wife) in the time after hours. He was wearing one shoe and one tennis shoe so that his rapid pace could be undetected. I was confined to quarters and given punishment hours for the offense, which caused me to miss my wife's cousin's Bar Mitzvah on Long Island. When I attended ICAF in 1984, Max Thurman, then the DESPER of the Army and a 3-star, was one of our speakers. I had not seen Max for twenty years. When I stood up to ask a question, Max interrupted me and asked if I was the gymnast from West Point. He also asked if I could please stand up when I addressed a senior officer—at 5'5" I was already standing but not high enough for Max. I forgot my question. I almost made stars my first two years—missing by two or three places in my ranking. This was after having only a B average in high school—so the academics agreed with me. However, my grades went down after meeting my wife my Cow year, but I ended up at 48th of 596 in the class and was the last person in the first row at graduation! I never expected to do so well at West Point. We had Jewish services in the Old Cadet Chapel and the Chemistry Laboratory during my years at West Point. Rabbi Soltes was an inspiration to us in maintaining our Jewish faith in such a predominately Christian environment. The annual Passover Seder at the Thayer hotel was always a treat—one to which I invited non-Jewish classmates.

[USMA tactical officers were supposed to wear shoes with hard heels on them so that cadets could hear them approaching. Max Thurman, a TAC, used a clever ruse to catch cadets unawares by wearing one tennis shoe.]

Sheldon J. Lustig, Class of 1953

One of my most memorable experiences involved the West Point Honor Code. As you may recall, many cadets in the Class of '53 (my class) were found on Honor arising from the "cribbing" scandal that occurred while I attended the Academy. During Plebe year, I roomed with three cadets, one of whom was a football player. At the end of Plebe year, we were informed that there would no longer be any four men rooms. After spending that difficult year together, we all wanted to remain together during our yearling year. In order to determine who would have to find other cadets to room with, we left the decision to the flip of a coin. I was the odd man out.

All throughout our yearling year, my plebe roommates seemed to give me the "cold shoulder." At the end of yearling year, I was shocked when their names were announced on the loudspeaker, along with others, ordering them to remain at West Point instead of accompanying the class on our summer field trip. This was the first indication that many of us had that a serious cribbing scandal was being investigated. It wasn't until after graduation, on my way to pilot training at Hondo AB, Texas, that I found out why my plebe roommates were essentially giving me the "silence" treatment the following year.

Two of the three former cadets were attending Texas University. I made a detour to Austin to see them. During an evening get-together in their apartment, they informed me that the reason they hardly spoke to me after plebe year was that they didn't want to slip up and possibly expose me to what was going on during our yearling year. I'll never forget their special effort to insulate me from the honor violations. As a result of a "flip of the coin," I never had to make that difficult decision whether to report honor violations that were being committed.

[Brigadier General Sheldon J. Lustig served in the Air Force for thirty years. He served in Vietnam and received the following awards: the Distinguished Service Medal, the Legion of Merit, the Bronze Star Medal, Air Force Commendation Medal four times, Vietnam Honor Medal First Class, and the Newman Medal awarded by the Society of American Military Engineers.]

Stacy L. Gervelis, Class of 2002

The story that stands out in my mind that I want to share isn't from West Point, but from my time in Iraq. During OIF II I was a military police platoon leader whose mission it was to coach, train, and mentor the

Iraqi police. The mission required us to work with the police everyday and spend at least eight hours with them training them how to police their country in a democratic way and not by using torture and intimidation. During the year there, I had the chance to get into many religious discussions with the Iraqis about Islam and other religions. In a world where the media portrays Islam as being very intolerant, surprisingly I had nothing but good experiences with them.

Inevitably the topic of religion came up and I would explain that I was Jewish and would wait for them to say something horrible about me or to stop talking to me. Remarkably they didn't. When I got more comfortable talking with my different police commanders I would ask them about their religion and why they fight all the time. Each one would tell me that Islam is a very tolerant religion and that they actually believe in the same prophets as the Jewish and Christian faith. Speaking with different people about their faiths opened my eyes a lot.

Not everyone in Iraq had a negative view of people who were Jewish; in fact I experienced a lot of religious tolerance. I also had waited to talk about religion until the people had gotten to know me, which may have helped. But my stereotype and preconceived notion of how I would be treated as a woman and as a Jew was shot down numerous times throughout my year in Iraq. I thought men wouldn't talk with me or do business with me, and I thought as soon as they found out my religious preference they would stop associating with me and I would be subject to harsh words or worse. Thankfully, none of that happened and instead I realized that I was the one who needed educating. I was being treated for who I was as an individual and not for what religion I fell under. It was an eye opening experience and a big learning point for me. I learned that I should not be so quick to judge other people or even not be so quick to expect to be judged. Whenever you go into a situation with your mind set of what other people think about you, you can miss out on a lot of very good friendships. I still keep in touch with some of the police commanders that I was fortunate enough to work with, and I'm glad that my eyes were opened.

[First Lieutenant Stacy L. Gervelis served in the Iraq war for two and one half years. She was awarded the Bronze Star for Valor.]

Aaron S. Attermann, Class of 2004

I found that the Jewish community at West Point was a much needed source of encouragement and inspiration. We were a very small group with the common attribute of religion to bind us together. I've also been enjoying that same bond out in the regular Army. The religious bond between Jews in the military is very strong as we are such a small population and so dispersed. When I was a new cadet we didn't have a rabbi for the first few weeks of Beast. About the 3rd week we finally got to meet the new rabbi. We all gathered in the chaplains office next to the mess hall and were just relaxing and enjoying some food during chaplains time. All of a sudden this huge man walks into the room with his fiancé and two daughters and is introduced to us as the rabbi. We look at the man who is smiling a huge smile and just overjoyed to be meeting us and we see that he is wearing airborne wings and has a Special Forces unit patch on his shoulder. We were simply amazed to have a rabbi who was in SF. We later leaned that he was the chaplain for SF while he was living in Israel and serving in the reserves. Of course Rabbi Huerta later led from the front and set the example for all of us as he deployed to Iraq at the kick off of the war, leaving behind his wife, and twelve children (one of which was newborn).

Arnold Winter, Class of 1949

I recall that as our Beast Barracks approached its end in late August (1945) we plebes in what was then Co. M-2 (to be later split into Co.'s L-2 and M-2) were ordered into the basements. It was there and in no uncertain terms that we were advised by a "Firstie" (whose name I prefer not to reveal in this insecure medium) that the first class—his class—had a member who was a "Negro" who was in flight training as a pilot and who would shortly be returning with his classmates for academics. We were instructed by this upperclassman that the "plebe system" did not exist insofar as our class conduct betwixt that upperclassman and members of our plebe class. I remember being taken aback by that direction from "authority." I am proud to say that insofar as I know the order was ignored by our classmates. I obviously do not have the perspective of the targeted upperclassman so I cannot be absolutely certain about how thoroughly that order (suggestion?) was carried out by our classmates; hopefully it was a wasted meeting and the suggestion" was totally ignored. The "black" upperclassman was later killed in an air accident—presumably he no longer pays a penalty for his ethnicity, wherever he may be.

Lawrence G. Michalove, Class of 1955

In September, 1954 the Jewish Chapel Choir was invited to New York City to sing at a ceremony marking the 300th anniversary of Jewish Settlement in the United States. As the ranking cadet, I was the chapel squad leader and choir director was classmate Norm Smith. We participated in the ceremony which took place at the Astor Hotel on October 20, 1954. A little known fact is the following: our choir was not the greatest, so to insure success, the "Supe" had our choir salted with a few members of the Corps of Cadets Glee Club. Needless to say, everything turned out just fine. No circumcisions were necessary.

Gary Bloomberg, Class of 1989

In my senior year, a group of my friends conducted a spirit mission prior to Army-Navy in which we took 45lb weights from the weight room and spelled out "Beat Navy" on the bottom of the Olympic Swimming Pool.

Steve Rotkoff, Class of 1977

The bottom line for me is that being a soldier and being a Jew have been compatible from the beginning. One of the things I love about both is that while neither is on the surface about social work and pulling up the less advantaged they both share this strong secondary theme. Judaism made me a better officer and the army made me a better Jew.

Barry Bort, Class of 1983

In late December 1982 Col Bernstein called me as CIC of Jewish Cadets to drive back to the Academy during winter break to participate in the ground breaking for the new cadet chapel. I consider that event as my fifteen minutes of fame in my life. I brought my father, a WWII veteran with me. The ceremony began at the Hotel Thayer for lunch. As CIC

I was interviewed by ABC television and a correspondent from the NY Times. Along with two or three other cadets, my photo was taken breaking ground and our photo appeared in the Poughkeepsie newspaper. That evening neighbors called the house to say they saw me on television. The next day my uncle called to say he was surprised during his train ride into NYC to unexpectedly read my quote in the NY Times. Thank you to everyone who contributed to the chapel fund drive and especially the anonymous last-minute donor who completed the necessary funding to beat the unquestionable deadline.

Eugene Fox, Class of 1956

The cadets need Jewish role models of officers still in service! Yesterdays heroes are just pictures on the wall. Take care of yourself. We are all getting older.

[Major General Eugene Fox served on active duty in the army for thirty-three years. His basic branch was field artillery. He served in Vietnam. He was awarded the Bronze Star Medal, Air Medal, Vietnam Awards, Distinguished Service Medal, Defense Superior Service Medal, Legion of Merit, Meritorious Service Medal, Army Commendation Medal, and the Parachute Badge.]

Kevin Price, Class of 1997

The Jewish Chapel was always a "safe haven" during the Beast Barracks Summer. The caretakers to local Jewish War Veteran groups took great care of us and made us look forward to each Friday night. The Passover Seder at the Hotel Thayer was one of my favorite events every year—it was encouraged to bring a non-Jewish friend, and it was a great time for them to learn about our customs and traditions. A lot of people have asked if I experienced any anti-Semitism at West Point or in the army. The answer is not really; I met a lot of people who "had never met" a Jewish person before, but mostly they were intellectually curious. As is the case with most minorities, once people get to know you, it makes very little difference what religion you are.

Irving B. Schoenberg, Class of 1948

West Point Off Broadway

Each year, as June Week and graduation draw nigh, the Corps of Cadets begins to salivate. First Classmen begin to think of class rings, new automobiles, officers' uniforms, graduation leave, first duty assignments and wedding ceremonies.

In the spring of 1947, all those happy thoughts got channeled into theatrics, song and dance that culminated in a cadet-written, cadet-produced and cadet-performed production called the 100th Night Show. It was the annual major project of the Dialectic Society. Two Jewish cadets of the class of 1947, Junius (Junie) J. Bleiman and Bernard (Bernie) J. Gardner, wrote the book for the 1947 show and they called it "Thumbs Up."

You may ask, why did they call it "Thumbs Up?" And why is this night's performance different from any other night? The answer lies in the fact that the show's plot is placed in the year 47 (get it?) BC, and at that time there is a fierce rivalry between the Roman Military Academy (RMA) and the Naval Academy of Annapolisia (NAA) in the not too-distant Kingdom of Annapolisia. The two academies have had a long-standing rivalry in all kinds of athletic activities, but none so contested as the meeting of the two gladiator teams in the highly hyped fall classic RMA–NAA game. To add to all that drama, the tyrannical King of Annapolisia has a beautiful daughter named Diana, who, much to the king's chagrin has fallen madly in love with a RMA first classman named Marcus Proficio.

Of course, the king is reluctant to have his daughter get romantically attached to anything associated with RMA, but she nevertheless manages to make a weekend trip to the RMA not only to observe the great game, but of course to spend time with her beloved Marcus.

The big game goes on and in the tradition of gladiator combat, the judges signal their decision on who wins and loses. Thumbs up is the sign for victory and thumbs down is the sign for defeat. It is thumbs up not only for the RMA, but for Diana and Marcus as well.

Could one call this a Jewish production? Perhaps. Not only were Bleiman and Gardner the book's authors, but Alan Gould, their classmate, was the Director of the Glee Chorus, which sang all the show tunes including "I Saw Love" with lyrics by Junie Beiman. Dick Littlestone (USMA

'47) played one of the judges who gave the thumbs up signal, and I played the part of the Greek general who was visiting RMA before the game was to be played. In addition to singing with the Chorus (composed mainly of the Cadet Glee Club), I was also part of a modern dance routine choreographed for the RMA cheerleaders.

My most unforgettable moment in the show came in Scene 2 of Act 1, as I made a grand entrance on stage wearing the helmet, armor and trappings of a Greek general making a diplomatic visit to the RMA. Cadets were always happy (even then) to have foreign dignitaries come visiting, because they usually got briefed during their visit about exercising their privilege of requesting the Academy's authorities to remove all punishment tours and confinements previously awarded the cadets by the Tactical Department.

It is important to note that the makeup for the Greek general's role was under the supervision of my Jewish classmate Joel Aron (USMA '48), head of the Makeup Department for the show. Using ether-glue, Joel carefully applied under my nose the large black mustache intended to demonstrate the Greek's military stature. When I entered onto the stage, the huge crowd was deadly silent anticipating my speech, which would liberate the punished cadets. I raised my arm in somewhat of a Hitlerian salute and was preparing to begin my oration. To gain the attention of the crowd and to lengthen the time of the proclamation I was to give, I inhaled as much air into my lungs as they would accommodate. In doing so, my mustache became unglued and was pulled into my mouth. I had no choice but to swallow hard so that I could bellow out my first few words, the signal for all hell to break out among the on-stage crowd. It was a scene similar to the popular show (in its day) "Hellzapoppin." Trying my best to carry on the theatrical tradition, the show must go on; I stayed in character for only the remaining minute as the curtain fell on the end of the act. I rushed backstage, stuck my finger down my throat, and as neatly as possible up-chucked the large black mustache. Joel, an academic "star man," who graduated number 2 in our Class of 1948, went on after he left the Corps of Engineers to become a very successful executive in IBM Corporation. He easily admitted that his skill as a makeup technician was not of the highest order.

Love Boat

The year was 1946. With WWII over, it was time for the military to take note of the lessons learned.

Military doctrine and training officials were in agreement: the landings in North Africa, the landing in Normandy on D-Day June 1944, and the many landings in the islands of the Pacific Area, proved that well orchestrated and executed amphibious assaults were critical to success in far-flung operations. One result: the training gurus at West Point decided that in the summer of 1946 the Class of 1948 needed to "get their feet wet," literally and figuratively while learning what amphib operations were all about.

Out of that decision grew Operation CAMID, joint training exercise involving the cadets (CA) of West Point and the Midshipmen (MD) of Annapolis. The USMA '48 cadets would function as infantrymen and wade ashore while the USNA '48B middies would function as the boat riders and watch from their dry perches up on the decks. Why the "B?" Because the Naval Academy decided to use a class numbering system different from that chosen by the Military Academy when the two schools split their original Classes of 1947. But before all of this watery adventure would take place down at Little Creek, Virginia, home of the Amphibious Fleet, the cadets and the middies scheduled to participate in the training would be allowed to go on summer leave.

I was home in St. Joseph, Missouri, enjoying life; sleeping late without an ear cocked to hear reveille. Mom's cooking, often specially ordered, was served cozily in the kitchen with the family. Nighttime was the time for merrymaking and fun. One evening I was out with a few of my long-time buddies at a favorite hangout. A couple of them had finished their military duty and were enrolled at the University of Missouri (Mizzu) trying to make up for the years spent in uniform. One of the Mizzu guys who was from Kansas City asked me if I knew a Jewish friend of his named Dick Rubenstein. Dick, he told me, had just finished two years at the Naval Academy, and therefore was a member of my counterpart class. "No," I said, "We've never met, but there is the possibility that we can meet later in the summer when our two classes are together at Operation CAMID." He gave me a good description of Dick Rubenstein:

a six-foot-one sandy-blonde who had starred in football at Southwest High School in Kansas City. I decided I'd do my best to find him among the other middies I might run into during the training. When the Mizzu boys got back to K.C., they'd tell Dick about me.

When we returned to the Academy from leave, we found cargo nets strung over the balcony rail overlooking the gym. They were put there to give us cadets the "opportunity" to go over the rail, carrying a full combat pack, and climb down the net, as we would be expected to do from a real live Navy ship onto a small landing craft which after loading would whisk up toward the "enemy shore." We were warned that a fall from such a net into the water between the big ship and the small landing craft could be fatal. The space between the big heaving ship and the small landing ship could quickly crush the fallen cadet.

Once we arrived in Virginia, we were quartered on board a troop ship along with all the middies. At sea, salt water is a deadly enemy to a M-1 rifle. Either clean it well and often, or the bore and its rifling gets rusty fast. Thus, were we cadets mandated to keep those rifles in good condition; they would have to pass inspection once we returned to parades and drilling at the Point.

CAMID was destined to be one of the most unforgettable episodes in my military life. It, more than anything else, convinced me that the Navy was not for me. But CAMID would reward me richly in a surprising way. One sunny afternoon out on deck, I was working on my "piece" (rifle), when I happened to glance up and see a middie passing by whom I thought might well be Midshipman Rubenstein. I identified him positively when I spotted his name stenciled on the back of his uniform. I could easily have tripped him using my rifle to prevent his getting away. Immediately, we both knew that the rendezvous predicted in St. Joe was about to happen. It was the meeting that would begin a life-long friendship . . . and more.

From that day on, Dick and I began a friendship that has lasted more than 59 years (as of this writing). We would renew our friendship on double-dates, and while still undergraduates after every Army-Navy game in Philadelphia. We would renew our friendship also in Kansas City or St. Joe while we both were on leave. His parents became my Uncle Leo and

Aunt Fan Rubenstein. My parents also "adopted" Dick. In 1949, I came to Kansas City from Smoky Hill AFB, Kansas, to be in his wedding.

On Christmas leave, 1954, I was invited to stay at Dick's house in Kansas City before returning to the University of Maryland where I was an Air Force ROTC instructor. When Aunt Fan found out I was to be in town, she invited me to join the dinner party for Dick and his wife, and Audrey (Dick's sister) and her husband. Included in the guest list was Dick's "little" cousin, Ann Hoffman, home for the holidays from Wellesley College, Mass. Ann and I met at the dinner. The following year, 1955, we were engaged, and in June 1956 we were married. Dick stood up for me at the wedding.

More information about Dick. In 1949, when his father Leo suffered a stroke and could no longer run his soft-drink bottle business, Dick was relieved from active duty in the Navy and given a compassionate discharge. The following year, when the Korean War began, Dick was recalled to duty and served for a couple of years at sea successively aboard two aircraft carriers: the Bon Homme Richard and the Kearsarge. He remained active in the Navy Reserve and finally retired as a "four-striper" captain.

If there is a moral to this story, it might be this: cadets and midshipmen can vigorously support their respective football team, can lose cadet bathrobes and midshipmen articles in their betting, but Jewish Academy graduates are loyal to their counterpart grads in another service. And it all happened because of a meeting on board what might be called The Love Boat.

The Congressman's Daughter

A professional soldier isn't trained to be a politician, although at times political influence could very well bring advancement in a soldier's career. In any case, it doesn't hurt to have friends or supporters in the Legislative Branch of government. So it was in 1946, in the spring of my yearling year, I decided to show my appreciation for having received my nomination to West Point from my hometown member of Congress, Representative Bill Cole of the 4th District of Missouri. One way to do that, I figured, was to invite his attractive daughter, Mary, to come to West Point for a weekend.

Should it be any weekend? No, it should be a special weekend, one which would allow me to impress Mary and her father. The weekend of the 100th Nite Show, in which I had an on-stage role, fit the bill. Mary Cole was a lovely, blonde young lady going to a finishing school in Washington, D.C. In my written invitation, I told her about the show, and suggested that she bring one of her friends along as a blind date for my roommate, John Delistraty. Mary responded quickly and wrote that she would be pleased to come to the Academy and would indeed bring one of her classmates as a date for John.

The show, called "Fantastica" borrowed freely from the old story of Rip Van Winkle who lived in the highlands around West Point, and added another modern twist. The main character was modeled after Marty Maher, the real-life retired sergeant who lived on the post for many years and taught swimming to cadets even though he himself could not swim a stroke. In the show, Rip Van Maher fell asleep and awoke 100 years later to find that things at West Point had changed radically in some ways, but in others not at all. The show was presented on a Saturday evening at the Post Theater, and Mary and her friend had excellent seats down front and center which had been given to me as a member of the cast. Mary's seat, it just so happened, was right beside Marty Maher's seat, and when Rip Van Maher was introduced on stage for the first time, Marty almost jumped out of his seat as he loudly proclaimed, "That's me!"

The following afternoon, I took Mary on a tour of West Point and we found ourselves on Flirtation Walk, of course. Passing below the rock with her accompanying cadet, if the "femme" fails to allow a kiss, then as the tradition states, "the Rock will rumble and the Academy will tumble to its very foundations." Mary couldn't bear the thought of destroying West Point, so she more than willingly obliged to carry on with the tradition.

Shortly after Mary and I had climbed the path leading up to the level of the Plain still hand in hand, I heard the call that every cadet dreads, "You man, halt!" It was Major Powell, one of the Tac Officers. I gave him my name and company as required and saluted knowing that I was in the initial stage of racking up a sizeable chunk of demerits. The next day on Company C-2's bulletin board was the unwanted noticed. I had been written up for (1) "holding hands in a public place," and (2) "wearing excessive lipstick." Beside my name was the dreaded symbol, the *, meaning that I was subject to punishment meted out by a board.

The next day, I was ordered to report to Lt. Colonel Robert Strong, a Tac who was also an Air Force pilot. I reported to him, was told to stand at ease, and awaited the bad news. He first asked me who the young lady I was escorting was. I replied, "My Congressman's daughter, sir." Then, to my surprise, he asked, "Was she pro" (cadet slang for proficient)? "Yes," I said, "2.85 (on a grading scale max of 3.0)." "That will be all, Mr. Schoenberg." I saluted and departed. My fate had been sealed. When the award sheet appeared on the company bulletin board, I found that I had been awarded a total of seven demerits, the maximum that did not entail either walking punishment tours or confinement to quarters. When my company mates read my "sentence," they wanted to know exactly how they could measure "excessive" lipstick the next time they were faced with the same situation. The story has a happy ending because Lt. Colonel Bob Strong showed that he had an understanding heart, and maybe also because he was also the brother of my classmate Gordon Strong. I figured that if the Air Force had other officers like him, I would willingly serve under them.

Cadet Usher, Ma'am

During its Cow Year, the Class of 1948 was exposed to a course in world literature. Time was allocated to the study of Edmond Rostand's inspiring play "Cyrano de Bergerac." Because Cyrano was a world-class swordsman, a poet and a soldier, those attributes made him an exemplary subject for study.

At the time that Jose Ferrer, the highly regarded actor, was starring in the play on Broadway in New York City, I was corresponding with a young lady who was a student at Connecticut College for women in New London. She had been struck by the acting bug and planned for a career in the theater. With a weekend pass at my disposal, I saw a great opportunity for not only making an impression on the Conn College lass, but at the same time enhancing my depth of understanding of Rostand's playwriting skill. So I sent out an invitation to Lois to come to the city and accompany me to the play. She couldn't resist, and the weekend plan was quickly set in motion. At the Saturday matinee performance, Lois and I were both thoroughly pleased with Ferrer's portrayal of Cyrano.

During intermission, we had gone to the lobby and I was waiting for Lois to return from the ladies' room. At this point, I must tell the reader that in 1946, although the end of WWII had been written into history, nevertheless the superintendent of the Military Academy decided that his cadets would continue to wear the uniform when away from the institution. So there I stood in the lobby, in my dress gray splendor, when a nice little old lady approached and stood before me.

"Young man," she said, "Could you tell me where I might find the ladies' room?" Having seen which direction Lois had gone, I told the little old lady where she would find the facility. She smiled at me, then opened her handbag and fished out a dime, which she offered to me with "thanks." Somewhat confused and surprised by her gesture, I said, "I'm sorry, ma'am, but I'm a West Point cadet." She quickly withdrew the coin, returned it to her purse, and replaced it with another coin, apologetically handing me a quarter.

A Lesson in Tolerance

In 1947, each of the cadet companies in the Corps of Cadets was made up of about 100 men from the four classes. In Washington Hall, where the cadets ate their meals, each company was assigned 10 tables to accommodate its 100 cadets. The table commandant was a first classman and he had with him one or more second classmen, one or more third classmen, and usually three fourth classman (plebes).

Cadets could expect to continue to sit at their assigned table for six weeks. At the end of one of the six-week periods, I was charged with organizing new table assignments, putting ten cadets at a table in the company area with the usual mix of classes at each table. Accordingly, I made the announcement at a company formation that at the up-coming Sunday dinner, the new table assignments would go into effect. The assignments and names were posted on the company bulletin board.

As table commandant of one of the tables, I had purposely put Second Classman Ed Howard at my table, because I was on the Editorial Staff and Ed was on the Photographic Staff of the Pointer Magazine, the Academy's cadet publication. Extracurricular activities had to be taken care of when time could be found, time that was not already claimed by academics, military training and other demands. Time was not to be squandered; it was precious. Ed Howard had come to West Point after two years at Dartmouth College, the prestigious Ivy League school. He was an excellent photographer, and a real asset to the Pointer Magazine. He was also black, one of only a few black cadets at the Academy at that time. Ed and I both knew that we could take care of many of the magazine's needs for photography by holding our "job conferences" during any or all of the three daily meals. It was an effective use of time.

Shortly after I made the announcement of the new seating assignments, two yearlings, third classmen, came to me and said they had a request to make. They asked to be assigned to a table at which my classmate Hank Stelling was commandant. I told them that I could probably arrange the switch by taking two yearlings from Hank's table and putting them on my table. I did, however, want to know what was behind the request. The answer I got from one of the two was, "Bill is from Alabama, I'm from Louisiana and we don't want to sit with Mr. Howard." I asked, "Is that the only reason?" Their joint reply was a firm, "Yes."

I told them their request was denied for several reasons. First, Ed Howard was a year ahead of them and would be an officer in 1949, a year before they would be commissioned as officers, assuming that they did in fact graduate in 1950. Secondly, Ed might well be their commanding officer at some point in their respective careers. Thirdly, they themselves might at some time even be the commander of an all black unit (it wasn't until 1948 that President Harry Truman signed the Executive Order which integrated the armed forces, resulting in black officers and men serving with whites, Hispanics and other races in one military unit). I told the yearlings they needed to change their way of thinking and adjust to matters over which they had no control.

The two southerners then told me that if I didn't move them to another table they would not eat. It was a stupid answer and they knew it, because there are no restaurants or other facilities at the Academy catering to cadets who would not be eating their meals in Washington Hall. Yes, there was the "boodelers" where cadets during their free time (of which there was very little) could buy ice cream, candy bars, etc. But of course meal formations were mandatory, and to miss one would subject the absentee to severe punishment. The conversation ended. I dismissed the two, curious to see what they would do when they came to my table for dinner on Sunday.

Naturally, they came. They sat at the table, but they didn't eat. Not one bite. They did give me looks that let me know they were not happy with my decision. At breakfast the next morning, we would see the next stage of their determination to abstain from food in Ed Howard's presence. The looks continued, but they made periodic stabs at the food on their plates. Only a portion of their meal did they consume. By lunch on that next full day, those two prejudiced third classmen were so hungry I was convinced they would devour the wooden table legs if there were no other edibles available.

There are some interesting facts to be told in the postscript to this lesson in tolerance. I've not had the interest to investigate what kind of careers those two members of the class of 1950 had in the years after they left the Academy. I do know that Ed Howard had a distinguished career in the Signal Corps, earned an MSEE degree from Purdue University, held several very responsible positions in the Joint Staff and other offices at the Pentagon, and retired as a colonel after thirty years of service. His youngest grandson, Scott Bostic, was scheduled to graduate from West Point in the Class of 2005. Scott's father, James Bostic, was a White House Fellow in the same class with General Colin Powell.

A Tale of Three Jewish Graduates

West Point is a hallowed episode in the life of a cadet. It is not just the three or more years of bonding and camaraderie, years during which a cadet is wrapped up in and bound by West Point's rules, regulations, physical demands, and Code of Honor. What affects does the Academy have on a cadet? What does the Academy plant in the mind and body of a cadet during those years within the Gothic walls, on its parade ground and athletic fields, in its classrooms, and out in the realms and reaches of military training? Those formative years in large measure determine the character, and, yes, even the future of each man or woman who treads those hallowed grounds. West Point molds more than individual character; it influences a cadet's outlook on life and even to a large extent the formed philosophy he or she will carry forward into the years after West Point.

This is the story of three Jews who graduated from West Point and whose lives were enriched and influenced by their relationships as classmates, as officers, as friends, and even as business associates. This is the story of Alan Henry Gould, Bernard William Abrams, and Irving Bernard Schoenberg.

West Point was Alan's ultimate goal. He was motivated to get the education he needed to gain admission to the Academy. Bernie was determined to gain recognition as a potential military leader in the Army ROTC program at Boys High School where he was the Cadet Colonel, the highest-ranking cadet in the City of Atlanta. Irv had the "chutzpah" to have his high school yearbook entry read that he would attend "West Point" where most of his classmates merely expressed their hope of attending college or trade school.

Alan came to West Point from Rochester, New York. Bernie entered West Point from Atlanta, Georgia. Irv came to West Point from St. Joseph, Missouri. Prior to coming to the U.S. Military Academy, all three had been university students. Alan had two years at the University of Rochester. Bernie had a semester at Georgia Tech. Irv enlisted in the Army reserve immediately after high school shortly after being nominated as a First Alternate for appointment to the Academy. During his first year of service, he was sent to the University of Kansas and then to Cornell University before entering West Point. All three had been nominated by a member of Congress and appointed cadets of the United States to the U.S. Military Academy by President Franklin D. Roosevelt. Those three and 744 other young men entered the Academy in July 1944, as members of the class of 1947.

Irv recalls the first time he met Alan and Bernie. It was during the very earliest days of their Beast Barracks in 6th New Cadet Company. The three of them were down in the "sinks" of Central Barracks engaged in "a technical military assignment," stenciling their names on the backs of their fatigue uniforms. Their determination not to fail but rather to meet and master the challenges of Beast Barracks carried them through those first six grueling weeks and they were assigned to Company C-2. For two years as Plebes and Yearlings they were company-mates surviving the demands of academics, the pressures of the tactical department, and the Master of the Swords' physical requirements.

In 1946, at the end of their first two years as cadets, the three cadets were part of a major separation. The allies had been victorious in Europe and the Pacific and WWII had ended. Army, in its wisdom, decided that the Academy should return to its long-standing, pre-war 4-year curriculum. To accomplish this major shift, the class of 1947 would be split into two parts, one part to graduate as the class of 1947 in June 1947, and the second part to graduate as the class of 1948 in June 1948. The Academy leadership, primarily on the basis of age, made the decision as to which cadets would graduate in 1947 and which in 1948. Those who were born in October 1925 or earlier were placed in the class of 1947. All others of the original class of 1947 were placed in the class of 1948. There were some exceptions. For example, where family hardships would result from placement in the class of 1948, a cadet would be allowed to graduate in 1947. Alan and Bernie fell into the "older" group, and would become members of the class of 1947. Irv, the youngest of the three, became a member of the class of 1948.

Along with that change in class designations came a major reorganization of the Corps of Cadets. In 1946, the number of cadet companies increased from sixteen to twenty-four. There would still be two regiments, but each regiment would consist of twelve companies rather than the previous eight. In that reorganization, Alan and Bernie were assigned to Company D-2 of the First Battalion of the Second Regiment, and Irv was assigned to Company F-2 of the Second Battalion of the Second Regiment. Because of the reorganization, no longer would the three cadets be in either the same company or the same battalion. Nor would they any longer be attending any of the same classes as before. As First Classmen Alan and Bernie would be taking courses that Irv, the Second Classman, would not be taking. As a Second Classman, Irv helped reinstate the "title" Cow, the designation that had been used for third-year cadets when the Corps followed a four-year academic schedule. Indeed the division into two classes and the reorganization separated Irv from Alan and Bernie. Although the three would no longer march in the same units at parades or attend the same classes, they were still together at Jewish Cadet Chapel on Sunday mornings, at "hops" (dances), and other social events. Their extracurricular activities did bring them together at times as seen in the listing of those activities below.

Alan Gould

Alan came to West Point having had two years of college in mechanical engineering. He also had training as a professional singer. With his great voice, it was only natural that as a cadet he was soon exercising his vocal chords and his knowledge of music for the benefit of the Academy. In the caption accompanying his picture in the 1947 *Howitzer* there was this description: "He loved music and put all his energies into making a success of the Glee Club." So it was not surprising that he became the Director of the Glee Club as well as the Director of the Jewish Chapel Choir.

He also applied his talent to the 100th Nite show for all three of his years at West Point. And as First Classman, he was one of a few cheerleaders who helped the cadets let the football players out on the field know that the Corps was behind them and lending their voices in support of gaining victory. The *Howitzer* also described him as "suave, polished, a gentleman in every sense of the word." It is an apt description of a man with Alan's ability and intelligence.

Bernie Abrams

Bernie came to West Point from Atlanta having completed one semester at Georgia Tech. At Boys High he had been the Cadet Colonel, the highest-ranking cadet in the Junior ROTC program in the city of Atlanta. His classmates called him "colonel" and no one disputed the title. In the *Howitzer*, accompanying his picture, is this description: "extremely conscientious and very efficient he was found to be successful in all undertakings . . . His good nature and courteous consideration of others has endeared Bernie to the hearts of all who knew him and earmark him to be a born leader."

He too was in the 100th Nite Show for each of his three years at the Academy. He was a "joiner" with membership in the Debating Society, Sailing Club, and Ski Club. He served on the Lecture Committee and as a *Howitzer* representative.

Irv Schoenberg

Like Bernie, Irv too was a product of the Army Junior ROTC program in his hometown of St. Joseph, Missouri. As a Cadet Company Commander he got his first real taste of leadership. With his father's overseas service in WWI, and his reading of all the books about West Point in the St. Joseph library, he was determined to compete for an appointment to West Point. Once at the Academy, he found many opportunities to exercise his interest and abilities. The write-up in the 1948 *Howitzer* is a fair picture of his four years as a cadet: " 'Ye Old Ed' shuffled his stack of letters from lonesome femmes and then, remembering a Hop Committee meeting, went dashing off. Only in the 8 (Cadet Brigade Headquarters) was more activity to be found . . ."

For three of his four cadet years, he sang, danced, and acted in the 100th Nite shows along with cast members Alan and Bernie. He suffered a broken arm in a toboggan accident during his Plebe winter, so he had to be excused from the first show that year. For two years on the editorial staff of the *Pointer* Magazine, he was editor of the Femmes Page. He served on the Hop Committee and on the *Howitzer* staff. He sang in the Glee Club and in the Jewish Cadet Chapel Choir (with Bernie) under Alan's leadership. And he was a three-year veteran of the Handball club.

The Great Separation

Irv was dramatically separated from Alan and Bernie on 3 June 1947, Graduation Day for the Class of 1947. Alan and Bernie pinned on their gold bars and became Army second lieutenants. On that same day, Irv added another stripe on the sleeve of his cadet dress coat signifying his advancement to First Classman in the Corps with still another year at the Academy before he too could pin on his own gold bars.

After graduation leave, Alan would be in Texas earning his wings as a pilot in the Army Air forces. Bernie would be making his mark as an infantry officer, first in Kansas and then in Germany.

Did their careers and their futures cross paths again? Yes, destiny would play its hand.

Alan Gould

Having won his wings, Alan flew B-29 aircraft in the 91st Strategic Reconnaissance Group, a part of the Strategic Air Command (SAC). His missions, many of them classified, took him to places not well known to most people. In 1949, the 91st Group was moved from McGuire AFB, New Jersey, to Barksdale AFB, Shreveport, Louisiana. There he and Irv would find themselves reunited as members of the 4th Air Division. But they would not be together long, because in 1950, the Air Force selected Alan to attend the Air Force Institute of Technology at Wright-Patterson AFB, Dayton, Ohio. Following that schooling, in 1951, he was awarded a Master's degree in Industrial Engineering.

His next assignment was with the Air Depot Group at Harmon AFB in Newfoundland, where the cold weather was a hazardous element of their air operations. To utilize his industrial engineering education, in 1953 the Air Force sent him to the Lockheed aircraft plant in Marietta, Georgia, a suburb of Atlanta. At Lockheed, he had oversight responsibility for millions of dollars worth of machinery and tools strategically placed there by the Air Force.

Because Bernie Abrams had been medically retired from the Army in 1952, for reasons to be explained later, he was in Atlanta working as an executive in Abrams Industries, the firm founded by his father in the early '20s. So, with Bernie in town and Alan assigned in one of the suburbs, they were reunited in Atlanta.

In 1955, Alan's wife Mimi was diagnosed with a serious heart problem. Soon thereafter, she became one of the first persons in the United States to undergo open-heart surgery. Putting her organizational ability to use, she was instrumental in founding the Mended Hearts Society and became the president of the Georgia chapter. The doctors told

Alan the physical demands that would be placed on Mimi as she moved with him from one military assignment to another would make it impossible for her to fulfill her role as a military wife. Captain Gould had no option other than to resign his commission and to seek employment in civilian life.

He was carefully considering, but had not yet accepted, a job offer from a large company in the mid-west, when Bernie asked Alan to join him as an officer in Abrams Industries (AI). At the time, AI was in the process of starting a new subsidiary, a company that would manufacture store fixtures. Alan's degree in industrial engineering and his military experience would play well together in establishing and operating the new manufacturing facility. The new company was called Abrams Fixture Corporation (AFC) and Alan was its president.

Within a few years, AFC was supplying well-designed and -constructed wood and metal store fixtures for such well-known merchant firms as W.T. Grant, J.C. Penney, Montgomery Ward, and Kmart. Later they would add Wal-Mart and Home Depot to their list of customers. Alan's reputation in the store fixture industry grew steadily and he was elected to the presidency of the National Association of Store Fixture Manufacturers, the organization to which belonged the most respected firms in the industry.

In 1971, Alan had a rare opportunity to enter into a partnership he helped create. As President of Winston Homes, Inc., he could employ his talents and skills in a start-up company producing modular housing. After he left AFC, he was in south Georgia working hard to prove that the modular housing was a viable and profitable concept. Unfortunately, during those few years with Winston the economy took a nosedive, and in 1977 Alan decided to apply his knowledge and experience elsewhere.

Again, Bernie offered Alan a chance to return to AFC as chairman of the board. Alan accepted the offer and the two were united once more. That combination lasted several more years until Alan decided that he wanted to be the master of his own destiny and began his business as a real-estate developer, a business he enjoys today.

Bernie Abrams

Following graduation from West Point and after a half-year of training in the States, Bernie was assigned to the 26th Infantry in Bamberg, Germany, where he served for two years. During those two years in Europe, Bernie's father had applied argument and pressure, urging him to complete his three-year obligation of service in the Army and then to resign his commission in order to begin assuming executive roles in Abrams Industries.

By the time he got on the boat bringing him back to the U.S. in 1950, he had practically decided that he would follow his father's desires and begin a career in Atlanta with Abrams Industries. It was while he was on the Atlantic Ocean that he learned of the North Korean army attack on the forces of South Korea.

The dialogue between Bernie and his father was not recorded, but it was Al Abrams trying to convince his son, Bernie, to accept his place in the family business. But Bernie's decision was to stay in the Army. His rationale: his country was at war. He had been trained as an infantry officer and his place was with the Army.

Having made the decision not to resign his commission, and following a short leave in the States, he was soon on his way to join the 15th Infantry Regiment of the 3rd Division. His first assignment was as a platoon leader in a 81MM mortar company. Promoted to captain in 1951, he was a company commander in the Regiment.

His company was heavily engaged in combat. With his key officers and non-coms gathered to prepare for action, a North Korean mortar shell exploded in their midst. Bernie was facing away from the explosion and was hit by shrapnel in both legs. Several of the men around him were killed and others badly wounded. Bernie was treated in the field and then evacuated to a hospital in Japan. For his service in combat he was awarded the Silver Star, the Bronze Star Medal (Valor), the Purple Heart (twice), and the Combat Infantry Badge.

Al Abrams got word that Bernie had been wounded and though it was unusual, he managed to get to Japan to visit Bernie in the hospital. The doctors told Al Abrams that for a while they were not sure that Bernie would survive his wounds. Later they told Al Abrams that Bernie came close to losing both legs, but they were able to save them. However, it was doubtful that Bernie would ever be able to walk without crutches or braces. Bernie was sent to Walter Reed Hospital in Washington, D.C., where he received rehabilitation treatment for more than a year.

While he was still a patient at Walter Reed, and because he had received so many units of blood during his treatment, the Red Cross asked Bernie to appear in a video with President Eisenhower. In his uniform with his decorations attesting to his combat record, he chatted with the President about the life-saving efforts of the Red Cross and the importance of the Blood Program. The video and still photographs of the meeting are historical documents.

In the summer of 1952, Air Force Captain Irv Schoenberg finished his tour of duty at Kadena Air Base in Okinawa. He had served as a member of the 307th Bomb Wing whose B-29 aircraft flew missions over Korea. His duty assignment was as Assistant Professor of Air Science in the Air Force ROTC detachment at the University of Maryland in College Park, Maryland. College Park was only a relatively short drive to Walter Reed hospital and Irv was able to visit Bernie on several occasions. During one of those visits, Bernie suggested to Irv that he might be interested in getting to know an attractive young lady hematologist who worked in the hospital and had assisted Bernie in his rehabilitation. Never one to pass up a good lead, Irv did take Naomi out to dinner and to the theater more than once. No great romance or marriage resulted from that encounter.

In 1952, Captain Bernie Abrams was retired from the Army for medical reasons. He returned to Atlanta and devoted his leadership and talent to the family business. He was highly instrumental in the growth of Abrams Industries and its several divisions. When his father retired and moved to Florida in 1972, Bernie was named chairman and chief executive officer of the company. He served the company until 1995 and when he retired he was named chairman emeritus.

But Bernie was a man of many interests and gave freely of his time and resources. He never stopped his devotion to the Army and his record so clearly reflects that devotion. Early on, he recognized the need for a strong and efficient USO in Atlanta. He served as Director of the USO

Council of Georgia and received its Patriot Award. The USO center at the Atlanta Airport is one of the busiest and is also considered one of the finest in the country, thanks in large part to Bernie's generosity.

He was appointed Civilian Aide to the Secretary of the Army in 1978 and held the appointment until leaving as Civilian Aide Emeritus in 1985, following a parade in his honor at Ft. McPherson, Georgia. He was awarded the Outstanding Civilian Service Award by the Secretary of the Army. The Association of the Army also recognized his contributions to the Army by awarding him the highly regarded Creighton W. Abrams Award. Bernie served as President of the West Point Society of Atlanta and was named a Distinguished Graduate of the Society in 1997. He held many national offices in the Association of the U.S. Army. In 1998, the Association of Graduates named him a Distinguished Graduate of the U.S. Military Academy.

In Atlanta's community affairs, Bernie was a recognized leader. He was the 1975–76 general campaign chairman of Atlanta's United Way that raised millions of dollars. As a long-time supporter of the Boy Scouts of America he served as president of the Atlanta Area Council and was presented the Silver Beaver Award, one of the highest in scouting.

He was also dedicated to Jewish causes. He served as president of the Gate City Lodge of B'nai B'rith and an active member of the board of his synagogue, The Temple. When the drive began to raise money to build a Jewish chapel at West Point, Bernie became one of the driving forces that lead to construction of the Jewish Cadet Chapel. He also contributed to the interior furnishings of the Jewish Cadet Chapel.

Convinced of the importance of Israel to the Jewish people, he personally financed a trip to Israel for a member of the U.S. Congress and escorted him on that trip. Bernie wanted the member to have a better understanding of the threat facing Israel in the Middle East.

Bernie died on 10 December 2001. He was buried with full military honors at Arlington National Cemetery. Had he been able to observe it (and maybe he did), he would have been absolutely pleased. He was a soldier to the very end.

Irv Schoenberg

When Irv took his graduation physical exam, the doctor told him that his eyes were not quite good enough to enter pilot training, but once he got away from academics and the books, there was a good chance that the eyes would come around and he could then shoot for pilot training. But the "new" Air Force beckoned and he was still going to employ his talents as a member of the flying fraternity, either in the air or on the ground.

As an historical note, the Defense Act of 1947 had created the U.S. Air Force and divorced it from the Army. Just prior to June 1948, when Irv and his classmates in the Class of 1948 were ready to graduate, the Army and the USAF correctly and courageously recognized that without an Air Force Academy there would be no Academy-trained officers being commissioned into the Air Force. So the "big guys" in Washington agreed to have 40 percent of the class of 1948 go directly into the Air Force. There was nothing in agreement saying that the 40 percent would remain constant. There was, it seemed, an unstated belief that eventually an Air Force Academy would be established. And it was, with the first class of cadets entering in 1955 at the Academy's temporary site at Lowry Air Force Base outside of Denver, Colorado. The USAFA class of 1959 graduated after six months at the newly opened Air Force Academy, Colorado Springs, Colorado. As another historical note: in 1949, a group of graduates of the U.S. Naval Academy were commissioned directly into the USAF.

Irv chose to accept the opportunity to become a part of the Strategic Air Command at Smoky Hill AFB, Salina, Kansas, out in the middle of the state. After a while he would take that physical exam and try to pass the eye requirements for pilot training. He tried several times, but the eyes never got much better. He was offered the chance to go into navigator training, but that had no appeal and he eventually decided that he would make his Air Force career down other paths.

Administration was the path on which he found himself. He started as a squadron adjutant at SHAFB and then Assistant Base Adjutant at Barksdale AFB, Louisiana. In 1951, with the war in Korea hot and heavy, he was assigned to the 307th Bomb Wing in Okinawa. The crews of the

307th were flying missions over Korea. Irv's job was Assistant Wing Inspector General. In 1952, near the end of his tour in Okinawa, the Air Force let it be known that it was looking for officers to serve as instructors in the Air Force ROTC program. Although Captain Schoenberg had requested duty at any school on the West coast, he got orders to report to the University of Maryland, College Park, MD to serve as Assistant Professor of Air Science. In 1954, he was selected by the Air Force Aide to President Eisenhower to be a White House Social Aide. It was a duty in addition to his teaching at the University of Maryland. His two years of serving the President turned out to be one of Irv's most memorable duties. Ike and Mamie Eisenhower treated the Air Force, Army, Navy, and Marine Corps aides almost as adopted sons.

By the end of his three years at Maryland, he had gotten a Master's Degree in International Relations and was ready for his next assignment. At that point, his Air Force mentor, Major General Joe Kelly (USMA class of 1932), Director of Legislative Liaison (L&L) in the Office of the Secretary of the Air Force, brought Irv to the Pentagon to serve under him in L&L. Irv's work with Congress was demanding but interesting. By 1959, Major Schoenberg was the Executive Officer in L&L.

Irv wanted the opportunity for command, and his wish came true with the help of a colonel friend in the Pentagon. With that help he was assigned to the 585th Tactical Missile Group in Bitburg, Germany. The group was equipped with the Matador and later the Mace missile, the very first tactical missiles deployed by the Air Force. Those missiles were actually radio-controlled aircraft positioned during the Cold War, and ready if needed to bring significant damage to the USSR in hot war. The missiles of his unit and the other units in the Group were on alert 7 days a week, 24 hours each day. He served first as Commander of one of the Group's three flights, and then as the Group Executive Officer.

On his return to the states in 1962, Irv was back in the Pentagon again, this time as Chief of Tactical Missiles in the Tactical Division of Air Force Operations. In that assignment he was involved with the removal from Turkey of the long-range Jupiter missiles targeted against USSR. When the Russians agreed to move their missiles from the Caribbean during the Cuban Missile Crisis, the Jupiters in Turkey were also removed.

In 1964, he was assigned once more to the Office of the Secretary of the Air Force, this time as Chief, Special Projects Branch, where he worked closely with Secretary of the Air Force Eugene M. Zuckert. When Secretary Zuckert retired, in July 1965, Irv, than a lieutenant colonel, was selected to be Deputy Executive Assistant to the Under Secretary of the Air Force. He left that position in 1966 to attend the nine-month course at the Industrial College of the Armed Forces in Washington D.C. He was promoted to colonel in 1966, and shortly thereafter earned a Master of Science Degree in Business Administration. In 1967, he was chosen to be Executive Assistant to the Under Secretary of the Air Force, a position he held until 1969.

Next, he was ordered to Wright-Patterson AFB, Ohio, to assume command of the Air Force Contract Maintenance Center, a worldwide organization with detachments in the U.S., Europe, the Middle East (including Israel), and Asia. One year later, he was moved to Robins AFB, Georgia, one of the five major Air Force depots where he became Director of Material Management (a job calling for a brigadier general). Finally, on Saturday, 31 June 1973, he retired from the Air Force after a total of 30 years in the Army and Air Force. Bernie Abrams and Alan Gould drove down to Warner Robbins from Atlanta for Irv's retirement ceremony and to be witness to his farewell to the Air Force.

Just as Alan had joined Abrams Industries (AI), Irv, too, was employed by the company, effective Sunday, 1 July, one day after his official retirement from the Air Force. Irv "reported for duty" on Monday, 2 July. For the next ten years he would serve as an executive in Abrams Fixture Corporation, and in the following eight years he would serve as a group vice president in the corporate offices of Abrams Industries. In 1990, at age 65, he retired from AI.

Community Service

Bernie set a pattern for community service by personal example. When he was Chairman of the Metro Atlanta United Way Campaign, both Alan and Irv worked as loan executives from AI. They and many others helped Bernie successfully raise millions of dollars to reach the highest goal ever achieved in Atlanta campaign. Alan and Irv would assist in subsequent United Way campaigns, each time filling important roles. With encouragement from Bernie, Irv was voted in as a member of the Kiwanis Club of Atlanta, one of the oldest and largest clubs in International Kiwanis. Irv would eventually be elected as President of the Club and designated a Distinguished President. He is still active in the club after 29 years of membership. Irv has served on the Board of Boys and Girls Clubs of Metro Atlanta for many years. He has also served for years on the Board of Hillside Hospital, the oldest charitable institution in Atlanta. Alan and Irv followed Bernie's lead in continuing their activity in the West Point Society of Atlanta. Alan and Irv and their families have held membership and leadership positions in Temple Sinai in Atlanta. They have also supported the Jewish Cadet Chapel at West Point, one of Bernie's cherished works. The classes of 1947/1948 Jewish Cadet Chapel Fund attest to that dedication.

Atlanta's Three Graduates

Many Jews in Atlanta found it hard to believe that Alan, Bernie, and Irv were not only Jewish graduates of the U.S. Military Academy, but classmates as well. When a Jew in Atlanta made that discovery, it usually brought a look of amazement and pride to his or her face. And it should have.

Epilogue

At West Point, friendships are born and the ties that bind classmates together for all of their lives may loosen over the many years, but they are never severed. Bernie Abrams died on 18 December 2001, but his memory and his influence remain strong in the minds of his classmates, Alan and Irv. Bernie's legacy, his dedication to West Point and its code of Duty, Honor, and Country, is carried on in the minds and actions of Alan Gould and Irv Schoenberg.

Jonathan Aaronson, Class of 1961, won the Eastern League Championship in the Flying Rings in 1959 and 1960. In 1960 he won the same event in the NCAA competition. The flying rings event no longer exists in gymnastics; the event is now the still rings. The flying rings were similar to a trapeze without a connecting bar between the two legs of the apparatus. The gymnast, grasping a ring in each hand, would execute a series of movements while swinging. He would increase the swing and terminate his routine with a flying dismount.

Bernard Greenbaum, Class of 1949

A few weeks before upperclassmen's Christmas furlough, I convinced my skeptical father to smuggle a bottle of wine to me for the "special event" plebes were expected to stage for the upperclassmen's last evening meal. For three weeks the bottle was hidden under my wall locker, then nervously sneaked out to formation under my arm and under my cape, and carefully squeezed during the march to the mess hall. Our table was located almost directly beneath the "poop deck" where the Cadet OD and the commissioned OIC were seated. I managed to slip the bottle out from under my arm to a spot under the table. Keeping it under the table, I poured a small amount into a GI coffee cup, and in the usual plebe-announcing voice I blasted, "Special beverage for the head of the table, sir!" then, "Special beverage for mister so and so, sir!" The head of the table received his cup, sniffed it, and with eyes wide as saucers, looked straight up to see if anyone on the "poop deck" was watching. He, and then all the rest of the upperclassman finished off the illicit drinks and passed their cups down to a table for a fragrance changing shot of coffee. We were all thinking the same thing: ten of us (including the plebes) were vulnerable to major slugs: nine months confinement and innumerable punishment tours for introducing an alcoholic beverage into the Cadet Mess, and then brazenly drinking it literally under the noses of the authorities. I enlisted the waiter to spirit away the bottle (in exchange for the small remaining amount in it) and the deed was done. It was a daring gamble that we had won! Of course the table commandant ordered the plebes to "fall out" and enjoy the dinner. A couple of weeks after the upper classes returned to West Point I was crossing North Area of Barracks in what was apparently a less-than-perfect plebe posture. Being a Central Area plebe, I might as well have been in a foreign country. Far behind me I heard an upper class voice: "You man, halt!" click, click, I halted. Then, approaching footsteps and, somewhat closer, the same voice, "Who are you mister?" My reply, in my most plebe-like voice: "Mister Greenbaum, sir." More footsteps and then a smiling upperclassman's face right in front of mine: "Oh, so YOU'RE Mister Greenbaum! POST!" The scene was repeated several times over the following few days and weeks in a variety of locations. Apparently reports of the "wine caper" had swept through the corps. Even certain upperclassmen in my own company who had apparently been intent on making a real cadet out of this gross plebe, adopted more gentle approaches. The "wine caper" had effectively ended my plebe year.

[Bernard Greenbaum spent eighteen years as the president (unpaid) of the U.S. Army Europe Retiree Council. He was awarded the Secretary of the Army Award for Exceptional Public Service, eight years concurrently as Member of Chief of Staff of the Army Retiree council. Colonel Greenbaum served in the Army for twenty-eight years as a Corps of Engineers officer, plus two years as an enlisted man prior to entering West Point. He served in Vietnam. He was awarded the Bronze Star Medal, the Legion of Merit, and the Service Commendation Medal. Bernie, my classmate, told me that during Beast Barracks, the rousing music of the Hell Cats—the drum, bugle, and fife group which played reveille and at lunch marches To the Mess Hall—kept him from resigning. They also stiffened my spine; one would have to be dead not to so react to their military music.]

Tatiana Blanc, Class of 2008

I won't forget when one Saturday we had a parade. I was tasked to march with another company and I felt really sorry for myself as these unknown upperclassmen were giving me a hard time. Then, that company's first sgt. said they didn't need me anymore and when I went back to my company all the ranks were filled. My training sgt. pointed to the Air Force tunnel and said, "Go and don't look back." I never scampered so quickly in all my life, afraid they might change their mind about letting me off from parading.

Daniel Dorchinsky, Class of 1992

Trumbull, CT is only about 1.5 hours away so my grandparents, parents, relatives used to visit as much as possible, which was a huge help during plebe year. I remember one Friday evening during Beast Barracks that at the last minute I thought about going to services. It was the night all plebes were going to be introduced to the congregation/community. Of course, I was tied up with some nonsense that I can't remember and ended up going late. I had the sense that my grandfather or father might be there. Because I was late, I sat in the back row until my name was called when I moved up to the pulpit. That's when my brother saw me for the first time since R. Day (he had been cussing my grandfather out for having dragged him up to the Academy to say hello to me and I wasn't even at services. After the ceremony, my brother tried to talk to me and all I remember was that there was food available (hot dogs). I ate six before I even acknowledged his presence.

Meagan Williams, Class of 2005

I grew up in a military family and I don't think that my parents ever expected that I would even want to join the Army, and certainly not even West Point. I had a great deal of support from the community at Fort Leavenworth, KS, where I spent all four years of high school. I had the chance to interact with many officers in that community, several of which were Academy graduates. I was impressed by the experiences I heard and their apparent dedication to the Army and the country. My parents are both (now retired) Army Officers and I have a great deal of professional respect for both of them. It was always encouraging to me to have that second "Army family" growing up. The Jewish Chapel at West Point has provided me with the strongest sense of family while I have been here. I have developed close relationships with the cadets, officers, and the Jewish community that continually and generously supports us. The past four years have brought me closer to my faith and have deepened my commitment to serving in the Army.

[Meagan Williams is currently serving as a military police officer in Iraq. She was virtually my right hand on the Jewish Community Council. Meagan is an outstanding young woman.]

Glenn H. Goldman, Class of 1984

During Beast Barracks my squad mates always encouraged me to go to services because they knew that the past Jewish services ONEGS always had great food. During Beast we were always hungry due to the "procedures" of the cadet tables. On several occasions I "smuggled" bagels, cookies, cream cheese, lox and the like back into the barracks. The items were always carried in my trousers or in my socks since anything visible or in my hands would be confiscated by upper classmen. As the only Jewish cadet in the platoon—my classmates "strongly" encouraged me to attend services in hopes that I would bring them back a snack. Thanks again—very much—to the Jewish War-vets who sponsored the ONEGS and took care of us cadets. I was there when they laid the corner stone for the New Jewish Chapel; prior to that Jewish services were held in the chemistry lab in Bartlett Hall, which also made for an interesting "setting" for services.

[Lieutenant Colonel Goldman has been on active duty in the Army field artillery for twenty-two years and continues to serve as I write this. He served in Operation Just Cause (Panama), Operation Desert Storm (First Gulf War), and operations in Macedonia and Kosovo. His awards include the Bronze Star Medal, the Army Commendation Medal three times, the Meritorious Service Medal four times, the Army Achievement Medal twice, the German Cross of Honor in Silver, the Armed Forces Expeditionary Medal with Arrow Head, "and others."

Jeffrey Marc Oettinger, Class of 1984

I experienced the building/completion and the first Aliyah at the Jewish Chapel.

Morton F. Roth, Class of 1957

Joined the Jewish Chapel choir as the only means a plebe had to leave the Academy grounds. Couldn't sing a lick, as true of most of the group. However the voices when combined in Hebrew song sounded pretty good to the groups we visited. On a trip to NYC (my family lived in Queens at the time) I visited my parents. My father drove me to the city to make the return formation scheduled for Sunday, 1600 hours. Traffic was heavy and I arrived at 1550, with time to spare, or so I thought. The bus to take us back was parked by the Astor Hotel. When I arrived there was no bus. I checked with a hotel employee who said the bus left a few minutes ago.

Apparently when roll call was taken on the bus there must have been a lot of noise (perhaps a little too much good cheer carried over from Joe King's Ratskeller) and the Cadet in Charge thought he heard a response when my name was called and had the driver leave early, thinking everyone was on board. My dad tried to catch the bus but we didn't spot it on the drive back to the Point. I made it to the Orderly Room at about 1715 hours and called the Cadet in Charge to tell him when he reported me to be sure to note that I made it back before 1800 hours—which I was given to believe was the magic hour after which you were considered AWOL. When I called there was a pregnant pause at the other end of the line, finally he said, "You mean you weren't on the bus?" He then said in a most unkind way that he would have to report himself for giving a false report. As a plebe I had no thought of asking this upper classman (a cow) why they had left me behind nor did I offer any more than a "No excuse, sir" at my board. I got the standard slug for missing a formation when off Academy grounds, something like 10 or 12 hours on the area and room confinement for some period, which I can't recall. The memory of that unjust punishment still rankles.

[Colonel Roth served in the Army Corps of Engineers for thirty years. He served in Vietnam for two years. His awards include the Legion of Merit, the Bronze Star Medal twice, the Air Medal, the Joint Service Commendation Medal, Meritorious Service Medal, Defense Superior Service Medal, and Army Commendation Medal.]

Ramona Fastow, Class of 2005

When I was a new cadet during Beast, one of my squad mates found out that I was Jewish. He said, "Wow, you're Jewish! Doesn't that mean that you can't eat pizza?"

During Passover 2005, there was a Thursday afternoon retirement parade for the Dean, BG Kaufman. Since the event was free, and they were off from school, thousands of Hasidim from the local Jewish community showed up for the parade. My friends and I were all surprised with the huge turnout. One of my friends, born and raised in Louisiana, was stuck in a throng of Hasidim, and looked to me for help. "Dan," I said, "Say slicha if you need to get through the crowd. It means excuse me in Hebrew." "Slicha?" he repeated, "Ok." Minutes later, he was at the other side of the street, clear of the crowd, and when I finally made my way over to him, he said, "Hey, Ramona, it worked! I just said slicha a few times and they cleared a path."

David Rokhlin, Class of 2005

I did CTLT (Cadet Third Lieutenant) with a light infantry company, Alpha Company 2/502 at Fort Campbell during the summer of 2005. I shadowed my assigned sponsor/lieutenant, Joe Presutto 03'. I wrote operations orders, conducted squad and platoon PT, I was the OIC for a company STX lane for NBC (Nuclear, Biological, Chemical) training, I helped the PL plan a company barbecue/picnic, attended a dining in, conducted a twelve-mile road march for time with the company, and I worked with the XO to help resource upcoming ranges. It was a great experience, and it was a prime factor in my decision to post at FT Campbell and to be a part of the Screaming Eagles. I was also "converted" to country music during my month in the South—prior to that I hated country music. After thirty or so days of continuous/consistent propaganda, *err* country-music listening in LT Presutto's car I came home and today probably upwards of 85% of the music I listen to is country. Amazing (still I enjoy NYs 92.3 and my Russian, Arabic, and Turkish music of course).

During the summer of 2005 I completed the Air Assault School (AAS) at Camp Smith. Thanks to my busy schedule that summer, I ended up taking the APFT for AAS while on AIAD in Chad. Granted it was still hot as hell at 0400 or so when I was doing the APFT, but I did relatively okay. Chasing goats and raising clouds of dust running around some random compound may not have raised my 2-mile run time, but it definitely raised some eyebrows—the locals there aren't fond of bare knees/legs and I was outfitted in my APFT uniform; they also don't seem to be very accustomed to others running around in circles about 8 times.

The AIAD to Chad, thanks to the Arabic department was great! Granted, I didn't learn too much Arabic (they mostly spoke a dialect I couldn't understand or French), but I really learned a lot about the country, it's people, and how our embassies and defense attaché operate. Being on the frontier of the Global War on Terrorism was also an eye-opening experience. Not to mention, being in an African country that had just come off an abortive coup-attempt. Being told our first morning (after no more than 3–4 hours of sleep) that we would have to use Motorola walkie-talkies because the government had shut down the cell-phone network to prevent the enemy from plotting was a great introduction to the Chad. My partner, Tim Brooks and I were treated like VIPs—we had a full 3-bedroom house, surrounded by a four-wall compound with barbed-wire and shards of glass on top of the walls, a gate, and a guard in a guard house that changed every eight hours. Forgetting to bring alarm clocks offered us daily language practice—how to explain to the guard to tell his relief to wake us up at such-and-such a time the next morning . . . needless to say, our other experiences (too many and some too sensitive to mention) were no less exciting. Low crawling on the dusty floor of a decrepit classroom to teach officers (including a general and a 1st SGT) about our military basic training and then standing up with all the dust displayed on your uniform was priceless. So was learning how to teach the officers English by way of demonstration—I collected silverware and other items from the kitchen in our house and took the phone off the wall to bring in to class. It was an amazing experience to say the least, and in my opinion only West Point, through its ambition, connections, and wisdom could arrange something like that for us!

My fondest/best memory/experience at USMA are many. For example, I am constantly reminded of my 2nd week of Beast Barracks when I "cut" the dessert pie. Granted it was not a fond memory then, but it is now. At least I can now say that my eyesight has been surgically corrected and now I truly have "no excuse." I might also be the only one who asked the First Captain during Beast where to put the soap (in the medicine cabinet) during room inspections—I stopped him in the hall (I had no idea it was him, because I yelled at the first person I saw in the hallway and he had his back to me) and asked him. Or perhaps the SAMI (Saturday morning inspection) before Acceptance Day when my roommates and I spent countless hours cleaning the room. I went to sleep around 0300. I'm not sure they ever went to sleep at all. All I know is that I woke up at around 0500, the overhead light was still on (of course today, thanks to Late Lights Policy this would never ever happen) and both my roommates were sitting at their desks. Perhaps they were zombie-like, but I didn't realize that it was still very early in the morning and jumped out of bed worried that I would be late to formation. Of course I quickly realized that they had never went to sleep or turned out the lights and that I still had plenty more time to sleep (a rarity since that day).

There are also other, more significant memories. Sandhurst memories from each of my first three years have always been great memories. The sheer exhilaration and excitement and pride of finishing the course with a great group of friends can hardly be replicated. Going to Uzbekistan yuk (sophomore) year with one of my best friends here and a Cow (junior) for the Foreign Academy Exchange Program was a great experience. Granted we were there at a sensitive time, just as the war in Iraq was announced by President Bush, we were treated like royalty and fired more weapons than in my entire four years at West Point. Besides AK74s, Makarov pistols, Dragunov sniper rifles, and their version of the M19 grenade launcher, we also fired RPGs and T72 tanks. I got lucky—I missed my first RPG shot so I was given an opportunity to fire a second. Each of us also drove their BMPs, BTRs, and T72 tanks. At that time, I didn't even have a NYS drivers license (I got one that spring after I came back to West Point), but they insisted I drive the tank so I did!

My worst/most challenging experiences were getting into a physical fight with one of my squad-mates (later kicked out of the Academy for other behavior) during Beast was not fun. We were both subjected to a Company Board (albeit pretty much a fake one). I treated it seriously though, and wouldn't sign the paperwork (sworn statements and such). Frankly, I believed that it was serious and didn't want to sign anything I didn't agree with (I argued I was just defending myself and not fighting) and the documents that had my personal information wrong, like the spelling of my name. My refusals to sign did not endanger anything positive with my Company Commander who was big lengthwise and widthwise and would charge at us like a bowling ball in a bowling alley during ultimate Frisbee games in the afternoons. I probably did get back at him when I asked to see legal counsel, perhaps a JAG. I was later told he almost had a heart attack, because he wasn't completely sure what to do and after all this was more just to "set an example" and impact some leadership training for him. To make it short, I had to move out of my room into my squad-mate's room (the one I had a fight with) and we had to be "Ranger buddies" for the rest of the summer. Ironically, after that, we actually got along relatively well and he was actually in my yuk year company . . .

My funniest/craziest USMA experience: Again, there are many. West Point has a tendency to make bitter, sweet, funny, etc. experiences and many of them. Although we were stopped before we could execute, plebe year we planned to chain a lockbox to a Squid's (Midshipman's) bed (underneath on the springs) which would be full of assorted alarm clocks (especially the hand-spun mechanical ones that shake violently and make an intensely irritating noise) that were set at 15 (or so) minute increments starting around 0300 in the morning the day before we left for the Army-Navy game (that we won, by the way!) While some upperclassmen became traitors and stopped us, it had the full potential to be very funny, and somewhat crazy indeed. I don't know what the Squid would have done—he'd either have to drag his bed outside of his room to the hallway, or go to CGR at 0300 in the morning asking for a bolt-cutter and having to explain what was going on.

West Point has been a rollercoaster ride, and while it's had ups and downs, I wouldn't for a moment forego the experiences, friends, and teachers, positive and negative (and all of which have taught me something important), for any other road in life. I think I may have come, at least part of the way, down what Robert Frost calls the "Road Less Traveled," but I wouldn't want it any other way and no way in hell would I turn around. I feel prepared and I'm excited to get out into what many affectionately call the "Real Army."

Yale Trustin, Class of 1945

As plebes we were advised to never volunteer, however my aunt Marie of Baltimore came to visit and attended our Sunday Jewish Service at the Old Chapel. She told the Rabbi (I believe Rabbi Unger from Newburgh) that I played the piano and organ. The next Sunday, of course, I became the Chapel organist, pianist and was instructed to form a Cadet Choir—I believe the first Jewish Choir (at least for quite some time) was never asked to perform on or off base except every Sunday.

All our Chapel services "drafted" plebes were less than wonderful—not concert material.

In the early part of my basic flying training at Stewart Field where we flew AT-6's, I had a traumatic experience—we made our first night landings (the first time I had ever been in any type of aircraft all night). We were to make five landings at an auxiliary field about 20 miles from Stewart Field and then return. I must have flown above a cloud going over Stewart Field because I didn't find the runway and got lost. We hadn't been briefed on any navigating or cross country procedure or any radio procedures or cross country flights. I flew in search of any landing field until my fuel was showing almost empty. I knew I must bail out any minute when all of a sudden a fighter plane flashed its lights and at the same time runway lights went on below—I followed them in the pattern and landed. I taxied to a hanger where a night crew was working on an airplane and I asked them where I was—he said Bradley Field—Hartford, Connecticut, at least 60 miles from Stewart. I parked the plane, got to a phone in operations and called my C.O. at Stewart, a major. He was still up flying looking for me. I was sure I would be "worked out." When he got back to Stewart and called me back he was so happy to hear that the plane and I were okay he said, "Get a good nights sleep, we'll fly over tomorrow and bring you home." They were so happy that I didn't bail out like the cadet did the night before (which ruined a costly AT-6) that I became more of a hero than a discipline case. Starting the next day they immediately taught us navigation and cross country radio procedures and I never got lost again! You can be sure I said a few "Sh'Ma YsRoel" during that flight and God was my co-pilot for sure!

Eric Jacob Roth, Class of 1987

Religion was not a very big factor in the choir. I, along with my company mate Marvin Walworth (blond hair, blue eyes, Protestant) joined the choir at the beginning of plebe year. It was a great way to get away from West Point and meet people. I occasionally got hazed by the upperclassmen for going on "get over choir trips," but I'm sure Marvin got it worse. Marvin wound up meeting his wife (Chinese American girl attending Goucher College) on a choir trip to Baltimore, Maryland. Singing ability was not a very big factor either. I remember a trip to NYC where we sang for Mayor Koch and the event was televised. I can't remember what songs we sang, but at one point in the middle of a song, nobody remembered the words so we would go from singing to humming and back to singing for the chorus. Another time for an Academy event we combined with the other religious choirs. Many of us didn't even know what to answer when asked the question if we were sopranos, baritones or tenors. It got even worse when they asked us to sing a few notes. Not to say some of us didn't have singing abilities, but at least half had none. But in the end the Jewish Choir was all about giving plebes an opportunity to get away from the Academy and form bonds of friendship. I switched over to the Air Force as a JAG in 1995 and was followed by my fellow Jewish West Point classmate Nate Berman in 1996. As we move up in the Air Force JAG Corp, we often have good chuckles about the fun times we had in the Jewish Choir.

[Lieutenant Colonel Roth is still on active duty (nineteen years) with the U.S. Air Force after eight years in the Army Corps of Engineers. He has been awarded the Defense Meritorious Service Medal, the Meritorious Service Medal twice, the Joint Superior Commendation Medal twice, the Army Commendation Medal twice, the Air Force Commendation Medal, the Joint Staff Achievement Medal, and the Army Achievement Medal.]

Lev Yampolsky, Class of 2002

First Russian Jewish cadet. Was born in Russia and immigrated to the US in 1988.

[Lev served in Afghanistan.]

David Malkin, Class of 1998

Some of my fondest memories are of the annual Model Seders during Passover. Each year, I would invite a handful of my close, non-Jewish friends to join me at Ike Hall for the Seder. It was a great chance to drink wine, share some laughs, and expose my friends to a Jewish tradition. We felt especially daring walking back to the barracks drunk as underclassmen! To this day, my friends still tell me how much they enjoyed the Seders.

Robert Siegel, Class of 1945

Dr. Goldberg Was Right

Dr. Goldberg was right. He knew he was right. Why else would he, a 65 year old doctor with terrible posture from slumping back in his desk chair, and with yellow nicotine stained fingers from chain-smoking Chesterfields without filters most of his life, go to 90 Church Street in early 1942 to fight for me?

I was completing my senior year at Andover, and had submitted applications to several colleges, including West Point which required a physical examination. The results were sent to my New York City address. The return address said, "War Department." Since I was away at school, my mother naturally opened the formidable looking envelope. She read that I had flunked the physical because the x-rays had indicated a spot on my lungs. She was more than slightly hysterical when she called Dr. Goldberg and demanded an explanation. Dr. Goldberg knew the army was wrong. He had taken an X-ray of my lungs two months before and knew there was no spot.

Shaking, she asked how he would override the army's findings (In those days, everyone still believed that anything the government said or did became etched in stone). He convinced my mother that he would do what had to be done and would be successful because he was right.

Dr. Goldberg grabbed a copy of my latest x-rays and headed for downtown New York. He demanded to see the x-rays the Army had based their decision on. He produced his. They produced theirs. A comparison was made. They realized that they were wrong. This, of course, meant that Dr. Goldberg was right. Something he had known all along. I was accepted to West Point. My mother was overjoyed. My father was happy. I was healthy again and going to West Point.

A Dangerous Order

After arriving in Japan at the end of 1945, my initial orders were to report to Cannon Troop, 5th Cavalry Regiment, and 1st Cavalry Division, stationed outside Tokyo. The regimental commander seemed glad to see me, a West Point graduate, although he kept me at attention while he questioned me for about ten minutes. Finally he dismissed me to go to the officer's quarters.

The first two months were not terribly interesting, mostly spent supervising Japanese laborers in beautifying the regimental headquarters especially building the new officers' club. Minimal time was spent with the troops, close order drill, some field exercises, no firing of cannons since those weapons had not yet been issued. We were really there as a reserve unit for the regiment.

Just before the officers club's opening, we were told that we were not invited for the first night, only field grade officers and VIPS from the area. Not too happy about this turn of events, we started collecting our own supplies for our own junior grade officers' celebration. As the evening wore on, our toast became louder, loud enough to be heard by the club next door. Apparently mine was singled out, perhaps as regular army I should have known better. The next morning I was told to report to the colonel's office, berated as I have never been berated before—not even Beast Barracks. I was ordered to report to Bomb Disposal School 200 miles to the south.

I thought at the time I was quite lucky, but later realized how little I knew about bombs and explosives from a short once-a-week course, lasting about six months, at the Academy.

The students at the school were being groomed to replace a group of Bomb Disposal civilians who were being paid $10,000 a year; they were formerly in the field, but now had desk jobs and filed reports to somewhere. I was presently making about $170 a month to do the same job of locating, disarming and disposing of ammunition scattered over most of Japan. My group was composed of many enlisted men plus four officers, one from each of the four American divisions performing occupation duty. They were all lieutenants, one of whom was a West Point classmate whose branch was Ordnance. We were about to spend six weeks learning everything known or unknown about explosives, both U.S. and Japanese. I remember little about what I learned, but it was important that I prepare very well for my immediate future. After leaving this school I would have no instructors to go to with problems. Failure in the field could be a lot worse than failure in a quiz in calculus at the Academy.

The course culminated in a final exam. We were given a field problem with various stations that we had to approach individually. We had to disarm a piece of ammo, a small bomb or mine. We all passed except for one officer, my West Point classmate. He flunked by picking up a Japanese land mine. He shouldn't have done that because it blew his head off. The funeral was the day after the final. After it, we departed, dispirited, to put it mildly, by the accident.

My squad consisted of myself, a master sergeant and three other enlisted men, all graduates of the school we had all just attended. We had two jeeps, one pickup truck, and thousands of dollars worth of disposal equipment left by the civilians group with the inflated incomes.

My new job went very well, I think. Like they say when you fly a plane—"any landing that you can walk away from is a good landing." I was my own boss, I think because nobody wanted to tell me what to do. If something I did turned out badly. No one wanted the responsibility. Early on I established a relationship with the Japanese Police, who knew where every unexploded US bomb was dropped, even though it might have been eight to ten feet below ground level. They would have Japanese laborers dig down to uncover it, let me know and I would disarm it by unscrewing the fuse in the nose cone. The first time I did it, I was shaking so hard I thought I might set it off. The manual said the disarming had to be done by an officer or the highest non-com present. As I mentioned, I had a master sergeant, a Texas born, 30 year old man, and I'd seen him at Bomb Disposal School. He was definitely very competent, an Ordnance non-com, who had several years experience in demolition. Tex-Leggett was five to six years older than I. I'd have loved to have him perform the final step but I was trained never to ask anyone in my command to do anything that I wouldn't do myself. I finally came up with a good solution. I'd go down with Tex and hold the flashlight while he disarmed the bomb. This probably saved several lives, including mine, since the bombs were mostly 2000 pounders.

In return for his service to me he would have the use of one of the two jeeps any night he wanted. He readily agreed to this. He was very self-assured, and confident that he could do his job without me and my flashlight, and now he had his own jeep. Problem solved!

Thornton Saferstein, Class of 1956

During Beast Barracks I spent an inordinate amount of time in the "laughing bag" because I smirked a lot (covered down below my shoulder in a laundry bag and forced to laugh continually).

[Lieutenant Colonel Saferstein served in the Army field artillery for twenty-four years. He served in Vietnam where he was awarded the Bronze Star Medal.]

Jack R. Hayne, Class of 1949

I guess I had better start sometime in 1934 or 35. My grandfather had a 160-acre farm near Livingston Manor, Sullivan County, NY. Our family would take the old Ontario and Western RR (O&W RR) from Weehawken, NJ up the Hudson River past West Point to what was referred to as the Jewish Alps. Each year when we made the trip I would see the military guards at the West Point RR station and that was when I first wanted to be like them—a cadet—not realizing that I was seeing soldiers. So at the age of 10 or 11 I began my interest in attending the Academy.

Jumping forward quite a number of years we were drafted in 1943 and served in the Army in the Coast Artillery, Antiaircraft, Field Artillery and Infantry. I was able to obtain an appointment as an alternate and somehow ended up filling the quota for Congressman Shepard of California.

On July 1, 1945 I met with my Army buddies Matt Lampell and Marty Hecht at a nightclub in NYC. It might have been Leon and Eddie's or the 21 club. It was our last evening of freedom. I suggested we take the train from Grand Central Station up the east bank of the Hudson River to avoid the harassment by the upper class men at the West Point Station. They opt to take the O&W RR (Marty was honorably discharged 6 August 1945 on account of physical discharge). I took the train out of Grand Central Station and met two officers reporting to the Corps of Cadets. One was a 2nd Lt Army and the other a 1st Lt. John Poulson. John became a classmate and graduate in '49 and the 2nd Lt. didn't make it through Beast Barracks.

We arrived early at around 8 AM at the station across from West Point, either Garrison or Cold Spring. I made a phone call to the dock across the river and asked for a boat to pick up two officers reporting to the Post. We were picked up by the Superintendent's launch and when we arrived at the dock there were cadets meeting the two new candidates. I was ignored and was able to find a staff car and driver and went to the Coast Artillery detachment near the old PX and Commissary. Reporting time was 11:00 AM at the East Sallyport of Central Area and I wasn't anxious to get started just yet. After a couple of hours of good GI coffee and delicious peanut butter cookies the 1st Sergeant provided a car to take me to Central Area.

That is when the fun began. Cadet 1st Class John Daniel Henry McDonough of Hempstead, Long Island, NY met me in the Sallyport. "Drop that bag" . . . "Pick up that bag" . . . screw in that neck tie etc. That bag was a little Red Cross issued bag that held my shaving kit, a bottle of shave lotion and a Baby Ben alarm clock. The clock never worked after that and I was out of a relatively new bottle of lotion.

After several hours I had to report to the 1st Sergeant of 4th Company. By the way, Matt Lampell was there ahead of me and had been suffering a few hours more than I. The upperclassman instructed me on the proper reporting procedure. (Hey, I knew how after serving 2-1/2 years in the Army . . . and I knew how to follow orders). I followed orders to the "T." I entered the Orderly Room of 4th Company, executed a proper and snappy hand salute, held the salute and reported exactly as instructed, "Sir, New Cadet Ducrot, BJ reports to the 1st Sgt of 4th Company, as orders." OH BOY DID I CATCH HELL. "Mister, get out of here and learn how to report properly." (The 1st Sergeant was Dick Ruble). Well, to make a long story short, after a couple of tries I realized I was Cadet HAYNE, J not Cadet Ducrot, BJ.

Then there was the experience at the North Athletic field during Bayonet training. Many of us reporting from the Army had been with the USMAP at Fort Benning, GA and had received excellent bayonet training under the tutelage of Major Bronkhorst. The Army's old field manual on the bayonet has a pen and ink sketch of a master posted with a rifle and bayonet that sure looks like the major.

Matt and I were in the same platoon and being short we were at the tail end waiting to run through the bayonet course. Matt whispered something to me and I told him to shush. Firstie Abraham Wolf of Brooklyn, NY heard me and asked, "Why are you talking, mister?" "NO EXCUSE, SIR," being the correct response. "Take a lap, Dumb Smack."

Well, I took a lap at high port in drill boots etc. As I approached the platoon I slowed to a walk and just then Wolf turns around and asks, "Why are you walking, Dumb John?" Once again with the proper response . . . "NO EXCUSE, SIR." "Take a lap, mister." So off I go again at high port on my 2nd lap. This time upon returning to the platoon I make sure I am in full view of that treacherous upper classman before I slow to a walk. Just then I hear my name called to run the course. Aha, now I can show my expertise. On the last dummy I goof and don't slide my hand up the rifle hand guard. The upperclassman monitoring that dummy exclaims, "Take a lap, Dumb Smack." And off I go on my 3rd lap around the quarter mile track at high port. Needless to say I am bushed.

By the time I return to the platoon and my DEAR FRIEND Matt Lampell, the training session is over and of course the last event is to have the entire platoon take a lap. That afternoon I reported on emergency sick call and entered the hospital for surgery.

Plebe year was an academic challenge for me inasmuch as I hadn't had much schooling in mathematics. In addition, I was scheduled to take Russian instead of the German I requested. I squeaked by in Math, and Russian by some miracle. In my Russian classes I would substitute Polish, Italian, Yiddish, Hebrew and German words for Russian words in the daily quizzes. Col. Hoffman would give me some credit.

Years later in North Korea, October 1950, I came across a supply of 40 mm antiaircraft ammunition in Navy canisters that the United States had supplied the Soviet Union during World War II. I was able to read the bill of lading in Russian and determine dates and route of shipment to Murmansk.

Then, of course, there was the mathematics to contend with. At the start of the academic year the plebes are assigned to math sections alphabetically. I started in the 9th section out of 23. The instructor was a basketball coach and wasn't a math genius by any stretch of the imagination. He worked all problems from the instructor's notebook and if a step in a solution of a problem was obvious and not included, he couldn't explain how to get from one step to the next. I dropped from the 9th to close to the last section. There I met Captain Roth, the diving team coach. Now here was an instructor quite knowledgeable in math. After several weeks with him I moved up many sections to a few above the 9th only to meet the basketball coach. On the next resection I was back with the Goats and with Captain Roth. After a few months of bouncing up and down the sections, each time meeting the same instructors, Captain Roth wanted to know what my problem was. I told him it was the basketball coach. He then told me he would give me grades to keep me in his section and make sure I learned my math. As a result, I became proficient and when I attended the University of Texas, El Paso, I was able to max all the exams in calculus and differentials. Captain, then Major Roth, had been the public relations man for NBC before WW II. To keep us awake in class he would place his hands on his desk and draw his knees up toward his chest and swing back and forth like a pendulum. Quite an amiable character.

As a Plebe, Sunday was the best day of the week. Mandatory Chapel Call. We marched from Central Area to the Old Cadet Chapel for services conducted by Rabbi Unger. I don't remember if we had a choir during plebe year. I joined the choir as a 2nd classman under classmate Chester (Chet) Trubin as choir director. The breakfast after services were memorable. I have yet to find an omelet as good as those in the cadet mess on Sunday after chapel. Through rain, snow, sleet, hail etc we walked to the Chapel. We didn't have a resident Rabbi so I joined my gentile roommates on Friday evenings to go to Protestant Chaplain Walthour's office for Bible classes on the Holy Scriptures (New Testament). We had a Passover Seder at the Hotel Thayer and I remember being asked to recite the four questions. I don't remember subsequent Seders. Rabbi Marcus Kramer of the Vassar Temple of Poughkeepsie replaced Rabbi Unger the next year.

At the end of Beast Barrack most of the cadets returned to the Academy from field trips and summer leave, except for those Air Cadets. All of us now departed for Pine Camp, NY with a layover in Cobleskill, NY. While a few of us were walking in town a farmer approached us and asked if we were interested in a home cooked meal. We jumped at the opportunity. I think there were eight of us at the meal in the farm house. What a terrific meal served family style. Loads of meat, fish, vegetables and home baked bread.

When at Pine Camp we were taken into the Watertown for a boat trip on the St. Lawrence River through the 1,000 Islands. At the first opportunity, I peeled off the group and headed down an alley more interested in roaming the town than boating the river. Apparently there was a nose count and it was determined that a couple of plebes were missing. 2nd Classman George Dell apprehended me. Someone from the class of 1945 who had been on the debating team had told me to make myself known to George and he would take care of me. Well this was not the way to get acquainted and all plebe year George Dell made sure I toed the line.

When Jim Steel and Lou Abele and I roomed together in the South Barracks above the Cadet Hostess' office I found out they were not aware of pizza. I had befriended Marshall, one of the barbers in the Central Area barbershop and found out that his town of Vails Gate housed a large Italian community and pizza was readily available. I made arrangements for him to bring in the pizza and hold it until after inspection of barracks. Then I'd pick it up and we could eat cold pizza but in the winter we could heat it on radiators.

During plebe Christmas I was restricted to barracks due to being deficient in English (a quick check of this document will certainly show you why). Spin the spurs on General Sedgwick's monument by the light of the moon at midnight in full dress under arms and go proficient. I did that and went "PRO." However, I picked a night without the moon, wore fatigues and used burnt cork on my face. I wasn't taking any chances.

In order to get away from that runt company, H-1, I joined the fencing team as soon as off-season began in September 1945. I had fenced since 12 years of age, in high school (and in the Army when the opportunity presented itself). Nothing like being a plebe and eating on the corps squad fencing team table. However that didn't last very long as there were only so many slots available for plebes. When I was bounced off the fencing table I went as far away from the large mural and H-1 Company. Flanker land was the place for me. I managed to get on the table of Star man Jack Schram. At the table were George S. Patton Jr, John (Jack) Frost and a yearling named Jones. Life on the flanker table was a breeze compared to H-1 Company. After about a week or two it was suggested that I invite some of my floating friends from H-1 to sit at the table. I invited a few classmates for the next meal. Big mistake. No sooner than we were seated the hazing began. Not a word was said to me, but they were raked over coals. After the meal I returned to my room to find a couple of unhappy classmates ready to skin me alive.

We had a few Jewish cadets on the fencing team starting in plebe year. Chet Trubin, Matt Lampell, Marc Jartman and me were representing in saber, epée and foil. Matt and Chet fenced saber all four years and Marc fenced epée for all four years. I started in foil but in the last meet as a second classman against NYU Coach Servando Velarde changed me to saber after only two lessons. During that meet I fenced both varsity foil and JV saber. The next year I fenced saber exclusively winning more bouts than I had won in foil. So in the 1948–1949 fencing season the first three fencers on the saber team were Jewish.

That year Dick Bowman, epée, Barney Cummings, foil, and Chet Trubin, saber, competed in the NCAA Fencing meet at the Academy and won the NCAA Championship, besting 28 other colleges. Dick Bowman won the Individual Epée Championship.

I first proposed marriage to Pearl while an enlisted man in the Army. Of course, we had to forestall getting married until graduation from the Academy. Early on we decided to request the use of the Old Cadet Chapel that was being used as the Jewish Chapel during our time at the Academy. We had no competition and were the first to be wed there on Graduation Day. Everything was well until my brother-in-law asked where my mother was. Oops! I forgot to pick her up in Highland Falls. Someone drove to get mom and the wedding was able to commence. Rabbi Kramer officiated and I don't remember much of what transpired. Classmate Bernie Rosen played the organ as he had done for four years as a cadet. Pearl and I exited the Chapel under an arch of sabers held by Chet Trubin, Jim Steel, Lou Abele, Lenny Shapiro (USMA '51) and Kim Kintz (USMA 51). Stan Shankman was to be the 6th saber man but was unable to attend (In 1952 Stan died in a commercial air crash on the way home from Korea). Boyde Allen was married next. Not too long ago while looking at movies taken at the wedding we noticed Ed and Nancy Marks in the background watching all the family congratulating us.

Graduation and the wedding occurred on Tuesday, June 7, 1949. The Korean War started on June 25, 1950 and that ended all chance of Pearl accompanying me to my assignment in Japan. She had received all her immunization shots and was eager to go but that was not to be.

In August I flew to Seattle and Ft. Lawton and joined numerous classmates in our trek to the Far East. Major Campbell, my plebe year English instructor, was plane captain. Dean McCarron, Fred Deem and Jack Burkhart were on the flight plus a few more.

Upon arrival at Haneda airport we were taken to Camp Drake and there met our classmate Lew Zickel. Lew had the job of call off the assignments for shipment out of the replacement depot. I don't think he cared for that job.

The next day at Camp Drake we lined up for our assignments and of fifteen artillery officer assignments 13 went to division field artillery and three went to antiaircraft units. The next day the assignments were reversed and Dean, Jack, Fred and I were assigned to the 10th AAA Group in Hiyoshi. We were offered assignments in either 90mm or 40mm battalions. I opted for the 40mm battalion figuring if I took the 90mm unit I'd be stuck in Japan. The four of us joined the 76th AAA AW Bn (SP) under command of LTC Charles L. Andrews, Spanish or Portuguese instructor at the Point. Four days later the battalion was aboard 4 LST's on the way to Pusan, Korea.

My battery became the advance unit of the battalion, always 100 or so miles in front of the battalion at some forward airbase providing air defense. Our battery got as far north as Sinanju, Anju and Kunu-ri in North Korea. After a while at K-29 airbase, the Battery Commander told me to reconnoiter the route to and the area at Sinuiju on the Yalu River. We were to occupy K-30 airbase at Sinuiju. I managed to get within 5 or 6 miles of the town when I realized the area was devoid of the usual garbage left by our troops. It appeared that we were well in advance of our lines. Discretion was the better part of valor and I had my driver turn the jeep around and we moved south to units of the 1st Cavalry Division. To my surprise I ran into none other than 1st Lt. Lewis Zickel. I always imagined him making assignments in Camp Drake back in Japan. We had a nice chat and I returned to my unit at K-29 on November 26 to find out that I had just been promoted to 1st Lt after 3-1/2 months in Korea (the Chinese started their major offensive on November 27). Later I found out that Colonel Andrews had visited the battery and ordered the battery commander to promote all the 2nd Lieutenants. Months later an officer from another unit told me that over a few drinks in Seoul with my commander he was told "I'm out to get all lieutenants, West Pointers, RA and those officers on competitive tours etc. . . ." Never did get to see my efficiency report.

More About Me

I have trouble carrying a tune. However, Chet put me between two tenors who could. I spent my time on the choir between Lew Zickel and Matt Lampell. I still can't sing alone.

Pearl got Lew a date with her 1st cousin Faye Halberg. Have you forgiven her? Faye lives in Las Vegas with her husband of many, many years.

As I mentioned earlier I took Russian unwillingly. My mother was born in Austria Hungary in an area that had been Poland and Ukraine at different times in history. She was quite proficient in Polish, Russian, German and Yiddish (also English). Whenever she came to visit I'd ask her to speak Russian. It did help a bit.

One day during Beast Barracks after we were allowed to have family visitors the CQ announced that my mother and sister were waiting for me in Grant Hall. That was a big surprise to me that my sister was coming to visit me. But, which one . . . the one from Baltimore or the one from Washington, D.C. I promptly went to Grant Hall and was greeted by my mother and none other than . . . guess who . . . Pearl, my OAO. Ouch, am I in trouble because a first classman from my company was approaching. My mom knew that she put me in jeopardy by bringing Pearl and quickly introduced my dark haired beauty as my sister before I could admit my guilt. When I got back to the barracks he tried to get a date with my sister.

On one of my mother's visits I tried to impress her with my recently acquired trivial knowledge by telling her that Evelyn Nesbit posed for

Lady Fame on Battle Monument. That was when my mom told me all about the scandal that was the talk of the town when she was a teenager around the turn of the century. That's my mom!!!

[Captain Hayne served in the Coast Artillery Corps in the Army for twenty-one years. He is credited with the development of a new technique for radar and missile site survey that was accepted by the U.S. Army Air Defense Command for use throughout the command. He also taught at the Air Defense School at Fort Bliss, Texas.]

Joel Kampf, Class of 1959

The first month in Beast Barracks on a Saturday my roommate Bob Roth and I convinced everyone they had to report to us for boot inspection and pretty well pulled a 1st class act on the plebes. We paid dearly when the platoon leader found out.

First class year we relocated a classmate's complete room to central area ready for inspection.

[Joel is a member of the West Point Jewish Chapel Fund.]

Peter Gleilhenhaus, Class of 1961

In 1957, when I was a Plebe, and not a member of the Jewish Chapel Cadet Choir, there came an invitation from Temple Emanuel at Parkchester in the Bronx to West Point. Temple Emanuel was the synagogue to which my family belonged; in fact my dad was the president a few times. The temple invited the Jewish Cadet Choir to come for a weekend, complete with hosted housing for the boys, etc. Although only a plebe, and not really part of the choir, I was permitted to make the trip (in those days, any trip for a plebe was a major event—plebes were there for 11 months, from R day to Yearling leave). I did have to promise not to sing, but rather to mouth the words when the choir "performed." The group performed on Friday evening at services, and then participated in the Saturday morning service. I was invited to sit on the "bima." When the Torah reading portion began, the rabbi stepped over to where I was seated and asked, "Which Cadet should be called for an aliyah?" One needs to remember that I was a naïve plebe, about two months into the academic year. I knew the first class cadets in the squad by sight, and a few by name.

I was totally oblivious to the fact that some of the upper class cadets were in the squad only to get out of mandatory chapel early on Sundays, and to take the trips. To the rabbi, I said, "Him, Mr. ____." As I said that Mr. _____ was called and came up to say the blessings. The rabbi again said, "Which cadet should, etc. . . ." I looked out and pointed to another first classman, and said, "Him." The object of my pointed finger became apoplectic. He waved and turned red. He shook his hand in front of himself, signifying, I thought, humility. In fact, he had never, until that day, experienced an aliyah. And, that was probably the first time Temple Emanuel had a Protestant cadet haltingly reciting the blessings.

In 1973, when I was in the DPE, I also was kind of the Jewish Lay leader. In January the courts announced that chapel would no longer be mandatory at the Academies. The next Sunday we had five people at services in the Old Cadet Chapel, my son and I, a civilian lady from Highland Falls, and two cadets. We had a little service and departed. The following week, the crowd was down to two, just the lady and me. Working with the commandant's office, the dean's office, and Chaplain Jim Ford, the cadet chaplain, we arranged to move the services to Friday night. The Dean allowed that we could use the Chemistry lecture room in Bartlett Hall. The Com and Dean's offices agreed we could have services right after the first class light in the mess hall. We got the word out, and what became a thriving event began. Every Friday we had our little service, with food brought by the supporting community. Once a month Rabbi Soltes came up and led the service. The other weeks, a cadet or officer did the duty. Very quickly the Jewish War Veterans posts from the area began to sponsor services, and when a post came, the food was wonderful. We continued to have the baccalaureate in the Old Cadet Chapel for a few years, but by 1978, were doing everything there on the third floor of Bartlett Hall. That included the Sunday school that continued throughout the period.

[Colonel Gleilhenhaus has served in the Army field artillery for twenty-nine years. He served in Vietnam and was awarded the Combat Infantry Badge, the Legion of Merit twice, the Meritorious Service Medal three times, the Army Commendation Medal three times, and the Vietnam Cross of Gallantry, "etc."]

David S. Niekerk, Class of 1978

My fiancée sent me a monthly Challah that I shared with my roommates. One month my roommate (Frank Hardy from Virginia) said, "Dave, I love it when you share this with us each month, but can you tell Toyel to put more sugar in this cake—it tastes almost like sweet bread." I had to explain it was bread, a part of a traditional Friday night dinner.

Jacob Kovel, Class of 1980

Spent four years in the Jewish Chapel Choir. Went on many excellent trips. After performances we would answer questions from the audience. As my class was the first with women in it, and there were two in the choir, we were often asked, "What is it like being a woman at West Point?" One night, after just such a question was asked, one of the men stepped forward and offered to answer. The audience had a good laugh and the cadet, Steve Soshkind, did an excellent job recreating the appropriate answer. My experiences with the choir made life a lot more fun. On another trip that year we were at a party and a friend of mine, who would later come to West Point, was sitting with me. One of the women in my class, Dana Maller, walked by in civilian clothes. I mentioned to my friend that she was a cadet. He commentated, loud enough to be heard, "That's a cadet?" At that point, Dana turned and responded, "Where? Where?" We all had a good laugh.

[Dana Maller was the first Jewish women to graduate from West Point.]

Roger Kaplan, Class of 1975

While a Beast Barracks platoon leader, several of my squad leaders and I spent some time speaking with tourists while the new cadets received training. The conversation was quite amiable, with the tourists asking many questions about the 4th class system. After about fifteen minutes, our new cadets started to exit Bartlett Hall. We excused ourselves and as we walked away the wife called to us and asked, "Don't forget to yell at the plebes for us!" It was difficult to keep a straight face (and one of the squad leaders obeyed). The tourists were happy.

[Lieutenant Colonel Kaplan served in the Army field artillery for twenty-two years and eight months. He was awarded the Defense Superior Service Medal, the Legion of Merit, Defense Meritorious Service Medal, Meritorious Service Medal twice, Joint Service Commendation Medal, the Army Commendation Medal four times, and the Army Achievement Medal three times.]

Richard D. Rosenblatt, Class of 1949

As a cadet I never once experienced any anti-semitism. I was in the Jewish Chapel Squad Choir because my best friend was the leader of the choir. He was Chester Trubin '49, a brilliant (star) student and a wonderful person. Years later, when we were both Air Force pilots, we had dinner in Munich with our lady friends. The next day, he had a flameout on landing (F-80, I think) and crashed short of the runway and was killed. We lost "the best of the best."

Oleg A. Gostomelsky, Class of 1990

I believe, although I cannot be certain, that I was the first cadet who was born in the former Soviet Union (now Ukraine). My parents immigrated to the United States when I was very young. For the oldest of reasons—political and religious freedom. I did, however, keep up with Russian as my parents spoke it at home and was completely fluent in the language (still am today). When the Soviet cadets came for a visit during the first exchange program, I was one of the USMA cadets assigned to chaperone them. The humorous aspect was that not being aware of my unique heritage, the Soviet cadets were very impressed with my fluency in Russian and assuming that it was the result of my Academy Foreign Language training became very impressed with the USMA language program.

Michael Romasa, Class of 1968

(1) Painting "Sink Navy" on roof of Cullum Hall 1966. (2) Attempt to paint "Beat Navy" on ships of Hudson River Reserve Fleet 1967—wet suits in the Hudson. (3) Official driver for picking up children for Sunday school. (4) Taking roommates to Seders at Hotel Thayer.

Milton A. Laitman, Class of 1939

At a plebe briefing in 1935, Col. Wheat explained the choices of chapel service available. Attendance was compulsory at either the Catholic Chapel or the Cadet Chapel (Protestant). When, at the end of the lecture, I inquired from him as to what chapel I would attend since I was Jewish, he replied, "You can attend the Cadet Chapel since it is non-denominational." I answered him, "Sir, it may be non-denominational for you but not for me!" He then proceeded to inform me that I could go to the Cadet Chapel and "Participate to whatever degree I chose." And so I attended Protestant Chapel for three years until we got our first Jewish Chapel squad in 1938.

David P. Warshaw, Class of 1989

Of great interest and fanfare to my plebe company-mates was the Friday night Sabbath service. Everyone knew to be in Warshaw's room after 2100 hours to take a break from getting ready for SamI and enjoy some bagels, cream cheese, and cake. These gatherings served as great morale boosters and put being Jewish at West Point in a positive light.

Jacob B. Cooperhouse, Class of 1942

When I came, it was required that we went to a religious service. For a few months I attended the Protestant service. Shortly after I arrived a Jewish service commenced and I was very happy about it, and attended regularly.

While we lived in Germany, the German community knew we were Jewish and, without being told, knew that I was taking our children to religious school every week. Also, every Sabbath there were flowers left for us on our doorstep.

[Colonel Cooperhouse served in the Army Signal Corps for thirty years. He served in World War II and was awarded the Legion of Merit twice and a myriad of other decorations.]

Eric Billig, Class of 1981

As a plebe, during 2nd semester term ends, a fellow plebe and I were returning from Eisenhower Hall on a Saturday night after a few beers to relax from the stress of finals. For some reason we decided to walk back through the train tunnel. When we were about half way through, a train came. We hugged the side of the tunnel, and although unhurt, were covered with soot in our white over grey. When we got to the barracks area, an upper classman, seeing our filthy state of uniform, yelled for us to halt. My friend did. I did not. Rather, I made a run in the barracks, hoping to outdistance the upperclassman and get into my room unnoticed. As I burst through the doors to the stairwell of the barracks, I ran into the captain of the wrestling team (or at least he should have been). Upon "apprehensions" I was "hazed" throughout finals week by the upper-class of my company, several of which stated their intent was to get me to fail my finals. Instead, while having to do all my studying from about 2300–0600 and getting no sleep for almost an entire week, my grades improved from my first semester and I made the Dean's list for the first time.

When I was first caught, the upperclassman's immediate suspicion was I had been smoking pot in the train tunnel, as about a week before several students were caught in the steam tunnel smoking pot. Then I was accused of fighting with civilians. Then I was accused of an honor violation of being off limits. Upon investigating of all these all the frustrated upper class could do was "slug" me for "gross lack of judgment." I got 45 and 45. Plus, as a result of this incident, the train tunnel is now off limits (the LTC that held my board told me how he and his classmates used to hop on the train and ride it through the tunnel.)

Ronald I. Karp, Class of 1972

I enjoyed being in the Jewish Chapel Squad, both for the religious aspect and the "escape" from Academy. During plebe summer, I remember looking forward to being with other Jewish members on Wednesday evenings where we could "hang out" and also consume treats like soft drinks and apples. I think we were the first plebes to go "off campus" when we departed for Rush Hashanah/Yom Kippur services in Long Island. Our sponsoring congregation treated us very well and, of course, being able to pray in place of like West Point had an even greater appreciation and significance. Every one of us automatically were in the Jewish Choir. It seems like our motto was, "If you can't be good, be loud!" I used to look forward to our choir trips as a way to leave West Point "behind" for a weekend and relax in a friendly atmosphere.

My "beating the system" on how I survived West Point: (1) I studied every chance I got to include (a) going to formation in the a.m. (mostly, but also lunch and p.m. too) and standing in my position in my platoon so that when it marched to the mess hall, I easily snuck out and walked back into the barracks to get in some early a.m. study. One of my friends would bring me cereal/milk, etc. back from breakfast. (b) I, almost every night, checked out a key at the Library that let me into a "Special Collections" room. There I studied with the privileges (even as a plebe) of a TV and an "auto von" phone where I daily called the AF at home and had them patch me into their "Civ" line to make free calls to my family and friends. (c) Going to AI in all my courses all of the time which meant I missed the dreaded parade rehearsals and, instead, could focus on raising my grades (I ended with an "A" average in everything). The irony of my quest for good grades and getting a good branch assignment was that I tore ligaments in my shoulder near the end of Firstie year and was medically disqualified for combat. I had to go CSS and chose "AG" (but I was the first to choose AG). (2) My girlfriend and I would meet during the weekday evenings at the ladies bathroom on the bottom/basement level of Thayer. There was a nice couch in an outer room just inside the entrance door that we locked so we wouldn't be caught. This was infinitely better than Lover's Lane—weather was a problem—and infinitely better than hanging out in her car (I had to balance meeting her and getting my homework done at the Library!). (3) I joined every club imaginable. Almost every weekend (it seemed) I had a choice of some trip if it was a "good" weekend to travel. I remember being in the Russian, German and French Clubs, but I took Spanish (during our "trip" summer, I was selected to be an exchange student at the Guatemala Military Academy)! (4) "On campus" I was in SCUSA, which meant we had our own table in the Mess Hall—a table run like any athletic table. When we had our conference, we were excused from classes, functions, etc. (5) I also was a DJ for WKDT (every Sunday I had a show) and traveled to broadcast Army Football games. (6) I was on the "lighting crew" and ran lights for every concert that came to campus.

Victor Olshansky, Class of 1997

Most memorable for me was the "Orthodox invasion" of West Point that would take place every year during Succoth. For this 8-day period each fall, throngs of black-hatted, black-suited, tsit-tsit laden gentlemen with their accompanying spouses, children, cousins, etc. all would wander from Trophy Point to the Jewish Chapel, enjoying both the autumn beauty of the Hudson Valley and the extended time off from work and school that the Jewish holiday season would bring to the towns of Monsie and Spring Valley, NY. One such family, of a prominent Jewish publishing house, befriended me plebe year as they stopped to ask me a question about Battle Monument. We have remained pen-pals to this day.

Avram (Avi) J. Isaacson, Class of 1996

At the Academy I had the opportunity to represent the Jewish Chapel and USMA in the press. Specifically, the question was posed to me by the American Jewish Committee of "What being Jewish means to me"? During the writing of it, I remembered back to my plebe year and contemplated the meaning of sanctuary and peace. The Jewish Chapel was exactly that to me . . . a sanctuary from a tough year and a place to contemplate history. Additionally, it was a base for me to gain strength to go through another week. When I wrote about shalom and the desire for peace, I never imagined that 10 years later I would serve in a military engaging an enemy in a war of ideas. Yet, each time I look back and read what I wrote in that article, the more I am thankful that the Jewish Chapel instilled feelings of peace, sanctuary, and reconstitution that my fellow classmates are bringing to places like Afghanistan.

Keith Samuels, Class of 1983

I met my wife in Cadet Chapel. I'm still laughing.

[Keith and his wife, Christy Bishop, were the first couple to be married in the Jewish Chapel.]

Christy Bishop Samuels, Class of 1984

I met my future husband during my first week of Beast Barracks at the Academy in Jewish Chapel. Those were the days when Chapel was held in

Thayer Hall. He was a yearling and I was a plebe—so we did not date the first year that I was at the Academy. As a matter of fact, I nicknamed him "The Obnoxious Yearling" because he was such a "nudge" during Jewish Chapel Choir practice—always trying to be funny. We began dating while I was a yearling and became engaged to be married my senior year. That was the year that the new Jewish Chapel was scheduled to be completed. Every week that year I visited the construction site to see how things were going—the construction engineer on site also discussed with me the progress of the chapel—he assured me it would be completed on schedule. The Jewish Chapel was finished in time for the Class of 1984 Baccalaureate Service and the first wedding to be held there—ours. I married that "Obnoxious Yearling" on Graduation Day in 1984—and we are still laughing and sharing fun times together 21 years later. Keith can still be a "nudge" however he is a terrific husband and father to our two children, Samantha Rose and Joseph Kyle.

[Lieutenant Colonel Samuels served in the Army Military Police Corps for twenty years and six months. She was awarded the following: the Defense Superior Service Medal, Defense Meritorious Service Medal, Meritorious Service Medal (4th award), Army Commendation Medal (5th award), Army Achievement Medal (3rd award), Joint Meritorious Unit Award (2nd award), National Defense Service Medal (2nd award), Army Service Ribbon, Overseas Service Ribbon (2nd award), Parachutist Badge, Joint Chiefs of Staff Identification Badge, Military Outstanding Volunteer Service Medal, Junior Officer of the Year, 21st Theater Army Area Command, General Douglas MacArthur Leadership Award, Junior Officer of the Year, Fifth United States Army, and United States Military Police Corps Order of the Marechaussee Medal.]

Jay Van Cleeff, Class of 1949

I guess my cadet history is rather bland! Except for one stupid mistake near the end of plebe year. There was an academic exam that I was not prepared for, so I put myself on sick call and missed the exam. Upper classmen found out about it and I ended up slugged with 6 months confinement and 132 punishment tours! So I spent yearling summer at Camp Popolopen confined to quarters and started punishment tours in Central

Area in September. Luckily some head of state came to visit early in the fall and all slugs were wiped out in an amnesty request from the visiting dignitary!

[Lieutenant Colonel Van Cleeff served in the U.S. Air Force for twenty-six years. He is a command pilot with 7,500 logged flying hours. He served in Vietnam, where he was awarded the Distinguished Flying Cross, the Air Medal four times, the Air Force Commendation Medal, and a variety of Vietnam Service Medals.]

Stephen David Spearman, Class of 1962

Steve Kott, a classmate, was a golden gloves champion from North Carolina, which we knew and the Corps did not. At the heavyweight open championship he faced a 1959 football player for whom the Corps was cheering. Kott demolished him.

Ms. Holland, the cadet hostess went to extremes to fix up Jewish cadets with Jewish girls and often came up empty. When I introduced her to a date, later my wife, still for that matter, Marion Gilman, Holland asked if she was a Gilman from Connecticut. Nope, a Gilman from the Bronx—we still laugh at that.

On a choir trip to Brooklyn I was asked to escort the wife of Mickey Marcus. She was very free with her thoughts and was incensed that he had been improperly portrayed in the film. That he had no girlfriend, and that she had not been consulted by the director or writers. Very nice lady. Forever maligned by Hollywood.

Max Kovel, Class of 1957

Born in Brooklyn, NY on 2 Nov 1934, to Russian immigrants. Studied Hebrew in a Lubavitch "cheder" and was Bar Mitzvah. Not really religious after that. Started thinking about West Point at that time and wrote to Senator Javits requesting information about appointment. Obviously, I was too young, but I thought that if I graduated from WP I would be accepted to any medical school in the country. I really didn't know much about WP or the Army. Graduated from Erasmus Hall HS in June 1951 and entered Brooklyn College, but maintained my interest in WP.

Joined AFROTC and won several military awards. I was given an opportunity by Senator Wagner to take exams in 1953 to compete for an appointment and ended up as a second alternate. I received a telegram on 24 June 1953 offering me entry in July as a Qualified Alternate (the principal and first alternate also entered—we all graduated) and decided to accept it. I graduated 12th in my class (Cdt Company 1st Sgt) on 4 June 1957 and was commissioned in the Corps of Engineers. I was married on 8 June to Bernice Cohen, whom I had been dating since September 1952 (I was in ROTC with her brother and sold her my history notebooks at Brooklyn College). I should mention that I had introduced Bernice's younger sister, Judy, to Irwin Mayer, USMA 56, and they were married when he graduated. He went to AF and was killed in a plane crash in Taiwan in 1970.

After the Engineer basic course at Ft. Belvoir I attended Jump School at Ft. Benning (Abn wings), and joined the 24th Engr Bn, 4th Armored Div, in Furth, Germany in Feb 1958. There, I was a platoon leader in a line company and then in the bridge company. Subsequently, I was the XO until December 1960 and then the Company Cdr of the Bridge Company (Co E) for the last four months of my tour in Germany. During that tour, my son, Jacob (USMA '80), and oldest daughter, Sarah (USNA '82) were born in the Army Hospital in Nuremberg. In 1960, I was selected by the Electricity Department, USMA, to get a MS in Nuclear Science from NC State, Raleigh, NC in preparation for a 3-year teaching assignment at WP. I attended NC State from June 1961 to June 1963, was awarded an MS, and reported to USMA in June 1963. My daughter Ruth was born in a civilian hospital in Raleigh, and is now an American Israeli.

During my tour at WP I took over from Maj. Gene Marder as the OIC of the Jewish Chapel Squad and Choir, working with Rabbi Soltes and conducting religious services when he was not there. He normally conducted services twice a month. My role with the Jewish program was also noted on my efficiency reports. My wife started the Jewish Sunday School (we needed one for our kids), with cadets as the volunteer teachers. We had some truly outstanding Jewish cadets and it was a wonderful experience, including some great choir trips. The choir even participated in the installation of Rabbi Soltes at his new Congregation in Great Neck, LI, which was attended by the USMA Superintendent. The Cadet Chaplain (he was later appointed the Chaplain for the House of Representatives) provided outstanding support, including funding for books, provision of classrooms, and funding for weekly Onegs that my wife set up at our quarters (we lived in the Lost Gray Ghost that was relatively close to the Old Cadet Chapel in the Cemetery) every Sunday morning. My daughter Rachel was born at the WP Hospital.

I was transferred to the Physics and Chemistry Department when the Nuclear Engineering course was transferred, and became an Assistant Professor in my third year. I revised several of the department supplementary texts and wrote a course outline for a new physics textbook.

At the end of three years I was offered a one year extension but the Corps of Engineers wanted me to go to the Career Course and I would have missed the beginning of the new semester, which was unacceptable to the Head of the Physics Department. Upon leaving WP I was told that my assignment after the Engineer Career course would be Thailand. I graduated as the Honor Student (#1 of 60). During that school tour I acted as the Cantor for the Jewish services at FT. Belvoir, which were conducted by Chaplain Stanley Davids. My daughter Rebecca was born at the Ft. Belvoir Army Hospital.

About October of 1966 my orders were changed and I was assigned as the S-3 of the 46th Engr Construction Bn in Vn. I met LTC McGuiness, who was going over to command that Bn in Jan 1967, and he started sending me information about the activities of the Bn while I was still at Ft. Belvoir. When I landed in Bien Hoa in March 1967 he met me at the plane and took me directly to 46th Bn Hqs and then 540th Group Hqs, and consequently I actually ended up in the job to which I was assigned. The 46th Bn was stationed at Long Binh, but we had projects in the Delta (Tan An Province), at Dong Tam, at Bearcat, and at Vung Tau. For the year I was there, I conducted Jewish Services at Long Binh and II Field Force. There was no Jewish Chaplain in country between the time that Rabbi Dimont (stationed in Saigon) left (except for one month) and a chaplain (Abn) arrived as an augmentee to the 101st Abn Div. However, while he visited my services in Long Binh on occasion, he spent most of his time traveling around the 101st firebases.

I remained the S-3 (two different Bn Cdrs) until Feb 1967, just after the Tet Offensive, and then finished the last six weeks of my tour as the XO (Air Medal and two BSM, 2 Meritorious Unit Citations, VSM, VCM with 5 campaign devices, during tour). While in VN I was selected to attend C&GSC, and reported to Leavenworth as a snowbird in June 1968. My family had lived in Brooklyn while I was in VN and remained there until the end of the kids' school year. They then joined me at Leavenworth.

At Leavenworth, I met Rabbi Lapp, who was also a student, and LTC Irv Jacobs, who was on the faculty. For the year I was a student, LTC Jacobs and I conducted the religious services for the military personnel at Ft. Leavenworth. I was selected for early promotion to LTC based on my performance in VN (I assume) in September 1968, but I didn't actually get promoted until October 1969. It was a long wait.

While I was at C&GSC I was offered the opportunity to return to graduate school for a PhD in Engineering Physics, with the school to be chosen by me (if they would accept me) and two years to do it. The UC at Davis agreed to accept me and I attended classes at their Department of Applied Sciences (known as "Teller Tech") collocated with the Lawrence Livermore National Lab in Livermore, CA. I did my research at the lab.

My son and oldest daughter were Bar/Bat Mitzvah in a civilian synagogue in San Leandro, CA, my son before I went back to VN and my daughter when I returned. With the benefit of a 3 month extension from the Army, I completed my research at Livermore and promptly returned to VN in Jan 1972. All US units were in the process of being drawn down at that time and I was assigned as the Senior Advisor to the 8th ARVN Engineer Construction Group, based just outside DaNang. The Group and one of its Bns occupied a former Seabee compound at the bottom of "Freedom Hill," and my team lived on the compound. I took the results of my technical research with me hoping to finish writing my dissertation, but didn't get anything done.

The Jewish Lay Leader at the DaNang Airbase left shortly after I arrived, but left me lots of wine and some kosher canned goods. There were essentially no US ground troops other than advisors and aviation people in the DaNang area and I didn't meet any other Jews. I spent a lot of time transferring US equipment and facilities to the ARVN, until North VN invaded South VN in about May of 1972; the fighting lasted until about September. The NVN troops were driven back by the ARVN with the help of US airpower. In November my team was pulled back into Saigon and I remained there, supporting the ARVN Logistics Hqs, until January 1973. I left VN the week before the armistice. (BSM, VNHM 1st CI, VN Technical Medal 1st Cl, VN Engineer Insignia).

After a two month leave, during which I completed, submitted and defended my dissertation (I was awarded my PhD in Engineering–Applied Science in June 1973), I reported to the Shock Physics Directorate of the Defense Nuclear Agency (formerly Defense Atomic Support Agency). I was told that this assignment was placing the round peg in the round hole, except for the location. I had requested not being assigned to the DC area. Supposedly, I was to stay at DNA for two years and then go to Ft. Lewis, WA to command an Engr Bn. I never left the DC area. In January 1976 I took command of an Engr AIT Bn at Ft. Belvoir (the Army ran out of PCS funds and offered me this alternative). (MSM from DNA). I remained in command until June 1976 at which time I was assigned to the Office of the Chief Scientist in the DCSRDA on the Army Staff. Shortly after that tour started I was selected for 06, and subsequently selected to attend the Industrial College of the Armed Forces at Ft. McNair. I was promoted to 06 in March 1977. I left DCSRDA in June 1977. (MSM and Army GS Badge).

From ICAF I was assigned as the Deputy Chief of the Office of Research and Development in Hqs, Corps of Engineers. However, a problem developed with the civilian selected to be the chief, a PL 313 position (later a GS 18 position), and I became the Acting Chief for the next fifteen months. Part of my task was to get a new chief. During that time I also co-Chaired a US-USSR working group under a HUD agreement on cooperation in the field of housing and other construction in extreme climates and unusual geological conditions. After a civilian was hired, I remained as the Deputy until June 1982 (LOM), and then returned to DNA as the Director of the Shock Physics Directorate, which was responsible for conducting research on the mechanical effect of nuclear weapons on targets, including the conduct of underground nuclear weapons effects tests and above ground simulations. I was also involved in the new program for the SDIO, which was established in 1984. I left DNA (DSSM) in December 1984 and became the Staff Director for Installation Services and Environmental Protection at the Defense Logistics Agency. I retired from DLA in August 1986 (DSSM) and went to work for a civilian contractor to support the SDIO program, continuing to live in the DC area.

From 1973 to 2003 I was an active Jewish Lay Leader at Ft. Belvoir. I was principal of the Jewish Sunday School for three years and a teacher for fifteen, teaching the confirmation classes. In 1975 I was inducted into the "Chapel of the Four Chaplains Legion of Honor." While Jewish Chaplains were assigned to Ft. Belvoir I volunteered as the Cantor for the Chaplains and frequently conducted services when the Chaplain was away. In 1990, the JWB awarded me their Military Lay Leadership Award.

In 1995, Ft. Belvoir lost its Jewish Chaplain and I became responsible for conducting or coordinating (with contract Rabbis or other Lay Leaders) all Jewish services at Ft. Belvoir. My wife became the Ft. Belvoir Director of Jewish Religious Education, a civil service position and the only one in the DoD, about 1978 and remained in that position until her retirement in 2001. The position was eliminated when she retired. During her tenure, she ran the Jewish Sunday school and the Hebrew school, and was the government individual responsible for coordinating all Jewish Activities.

Ernest Randall Smith, Class of 1985

In a nutshell, I went to West Point with Judaism as the last thing on my mind. It was not an active part of my life anyway, so there was no loss expected. Growing up, my family followed the basic (reformed) Jewish traditions, though we belonged to a conservative synagogue in Patchogue, NY. I went to Hebrew school, had a Bar Mitzvah etc. and felt very strongly about being a Jew. But I never really experienced any Jewish or spiritual energy at gatherings of any sort. I was a Jew at heart but that is where it ended.

Amazingly, this changed at West Point! In my era, the Jewish cadet population was dynamic and close knit and we had a fantastic local community. With my friends, I went to services every Friday, starting with Rabbi Soltes in an auditorium and ending at the new Jewish Chapel (built during my tenure—I attended the groundbreaking with you, probably!). I was very involved in the Jewish Choir, the co-cadet in charge as a Cow. At these gatherings, I felt a wonderful, magical Jewish energy for the first time in my life. Singing the prayers and songs at services and performances, I was spiritually moved. So, I thank West Point for giving me an incredible Jewish experience—who would have thought.

Bruce Ressner, Class of 1973

I was the CIC of the Jewish Chapel Squad in 1973 when chapel services became voluntary. There is one anecdote I'll relay. When worship went voluntary, we began Friday night services in Barclay Hall in a chemistry auditorium. However, since it was an academic night, worship for those on restriction for academics had to terminate by 1920 Call to Quarters. A few members were affected. The OIC informed me that he would take responsibility for any repercussions if they stayed. I received a "slug" for dereliction of duty from my TAC within the week and referenced my OIC. I did not get the "slug." I found it very odd that the armed services had insisted for so long all the way to the US Supreme Court that mandatory chapel was necessary and then volte face and tied to inhibit voluntary prayer.

Sherri Langston Whiteman, Class of 1989

Sherri Langston Whiteman sent me a series of newspaper articles from newspapers in Warrick, New York, New York City, and Delray Beach, Florida on her Bat Mitzvah, the first Bat Mitzvah in the then 186 years of West Point history. It took place in 1988. Chaplain (Major) Kenneth Leinwand taught her and officiated. She was attended by family, friends, Jewish and non-Jewish cadets.

Sherri had not attended a service in a synagogue before coming to West Point. She volunteered to teach Sunday School in the chapel but felt she lacked the basic knowledge of Judaism and asked the rabbi to teach her. The articles tell about non-Jewish cadets joining the choir and attending chapel with the Jewish cadets. She emphasized that she never experienced anti-Semitism at West Point. She found her spirituality in the religious activities there.

Jacob E. Bloom, Class of 1873

Born in Ohio. Field Artillery. Served in the French Indian War in 1877. Resigned in 1880 as a first lieutenant. He joined the U.S. Volunteers as a captain, 1898–99. Captain, U.S. Army '01, 1904–1906. Retired disabled in 1911, Major Assistant Deputy 1916–1918. He died in Spokane, Washington, 8 February 1939 at eighty-seven years of age.

As a second lieutenant, Bloom sought an assignment with Colonel George Armstrong Custer's Seventh Cavalry Regiment. He was turned down along with other applicants. He was reprimanded for not following the procedure for such requests.

Bloom may have testified at the court martial of Cadet Henry Ossian Flipper, the first black graduate. A Jewish cadet is known to have testified, as is apparent from the documentary articles shown on television some time ago. This is clear from the fact that when the Jewish cadet took the stand, he was unable to swear on the Bible for religious prohibition and had to "affirm" his testimony.

EPILOGUE

I have a friend in the local Jewish community who intentionally discouraged her son from accepting an appointment to West Point. On the other hand, two alumni who submitted their questionnaires for this book reported that their rabbis had urged them to attend. Late in the 1930s, my family and I visited the son of our kosher butcher from Newark, who was a second lieutenant on active duty at Fort Dupont, Delaware.

I cite these varied approaches to military service by Jews. Yet the prevailing stereotype of the American Jew is one of avoidance. Chaplain (Major) Carlos Huerta quoted an apparently widespread belief that "Jews are consumers of freedom, they do not manufacture it." This is in part only a perception and partly true.

The question relevant to this book is why there is a reluctance to send your child to West Point. It cannot be solely rooted in lifetime earning potential. Regular army officers earn as much as or more than many Jews who enter fields like social work, art, teaching, and philosophy. Is it a perception of a low intellectual environment at West Point? One needs to look closely at the Academy to become familiar with its opportunities for the intellectual development of the cadet. West Point's academic program offers forty-four majors on a thirty-subject science GRE curriculum. We have had great success in producing Rhodes Scholars, East-West scholars, and other distinguished graduates.

West Point's engineering curriculum earned it a rating as the fourth highest college of engineering curriculum in the United States.

West Point is also considered to be the premier leadership school in the country, if not the world. The corporate world competes with the Army for its graduates.

The Army sends many graduates for postgraduate studies in medicine, law, and a broad menu of esoteric subjects. We are blessed with a highly educated officer corps. It needs Jewish officers and must always have them.

Tuition is free at West Point. In addition, cadets are paid $845.57 per month for expenses.

Those who serve for twenty or thirty years are well equipped and young enough for second careers, augmenting their retirement pay.

With respect to the religious effect of West Point on our Jewish cadets, it has been quite positive. We have had a number of Bar and Bat Mitzvahs. The rabbi will also accommodate a cadet who asks to study for these ceremonies. Hebrew is taught as an elective (usually selected by Christians). Grads have been vocal about the positive effect that Jewish activities have had on them both as Jews and as soldiers.

Finally, there is an obligation hanging over us. American citizens need to evaluate their attitude toward their obligation to the nation that has offered them so much.

West Point will not countenance discrimination or demonstrations against Jews, Israel, or other issues dear to the Jewish American community.

INDEX